THE CHINA
MATRIX

THE CHINA MATRIX

The Epic Story of How Donald Trump Shattered a Deadly Pact

LEE SMITH

CENTER
STREET

New York Nashville

Center Street

Hachette Book Group

1290 Avenue of the Americas, New York, NY 10104

centerstreet.com

@CenterStreet

First Edition: October 2025

Center Street is a division of Hachette Book Group, Inc. The Center Street name and logo are registered trademarks of Hachette Book Group, Inc.

The publisher is not responsible for websites (or their content) that are not owned by the publisher.

Center Street books may be purchased in bulk for business, educational, or promotional use. For information, please contact your local bookseller or the Hachette Book Group Special Markets Department at special.markets@hbgusa.com.

LCCN: 2025939186

ISBNs: 9781546008408 (hardcover), 9781546008422 (ebook)

Printed in Canada

MRQ-T

1 2025

For Richard Chen, 1970–2025—warrior, teacher, friend

Contents

CHAPTER ONE

The Deadly Pact

"I'VE TAUGHT PEOPLE A LOT ABOUT CHINA," SAYS DONALD TRUMP. "China and the threat it poses to America."

The president is guiding me on a brief tour of his Palm Beach home, Mar-a-Lago.

"China has been ripping us off for many, many years and nobody ever did anything about it," says Trump. "Whether it was because they were intimidated, or whether it was for other reasons, China has taken advantage of us and we, through corruption or incompetence, have allowed that to happen. We have been losing hundreds of billions and even trillions of dollars to China over a period of many years. A steady stream of $500 billion a year and more in the trade deficit alone. Our wealth has been shattered."

Secret Service agents follow the president as he checks in with aides. I meet one woman who unfurls a thirty-yard-long printout of all the emails that have been sent to Trump in the last twenty-four hours. "They're all Americans writing President Trump to thank him for what he's done," she says.

Americans chose him, among other reasons, to defend them from China and a predatory US ruling class whose ties to the Chinese Communist Party (CCP) had become the source of its wealth, power, and prestige. Trump had identified the problem decades before his 2016 run for president.

"Though we have the upper hand, we're way too eager to please the Chinese," he wrote in his 2000 book *The America We Deserve*. "We see them as a potential market, and we tend to curry favor with them even at the expense of our own national interests. Our China policy under Presidents Clinton and [George H. W.] Bush has been aimed at changing the Chinese regime by incentives both economic and political. The intention has been good, but it's clear to me that the Chinese have been getting far too easy a ride."[1]

What it looked like on the ground for working Americans was ruin and misery. But according to the men and women Americans elected to protect their peace and advance their prosperity, there was nothing to be done about it. Even the president of hope and change said he was helpless when it came to China.

Barack Obama was referring to Trump when he said, "When somebody says...that he's going to bring all these jobs back, well, how exactly are you going to do that? What are you going to do? There's no answer to it. He just says, well, I'm going to negotiate a better deal. Well, how exactly are you going to negotiate that? What magic wand do you have?"[2]

The truth was plain to see: Beijing hadn't outplayed the top lawyers that White House after White House sent out to negotiate against the Chinese; the US establishment had just sold out America. It was to the advantage of the movers and shakers from Capitol Hill and Wall Street, Silicon Valley and Hollywood, media and the fashion industry, and they didn't care how it hurt their countrymen and elevated foreigners.

So middle-class Americans hired an outsider who promised to take on China. Trump moved quickly. He invited Xi Jinping, the president of the People's Republic of China (PRC) and the general secretary of the CCP, to meet him here at Mar-a-Lago in April 2017.*

"Until the China virus came, I liked and greatly respected Xi," Trump says. "I got along with him very well. But they had this slogan, 'China 2025,' and I said to him that it's a very unfriendly term. I said, 'I really don't like that term because you're basically saying that you're going to dominate us by 2025, and I don't believe that's going to happen.'"

Half a year after their US meeting, Trump visited Xi in Beijing and described it in a speech he gave a few days later in Vietnam.[3]

I recently had an excellent trip to China, where I spoke openly and directly with President Xi about China's unfair trade practices and the enormous trade deficits they have produced with the United States. I expressed our strong desire to work with China to achieve a trading relationship that is conducted on a truly fair and equal basis.

The current trade imbalance is not acceptable. I do not blame China or any other country, of which there are many, for taking advantage of the United States on trade. If their representatives are able to get away with it, they are just doing their jobs. I wish previous administrations in my country saw what was happening and did something about it. They did not, but I will.

From this day forward, we will compete on a fair and equal basis. We are not going to let the United States be taken advantage

---

* Communist China's top leaders traditionally fill three roles at once: head of the regime; president of the People's Republic of China, head of state; and chairman of the Central Military Commission, head of the military. Throughout, I generally use People's Republic of China (PRC) to refer to the Chinese state and Chinese Communist Party (CCP) to designate the communist regime that rules it.

*of anymore. I am always going to put America first the same way
that I expect all of you in this room to put your countries first.*

"We had 164 million people working," Trump tells me. He
considers it one of his greatest achievements as president—to get
Americans jobs. "We had everybody from every segment doing
well—poor, rich, middle-class, it didn't matter. African-Americans,
Hispanic-Americans, Asian-Americans, women, men, people with
degrees from MIT and the Wharton School of Finance, people
that didn't have a high school diploma. There wasn't one group that
wasn't doing great. Welfare was way down. Everything was going
good. Food stamps were down because people had great jobs and
they were happy, they were thrilled."

It was evidence that Trump had kept his word. Returning the
jobs to America that the ruling class had exported to China was the
core promise of his 2016 campaign. In office Trump and his aides
came to understand that this meant taking on a vast network of
American elites keen to protect their relations with China, a multi-
generational matrix of public and private sector interests from the
political, corporate, and cultural establishments that occupied the
space carved out more than a half century ago by Henry Kissinger
when he served as President Richard Nixon's national security advisor. With his 1971 secret trip to prepare for Nixon's historic visit, he
opened China to the world, again—Kissinger was the Marco Polo of
the globalism era.

"Henry Kissinger was a smart man," says Trump. In October
2017, he visited Trump in the Oval Office. "Mr. President, I didn't
expect this opportunity," said Kissinger. "It's always a great honor to
be in this office, and I'm here at a moment when the opportunity to
build a constructive, peaceful world order is very great."[4]

"He wasn't helpful or unhelpful," Trump says of the former official who died in November 2023, revered as one of the "wise men" of Washington. "But he loved China. He loved China for a reason."

THE KISSINGER CONTINUUM

The opening to China was celebrated by the foreign policy elite as well as the cultural establishment, high and low, from sports to high art, including an opera, *Nixon in China*, and a famous series of Andy Warhol paintings of Mao Zedong. Nixon later came to reconsider the wisdom of the opening to China, but for Kissinger it became the cornerstone of his historical legacy as a statesman, and then as a corporate leader. His postgovernment career coincided with the rise of globalism, the new world order that saw national borders and even national sovereignty as a hindrance to free trade. China, with an enormous pool of cheap labor, often slave labor, was seen as the centerpiece of the new system. And as the statesman who opened China to the West, Kissinger became the model for the new American establishment, a network of political, corporate, academic, cultural, and media elites that profited personally from the US-China relationship.

They made money by doing business with China, by opening doors for others to profit there, too, and by paving the way for China to enter what they euphemistically called the rules-based international system. The result, according to forecasts delivered by US policymakers throughout the 1980s and 1990s, would be China's eventual democratic evolution. Instead, Beijing's techno-autocracy rubbed off on American elites. Thus, what they meant by "international system" was just a series of political and economic arrangements through which communist elites became further entrenched thanks to the money they and their US partners accumulated on the back of Chinese labor and at the expense of the American workforce.

Kissinger became the role model for a networked US elite

regularly scrambling to hide China's depredations from plain view and thereby protect their riches and avoid blame themselves. Whether it was after the People's Liberation Army (PLA) air force brought down American planes in the South China Sea, or Trump declared a trade war with the PRC, or the PLA lied about its role in a pandemic that killed hundreds of thousands of Americans, turned millions more into paupers, and left the US economy in ruins, the former top diplomat stepped forward to make Beijing's case.

He built communist China the biggest and costliest lobby in world history, consisting of the ruling establishment of the most powerful country in world history. Everyone on the inside was in on it. All they had to do was make sure China stayed open for business.

In the early 1980s Kissinger started a consultancy, Kissinger Associates, whose roster over the years included former secretaries of State, Treasury, and the Department of Energy; national security advisors; ambassadors; and CIA officers. Kissinger managed to avoid having to register as a foreign agent because even though he lobbied openly on behalf of China for forty years, he wasn't paid directly by the Chinese. Rather, he drew his income from the major US industries that he vouched for in Beijing, under the tacit agreement that in return for access to China they would make the calls and demand the meetings with DC lawmakers and the White House to lobby for China. It's a loophole that serving US officials never dreamed of closing, since they saw it as a useful paradigm to pursue their own postgovernment ambitions.[5]

The list of former officials from Democratic and Republican administrations who have run strategic advisory firms, think tanks, or otherwise emulated Kissinger to profit from promoting US ties with China reads like a Who's Who in Washington of the last half century, comprising both Democrats and Republicans. There's Ronald Reagan's Secretary of State Alexander Haig, a former Kissinger aide; George H. W. Bush's national security advisor, Brent Scowcroft, and Secretary of State Lawrence Eagleburger, also both former Kissinger aides and then employees; Bill Clinton's Secretary of State Madeleine Albright, his Defense Secretary William Cohen, and his national security advisor, Sandy Berger; George W. Bush's Treasury Secretary Henry Paulson and US Trade Representative Robert Zoellick; and former Barack Obama aide and Joe Biden aide Kurt Campbell; as well as Biden's Secretary of State Antony Blinken, Director of National Intelligence Avril Haines, and CIA Director William Burns.

To support the industry he built to advance the US-China relationship, Kissinger curated the intellectual apparatus to ensure his heroic version of the opening and all that came after dominated the narrative as the mainstream account. Centers and institutes were named after him, like the Wilson Center's Kissinger Institute on China and the United States, and the Henry A. Kissinger Center for Global Affairs at Johns Hopkins University; and chairs bear his name at the Library of Congress, the Council on Foreign Relations, and the Center for Strategic and International Studies, as well as fellowships given at Johns Hopkins and Yale.

Kissinger's central role as éminence grise of the US-China relationship made him something like a dark-mirror version of Gandalf, the sage wizard in J. R. R. Tolkien's *Lord of the Rings* trilogy, who guides a band of searchers on their quest. Except, where Gandalf's charges were tasked to destroy a ring of absolute power that corrupted all who touched it, Kissinger's charges—corporate titans, Wall Street bankers, leading politicians, university presidents, sports stars, and Hollywood moguls—wanted the ring of power forged in the Middle Kingdom for themselves. Naturally, they became corrupted by it and brought devastation and ruin to their own country.

Because Trump's mission was to break the spell Kissinger had cast, the forces from every sector of the political and corporate establishment that over two generations had coalesced around it fought back. They joined China's long war against America.

THE CHINA CLASS FIGHTS TRUMP

It's not surprising China turned its weapons on Americans immediately after the revolution. Washington had supported Chiang Kai-shek's Nationalist forces against Mao, and Mao won. To contain the spread of communism, the US fought PRC allies in Asia, where the Chinese killed and aided in the killing of thirty-seven thousand Americans during the Korean War, and more than fifty-eight thousand in the Vietnam War.

The long war against America continues, through subtler means. The Chinese are responsible for the manufacture and distribution of fentanyl, which is illegally pushed across our southern and northern borders and typically kills as many as seventy-five thousand Americans yearly.[6] More than a million Americans died during the Covid-19 pandemic, which originated with a leak from a Chinese government lab in Wuhan where the PLA runs biowarfare programs. There's no evidence the pathogen was leaked intentionally, but China's lies about the nature of the virus's origins, lethality, and how it was transmitted are evidence that Beijing opportunistically used it as an instrument in an information warfare campaign to weaken its Western rivals, primarily America.

China's depredations are typically ignored thanks to the efforts of a well-funded propaganda machine. Beijing pours money into various American intellectual institutions, including universities, think tanks, and media. It also pays US academics directly, as well as social media influencers on all the major platforms, Twitter, YouTube, and Facebook, to smear America and dismiss reports of China's human rights abuses of its own population, particular minority groups, like

Tibetans and Uyghurs. The CCP also cultivates ties with subnational actors, including American minorities, mostly but not exclusively African-American, as well as state and local governments, to undermine US interests.

But far and away the most powerful asset deployed by the PRC is what I call the China Class, leaders from the political, corporate, cultural, academic, and media establishments that have gotten rich off making China rich. Virtually all of what the PRC now makes, from state-of-the-art hi-tech to advanced military hardware, has either been stolen by them or transferred to them by American elites in exchange for future favors. China's leaders from Mao down to Xi Jinping are typically credited with raising hundreds of millions of peasants out of poverty, an economic miracle like nothing before it, say admirers. But the reality is that it was the policies of the Chinese Communist Party that plunged the Chinese into misery and poverty in the first place.

It wasn't Beijing that built China's prosperous new middle class. The Chinese are hardworking and intelligent people but the type of people who have risen to the top of the communist regime have crawled over corpses to get there—over 70 million Chinese killed under Mao alone.[7] It was America's political and corporate elite, the China Class, who largely through trade and financial instruments made this murderous regime what it is today, a peer adversary of the country they call home. And they did it to augment their own wealth, power, and prestige at the expense of impoverishing the American middle class.

The China Class appeared at first to be a random assortment of personalities from various industries and institutions who seemed to have little in common, outside of the fact they were excoriated by the newly elected president. But Trump's resolve to take on China, and his relentless attacks on them, gave the elites collective self-awareness, or what Marxists call class consciousness. Together, they saw that they represented a nexus of public and private sector interests that shared not only the same prejudices and hatreds, cultural tastes, and consumer habits, but also the same center of gravity, the US-China relationship.

Connections that might have once seemed tenuous or nonexistent became lucid under the light of Trump's scorn, and the reciprocal scorn of the elite that loathed him and the Americans who elected him to fight on their behalf. A decade ago, no one would've put, for instance, NBA superstar LeBron James and Apple CEO Tim Cook in the same family album, but there they are, linked by their fantastic wealth owing to cheap Chinese manufacturing. Miramax Films and Harvard's Kennedy School? They both produced propaganda that assisted the PRC's rise to global primacy. The Black Panthers and Goldman Sachs? Both hitched their fortune to Beijing's ascendancy.

Some did warn about the dangers of China. Labor unions were against admitting China to the World Trade Organization (WTO). In 2000, AFL-CIO president John Sweeney called "the fevered rush to admit China to the WTO a grave mistake."[8] And four years later the AFL-CIO submitted a petition, arguing that China's labor practices, including the suppression of workers' rights, were unfair trade practices that harmed American workers.[9]

Human rights groups like Amnesty International, Human Rights Watch, Freedom House, and pro-Tibet activists swam against the tide of pro-China sentiment. Sometimes they were joined by famous celebrities, like actor Richard Gere, and even US policymakers, like former House speaker Nancy Pelosi, who as a young California congresswoman attended a rally at Tiananmen Square two years after the 1989 massacre there and waved a banner in support of the victims of the PLA's depredations.[10]

Democratic House Representative Dick Gephardt, who ran for

president in 1988 and 2004, opposed granting China permanent normal trade relations (PNTR) status, also known as most-favored-nation (MFN) status, because it would hurt American workers, while ignoring China's human rights abuses. "Only when there is real progress that addresses our concerns," he said, "should it be granted."[11]

One of the most vocal critics of US trade policy was Ronald Reagan's onetime deputy US trade representative, Robert Lighthizer. "Giving China most favored nation treatment for trade," said Lighthizer, "was a tragic mistake."[12] Lighthizer was US trade representative in Trump's first term, and perhaps the most important piece in Trump's China policy.

And there was Trump himself. "I think we need to take a much harder look at China," he wrote in 2000. He was critical not only of China's trade practices but also its human rights abuses—and he knew the corporate establishment was protecting China. "There are major problems that too many at the highest reaches of business want to overlook. There is, as I mentioned, the human-rights situation," he wrote, citing a report: "'Abuses included torture and mistreatment of prisoners, forced confessions, and arbitrary and lengthy incommunicado detention. Prison conditions remain harsh. The government continues severe restrictions on freedom of speech, the press, assembly, association, religion, privacy, and worker rights. All public dissent against the party and government was effectively silenced by intimidation, exile, the imposition of prison terms, administrative detention, or house arrest.'"[13]

He'd pinpointed the source of corruption in our elite, the reason for the impoverishment of the middle classes, and the threats to our peace. But even he was surprised to find how bad it was when he first came to office.

"They're partners with China on virtually everything," Trump says. "I mean, they just drop to their knees when China speaks. I've never seen anything like it. And they may be afraid of China. It's not just business. It seems like they're afraid of China."

Among other things, they're afraid of forfeiting the financial benefits. "I know one man who was very opposed to China," says Trump. "All of a sudden, he comes in and he's talking to me and I said, 'Whoa! What happened?' He's talking so positively about China. I said, 'I've never seen anybody go from being so brilliantly against something to being so brilliantly in favor of it.' I said, 'They're paying you, aren't they?' He said, 'Yeah, they paid me a ton of money.' They pay people a fortune."

Even if it wanted to, the China Class can't cut itself off from its life source. "It's like a fix," says Trump. "And China knew that I was willing to get off the fix. It's like drugs."

So they fought Trump on China. They fought him on trade and the tariffs he imposed on Chinese goods during his first term and again when he tariffed China at the start of his second term. And they fought him on national security issues related to China. They fought him when he ordered restrictions on travel from China after a virus swept out of a city hosting a Chinese government lab funded by America's biodefense czar Anthony Fauci in the fall of 2019.

AMERICA POISONED

Covid was the real-world manifestation of a decades-long truth, the metaphor employed to describe the relationship merging US and Chinese elites had come to life: China's communist party had poisoned America. The pandemic dramatized just how profoundly the relationship had transformed the country's ruling class, now employing the same tactics as the CCP and mirroring its cruelty. Covid became an instrument to demoralize Americans and imprison them in their homes; lay waste to small business; leave them vulnerable to rioters free to steal, burn, and kill; keep their children from school and the dying from the last embrace of their loved ones; desecrate American history, culture, and society; and defame the country as *systemically racist* in order to furnish the predicate for why ordinary Americans *deserved* the hell that the elite's private sector militias like BLM and Antifa and the FBI and other intelligence services had prepared for them.

US political and corporate elites used the pandemic to disintegrate American norms, including election laws that were unconstitutionally altered to favor a candidate whose financial ties to CCP elites were uncovered a month before the election. But like communist party censors, dozens of US intelligence officers arranged with social media platforms and prestige press outfits to block reports of Joe and Hunter Biden's corrupt relations with Chinese officials.

The election of Biden represented the hegemony of an American ruling class that sees its relationship with China as a shield and sword against its own countrymen. To those most dispirited and demoralized, it resembled the installation of an occupation government ruling on behalf of a hostile power. With Trump gone, there was nothing impeding the political and business establishment from restoring its cozy relations with Beijing and accelerating the betrayal of American sovereignty.

During a trip to Vietnam in September 2023, Biden explained:[14] "I don't want to contain China." He continued: "I just want to make sure that we have a relationship with China that is on the up and up, squared away, everybody knows what it's all about." It was a far cry from Trump's Vietnam speech nearly six years earlier when he asserted he would pursue the interests of the voters that made him president. Biden was most concerned to soothe Chinese anxieties—and US donors with a portfolio staked to China's success. "It's not about isolating China...I want to see China succeed economically," he said. "We're not looking to hurt China...We're all better off if China does well...We're not looking to decouple from China."

He immediately began rolling back Trump initiatives to keep China in check. For instance, he ended the Trump Justice Department's China Initiative to root out CCP espionage. After the PRC's foreign ministry complained it was racist, Biden compliantly shut it down.

And he made Americans more vulnerable to China. When Biden reversed Trump's border policy, among the millions who entered illegally were large numbers of PRC nationals who, according to a former US intelligence official, are attached to a special PLA unit.

With America's borders open, fatal overdoses of fentanyl peaked above 112,000 deaths.[15] Other drug problems got worse, too. Chinese gangs with ties to the PRC government are responsible for much of America's illicit marijuana trade. Chinese organized crime, say Oklahoma law enforcement authorities, has "taken over marijuana in Oklahoma and the United States." According to one report, Chinese mobsters are "illegally moving money overseas for the Communist Party elite and spy on and intimidate Chinese immigrant communities."[16]

And the Biden administration failed to secure the drugs that keep Americans alive. The Covid pandemic showed how reliant the United States had become on Chinese-made pharmaceuticals, with the United States importing $2.1 billion in pharmaceutical products. After Biden had three years to reshore pharmaceuticals, by 2024 imports had more than tripled, with the US spending more than $7.8 billion on drugs manufactured in China.[17]

In the early winter of 2023, a PRC spy balloon entered US territory in Alaska. After a week during which it had traversed the continental United States, it was shot down off the South Carolina coast. The fact that it was carrying US-made technology, including a satellite communication module, sensors, and other sophisticated surveillance equipment, only underscores how American corporations prioritize profits over US national security.[18] It also showed how Beijing controlled an administration led by a president whose family had clear ties to China. Indeed, as we'll later see, as Obama's vice president Biden had opened Wall Street up to Chinese fraud that netted Beijing trillions while exposing US investors to financial ruin. Then his family reaped the benefits.

As president, Biden continued to make the Chinese richer and Americans poorer. He revoked tariffs worth $8.5 billion that Trump imposed on Chinese solar panel manufacturers.[19] One study showed that Biden's 2022 Inflation Reduction Act—legislation pushing the climate agenda—showed that Chinese manufacturers could earn up to $125 billion in tax credits under the Biden law.[20] Further, by hiking up energy prices to satisfy climate ideologues and lobbyists, Biden made the United States less competitive and China stronger by comparison.

On the national security front, Biden's withdrawal from Afghanistan gave China Bagram Air Base, a listening post where the United States had kept tabs on Beijing's military activities. "We would have kept Bagram because of China, not because of Afghanistan," says Trump. "This is one hour away from where China makes its nuclear weapons."

Biden, says Trump, damaged the US alliance system to help China. "Their stupidity with Saudi Arabia was unbelievable," he says of his predecessor's White House. Trump had defended the Saudis when he was pressured to relinquish the decades-long relationship with the world's top oil producer. But he fought back: Saudi kept oil prices low, which is good for global markets, and invested in the United States, which is good for American workers. "They treated Saudi terribly," Trump says of the Biden team. "They pushed them right into the hands of China."

While Riyadh flirted briefly with Beijing, Saudi Arabia did not realign with the Chinese—or else they would've risked not only a long-standing alliance but also one of the pillars of the post–World War II order, which has made the United States the wealthiest, most powerful country in world history.

Because of the Biden administration's recklessness, many began to wonder if the US was on the verge of losing its dominant position. After all, the dollar's status as the world's reserve currency is owing among other things to the arrangement Washington policymakers made with the Saudis at the end of World War II: The world buys American bonds and invests in US real estate because the United States is the chief guarantor of security around the world, a large component of which is making sure that Persian Gulf oil gets safely to market.

Among other dangers in that strategically vital region is the anti-US terror regime in Iran, which has joined forces with China and Russia. "Biden forced China and Russia together and now they have Iran," says Trump. In March 2024, the three conducted joint naval exercises in the Gulf of Oman.[21] "How could Biden have let so many things get so bad?"

When Trump first came to the White House in 2017, he was hopeful that his administration could force some distance between Beijing and Moscow, but Trump's domestic opponents made that impossible. The Hillary Clinton campaign's dirty trick smearing the 2016 GOP candidate as a Russian agent was retooled by Obama's spy chiefs and turned into a weapon to undermine Trump's presidency.

With false allegations of Trump's ties to Moscow, the "Russia collusion" narrative had effectively become an instrument to redirect the public's attention away from China, Trump's priority. Russiagate protected China and its US partners from scrutiny and prevented Trump from shaping a more comprehensive foreign policy to deal with the threat from Beijing. Instead, says Trump, Russiagate "put us into a hostile environment with a powerful country."

Who knows if the Trump team would have succeeded in isolating China with a US-Russia partnership, but the Russia collusion narrative obstructed the policy of the man elected to conduct US foreign relations.

"We might have had a good relationship with Russia," he says. "Russia has very valuable land with minerals and things that we could have used, and we have things that they were desperate to have. And I said to Putin, 'You probably know . . .' And he said, 'I do know without you even saying it.' He said, 'It's virtually impossible for you to do anything with us.'"

From Trump's perspective, Russiagate was a geopolitical disaster with the final bill still yet to come. "One of the things that I learned very early on from a lot of very smart people is, don't let Russia and China get together," says Trump. But the Americans fighting Trump helped force them together. Trump says: "They pushed Russia to China."

That formula is an inversion of how the US-China relationship began more than fifty years ago, with Kissinger's secret July 1971 trip to Beijing to prepare the ground for Nixon's state visit. Nixon and Kissinger set about to leverage China against the Soviet Union. They called it "playing the China card," but it was among the worst bets American leaders ever made, for their strategic gambit evolved into the devastation that Trump was elected to repair.

From Trump's perspective, the long line of American presidents dating back over half a century are all responsible for the carnage.

"They were all really bad," Trump says of his predecessors' records on China. "But Richard Nixon is the one who opened up China. It was a terrible mistake. A lot of people praise him for opening up China. But I think they're stupid people, too. It was a very bad day for the United States. He let them in, and other people let China take advantage of us. There were other presidents who followed and other presidents who allowed the rape of the United States to go on and on." But it was Nixon, and Kissinger, who initiated it.

"The worst thing Nixon did wasn't Watergate," says Trump. "It was allowing China to take advantage of this country. He and Kissinger are the ones that opened up China. And it was a terrible mistake. It didn't have to be this way."

This is the story of the US ruling class's deadly pact with China. It shows how the career of one man, Henry Kissinger, shaped the world as well as the country we live in today. And it's the story of the man twice elected to undo Kissinger's spell. Trump and Kissinger, antagonist and protagonist, are the two poles around which this epic account of the last fifty years of American politics, culture, and society revolves.

CHAPTER TWO

Unbalancing America

It is no longer possible to think that one
side can dominate the other.[1]

—Henry Kissinger

THE MANCHURIAN CANDIDATE IS A COLD WAR THRILLER ABOUT communist powers infiltrating American political circles at the highest levels. Starring Frank Sinatra, the 1962 film tells the story of Korean War veteran Sgt. Raymond Shaw (played by Lawrence Harvey), who is taken prisoner along with his platoon. Their communist captors brainwash them all and formulate a plan to use Shaw in their secret war against the United States. Freed from captivity, the men speak of Shaw's heroism and gallantry, qualities they attribute to him based only on a false memory implanted by their captors along with the rote phrase, "Raymond Shaw is the kindest, bravest, warmest, most wonderful human being I've ever known in my life."

In fact, he's cold and distant, having been raised by a psychopath for a mother, played by Angela Lansbury. She's secretly in league with the communists who mangled her son's body and psyche and vows revenge against them for making her child the instrument of their design. Still, she presses on with the scheme to enslave America. With her husband, a voluble and dimwitted anti-communist US senator (modeled after Senator Joe McCarthy) nominated to the number two spot on the presidential ticket, he's only a sniper's bullet away from the Oval Office, where he'll become the avatar through whom she and her foreign coconspirators will collapse the free world.

The story of betrayal related here begins nearly a decade later in 1971, and it's notable how many themes it shares with the fictional Hollywood account. Hailed as a Cold War classic that captures the period's paranoid sensibility, the movie's representation of propaganda and brainwashing might have prepared the American public for the messaging that accompanied the strengthening of ties between the United States and the People's Republic of China. As false as the stock praise for Raymond Shaw's character is the broad assertion, relayed by every US president since Richard Nixon—except for Donald Trump—that the rise of China's communist party is good for America and conducive to world peace.

Here's how Nixon put it: "What brings us together is a recognition of a new situation in the world and a recognition on our part that what is important is not a nation's internal political philosophy," he told Mao during their historic meeting. "Therefore, we can find common ground, despite our differences, to build a world structure in which both can be safe to develop in our own ways on our own roads."[2]

With Mao's death, Gerald Ford said: "I am confident that the trend of improved relations between the People's Republic of China and the United States, which Chairman Mao helped to create, will continue to contribute to world peace and stability."[3]

Jimmy Carter said: "the United States and China need to build their futures together."[4]

In Ronald Reagan's words, "We can work together as equals in a spirit of mutual respect and mutual benefit... America and China are both great nations. And we have a special responsibility to preserve world peace."[5]

According to George H. W. Bush, "One of my dreams for our world is that these two powerful giants will continue working toward a full partnership and friendship that will help bring peace and prosperity to people everywhere."[6]

Bill Clinton wasn't worried about the rising communist juggernaut: "Our objective is not containment and conflict; it is cooperation. We will far better serve our interests and our principles if we work with a China that shares that objective with us."[7]

George W. Bush agreed: "China is on a rising path, and America welcomes the emergence of a strong and peaceful and prosperous China."[8]

So did Barack Obama: "Our goal is not to counter China. Our goal is not to contain China," he said.[9] "We want China to succeed."[10]

And in the words of Joe Biden: "China is going to eat our lunch? Come on, man. I mean, you know, they're not bad folks, folks. But guess what? They're not competition for us."[11]

US presidents should always seek to avoid conflict with foreign powers and hence allay the electorate's fears lest the country be swept up in a wave of mass panic. But the ongoing efforts, for more than half a century, to obscure the threat that China poses to our national security, economy, and way of life suggests that Washington was propagandizing Americans to distract us from the all-too-apparent fact, highlighted by the transparently mendacious denials at the highest levels of government, that China is indeed a threat.

Why did our elected officials mislead the American public for so long? It seems at first they believed that relations with communist China would lead to stability and even peace. Later, more cynically, the political class protected China to satisfy corporate campaign donors that drew their wealth from doing business with the PRC. And eventually, it became impossible to imagine any other way to relate to China but appeasement. As *The Manchurian Candidate* dramatized, the real threat to our constitutional republic isn't the communists from across the ocean but the Americans working with them to advance their own causes. The threat to America is coming from inside the house.

And so, like *The Manchurian Candidate*, our story begins in secret: The president of the United States has opened a secret channel to initiate relations with the People's Republic of China and set in motion a chain of events that has led to our present circumstances.

But this story is not about a lone sleeper agent, or a spy ring that infiltrated the State Department or the Pentagon or the CIA. Rather, it is the history of an entire ruling class that over a fifty-year span was guided then inspired by the policies and preferences, the actions and opinions, of America's most famous statesman, one of the rare Washington bureaucrats who rode reputation all the way to fortune and celebrity, dining in New York's most exclusive restaurants, with gorgeous women hanging on his arm and the political, corporate, and media establishment hanging on his every utterance. Henry Kissinger's secret trip to China is the opening scene in an epic account of American corruption and Chinese subterfuge that shows how the corporate establishment—industry and finance—as well as the worlds of media, entertainment, sports, and academia, joined forces with the political class to betray America and make it poorer, divided, and prey to a totalitarian regime.

THE SECRET TRIP

Kissinger was thinking about the time in 1954 when then US Secretary of State John Foster Dulles refused to shake Zhou Enlai's hand.

Kissinger imagined the snub was still on the mind of the Chinese prime minister decades later, so when they first met in the Chinese capital on July 9, 1971, the American envoy made a broad show of extending his hand. Kissinger was right: Zhou still felt the slight from decades past. Kissinger later remarked that "it was the first step in putting the legacy of the past behind us."[12]

In exchange, Zhou offered Kissinger a cigarette. The Chinese premiere was surprised that neither Kissinger nor any of the aides traveling with him wanted one. "I have found a party that doesn't smoke," said Zhou, and welcomed them to China.[13]

"Many visitors have come to this beautiful, and to us, mysterious land," said Kissinger.

"You will find it not mysterious," said Zhou. "When you have become familiar with it, you will find it not as mysterious as before."

"For us this is a historic occasion," said Kissinger. "Because this is the first time that Americans and Chinese leaders are talking to each other on a basis where each country recognizes each other as equals. In our earlier contacts we were a new and developing country in contrast to Chinese cultural superiority. For the past century you were victims of foreign oppression. Only today, after many difficulties and separate roads have we come together again on a basis of equality and mutual respect. So we are both turning a new page in our histories."[14]

Kissinger spoke self-consciously. Flattering one's host is standard diplomatic protocol, but Kissinger was speaking like a figure from a historical romance because he had an eye to future accounts of the moment.

Zhou's place in history was already secure. He was a veteran of the 1949 revolution and the subsequent struggles led by paramount leader Mao Zedong. Zhou's responses during the course of Kissinger's trip to the city Westerners still spelled *Peking* indicate he knew he had the advantage. The Americans had given it away freely by casting themselves as the supplicant.

They had implored the Chinese to keep the visit secret. In correspondence with President Richard Nixon, Zhou had suggested they make it public, but Nixon and Kissinger insisted on secrecy.[15] The Americans didn't want to be embarrassed. Part of what drove Nixon to visit China was to get there before Ted Kennedy or George McGovern or other potential 1972 candidates for the Democratic Party's nomination. Nixon wanted to impress the liberal elite he loathed, and he must have dreaded the prospect of the media mocking him if Mao rebuffed him. On the other hand, both his own party and the "silent majority" of mainstream American voters that backed him were proudly anti-communist. So, Nixon wanted to be certain of success before making his plans clear. The opening to China was to be a crucial part of his reelection campaign and the fulfillment of a promise made during his successful 1968 run to bring China in from the cold.

In preparation for his 1968 campaign, Nixon had written a well-received article on China for *Foreign Affairs* to show the Washington establishment he wasn't just Dwight D. Eisenhower's former vice president.[16] Ike ended the Korean War in 1953 by threatening to use nuclear weapons against North Korea and its patron, China, unless they came to terms.[17] With Joseph Stalin's death two months after Eisenhower's inauguration, the North Koreans lost crucial backing, and the armistice was signed in July.

The geopolitical landscape had changed in the intervening years. In 1964 China first successfully tested a nuclear bomb, and America's war in Asia was against a different Chinese ally, North Vietnam. Nixon warned in his 1967 article "Asia After Vietnam" that the "world cannot be safe until China changes." Americans couldn't "afford to leave China outside the family of nations, there to nurture its fantasies, cherish its hates and threaten its neighbors."

But Nixon wasn't going to roll over to accommodate the PRC. "Coming to grips with the reality of China," he wrote, "does not mean, as many would simplistically have it, rushing to grant recognition to Peking, to admit it to the United Nations and to ply it with offers of trade—all of which would serve to confirm its rulers in their present course."

Nixon's plan, as he'd explained in the article, was to "persuade China that it must change." He wrote "that it cannot satisfy its imperial ambitions, and that its own national interest requires a turning away from foreign adventuring and a turning inward toward the solution of its own domestic problems."

America's evangelical habit of instructing foreign states in what is good for them is part of the legacy of the late nineteenth- and twentieth-century missionary movement, when the hardiest members of Protestant congregations were sent to convert the masses in hard places like the Middle East and China. Though they largely failed in bringing salvation to the heathens, their children came to play important roles in shaping Washington policy in those regions. Having mastered the difficult local languages, acquired extensive knowledge of the locales, and formed sentimental attachments to their inhabitants, they filled the US diplomatic corps and other government positions as military and intelligence officers. If their parents had not saved the foreigners' souls, the next generation of Americans were devoted to teaching them the social gospel and how to live best, how to live like Americans.

The most famous scion of the nineteenth-century missionary movement was Henry Luce, founder and publisher of *Time* magazine, who was born in Shandong province in 1898 to missionary parents. After studying in England and the United States, Luce started *Time* in 1923, and later its sister publications *Life* and *Fortune*, establishing a media empire that made him one of the most influential men in the world and whose magazines inoculated the US public against communism.[18]

Luce visited China for the first time in two decades in 1932 and met Chiang Kai-shek, head of the Nationalist Party, or Kuomintang, who'd been leader of the Republic of China since 1928. His wife, Soong Mei-ling, was from a prominent Christian family, and Chiang converted in 1930, baptized by an American missionary.[19] His newly adopted faith gave him a strategic advantage, making him more appealing to Western nations, especially the United States. Luce used his publishing empire to promote Chiang as a future American partner in what was certain to become, as the proudly patriotic Luce put it, "the American Century."

But on the ground, Chiang's forces were inept against both the Japanese and, when World War II ended and the civil war resumed, Mao's forces. After spending $1.5 billion to support Chiang against the Japanese, the United States poured at least $2 billion into Chiang's coffers to fight the communists, with nearly half of it lost to corruption and waste.[20]

The State Department and other US agencies were staffed by plenty of Mao sympathizers. Some were committed communists while others believed, along with Luce's China correspondent, Theodore White, that the corruption and cruelty of Chiang's cadre meant there was little chance for a Nationalist victory. Regardless of their political leanings, the analysts assessed there was little more they could do to sustain Chiang. According to a thousand-page 1949 State Department document known as the White Paper, "A realistic appraisal of conditions in China leads to the conclusion that the only alternative open to the United States was full-scale intervention in behalf of a Government which had lost the confidence of its own troops and its own people."[21]

With Chiang's government fleeing to Taiwan in 1949, the great

Washington, DC, debate over "Who lost China" began. Luce's publications blamed the Harry Truman administration and argued that US officials had undercut Chiang by withdrawing support. For a time, Luce's interests intersected with those of Senator Joe McCarthy. But as the firebrand legislator's anti-communism devolved into paranoia, the media mogul began to tire of McCarthy's typically unsubstantiated rants. After a 1951 speech during which the Wisconsin lawmaker accused Secretary of State Dean Acheson and Defense Secretary George Marshall of "craven, whimpering appeasement" of the communists, Luce cut McCarthy from the herd.[22]

A subsequent *Time* cover story argued that the antics of "Demagogue McCarthy...foul up the necessary examination of the Truman-Acheson foreign policy." From Luce's perspective, McCarthy's outrages had effectively covered up the real mistakes the Truman administration had made, errors of judgment and policy that needed to be studied and corrected for the sake of US power and prestige in the midst of the Cold War confrontation with communism.[23]

Almost as bad as Mao's victory was the fact that McCarthy had given anti-communism a bad name. According to one young China scholar, McCarthy's attacks moved the "center of gravity" on China issues leftward. Maoist sympathizers, some flushed out of government, dominated the universities and made China scholarship and analysis "more often than not spectacularly wrong on the essentials."[24] For instance, one pro-China historian claimed that an estimate of one to two million deaths from the famine caused by Mao's Great Leap Forward was "extreme."[25] As the world later discovered, the true number of deaths—most from starvation or disease, though many were executed—might be as high as fifty-five million.[26]

The pro-Mao professoriate held that the "revolution was the best thing that ever happened to China," and it was America's fault for bad relations with the PRC. In sum, according to America's red consensus, Washington owed the Chinese Communist Party an apology.[27]

This was the mainstream intellectual current that the proudly anti-communist Richard Nixon and his aide entered as they prepared to win over communist China.

UNBALANCING POWER

Kissinger, too, went to China to convert the Chinese. As Nixon had written in his 1967 article, the key to diplomacy with China was to persuade them to understand their national interest. And even long after it became clear that Beijing kept its own counsel, Kissinger would continue to insist that the purpose of engaging the PRC was to liberalize and reform the party.

Kissinger was also, perhaps primarily, interested in the part China might play in his conception of the post-WWII world. The prospect of brokering relations with the Asian giant appealed to Kissinger's self-image as a visionary statesman. He wasn't a starry-eyed dreamer but a realist. Only he was clear-eyed enough to see through Cold War clichés and treat with a regime that Washington had cut off after the 1949 revolution.

He came to politics from Harvard University's Department of Government, where he studied grand strategy, a real-world version of international chess in which nations plot to achieve their long-term objectives and deter, or destroy, rivals. The discipline is best suited for regions like Europe or the Middle East, where small states or large clans find themselves surrounded by hostile and then more hostile powers. The United States hadn't needed a grand strategy before World War II. The Monroe Doctrine dictated American supremacy in its own hemisphere, where America's northern and southern neighbors are usually friendly and much weaker, and to our east and west are oceans.

But with victory in Europe and Asia, America became the dominant power in the Atlantic and Pacific while facing down a Soviet rival occupying a huge part of the Eurasian landmass. Even before Moscow tested its first bomb in 1949, American academics and statesmen began formulating plans for preventing the two nuclear-armed powers from an apocalyptic exchange. Most famous among the grand strategists was State Department official George Kennan, whose 1946 diplomatic cable, known as "the Long Telegram," outlined a policy of "containment" to box in the Soviets and stop the spread of communism without risking full-scale war.

For Kissinger, stability came from the balance of power, like the arrangement struck by European states that kept the peace on the continent after the Napoleonic Wars. The Congress of Vienna was convened in 1814-15 and gave rise to what's known as the Concert System—and this, the subject of Kissinger's dissertation, was his model of stability, a multipolar system in which all powers agreed to pursue their interests in moderation. He credited the Europeans for "inventing" the balance of power, which he regarded almost like a mystical concept.[28]

"The order established at the Congress of Vienna was the closest that Europe has come to universal governance since the collapse of Charlemagne's empire," he would write later. "It produced a consensus that peaceful evolutions within the existing order were preferable to alternatives; that the preservation of the system was more important than any single dispute that might arise within it; that differences should be settled by consultation rather than by war."[29]

Kissinger's interpretation gave the parties too much credit. With Austria, France, Prussia, Russia, and Great Britain vowing to respect each other's borders and spheres of influence, the Concert System expressed not comity but exhaustion and the inability to return to armed conflict. And even then, Europe's peace lasted only until 1853, when Russia contested with France and England in the Crimean War.

Still, Kissinger believed that the brief respite from war represented one of history's golden ages, when the civilized world was united under one order. So, he envisioned a modern-day Concert System as the foundation for a new order, and with the split between the two communist regimes threatening to turn hot, he and Nixon believed the time was right.

What's known as the Sino-Soviet split started as an ideological contest between China and the USSR that later threatened to go nuclear. After Stalin's death, his successors began to reevaluate the legacy of the man who was responsible for the deaths of millions of Soviets. At the Twentieth Communist Party Congress in 1956, Soviet leader Nikita Khrushchev delivered a long speech denouncing Stalin's cult of personality and the purges that marked his pathological regime. "The negative characteristics of Stalin, which, in Lenin's time, were only incipient, transformed themselves during the last years into a grave abuse of power by Stalin, which caused untold harm to our Party," said Khruschev. "He discarded the Leninist method of convincing and educating, he abandoned the method of ideological struggle for that of administrative violence, mass repressions and terror. He acted on an increasingly larger scale and more stubbornly through punitive organs, at the same time often violating all existing norms of morality and of Soviet laws."[30]

For Mao, this was heresy. He and Stalin had an uneasy relationship, and the two totalitarian regimes had held different visions of the communist project drawn from the character of their respective societies—for the Soviets, Marxism drew its power from the urban proletariat, while the Chinese believed that the peasantry represented the revolutionary vanguard. But publicly degrading one of the giants of the age was too far for Mao. And by exposing the

USSR's dirty laundry to the capitalist powers, Khruschev had made the entire communist project vulnerable. In defending Stalin, the CCP defended "the prestige of the international communist movement among working people throughout the world" and "the theory and practice of Marxism-Leninism."[31]

And thus, Mao laid claim to the revolutionary legacy of Stalin that the Soviets disavowed. Khruschev's expressed desire to steer Moscow toward accommodation and coexistence with the Western powers was belied by Soviet actions, like the deployment of nuclear missiles in Cuba, which nearly led to war with America in October 1962. But the CCP was proudly disruptive, inspiring and often supporting revolutionary movements throughout the world, and it seems the American side never fully considered the consequences of raising the more radical communist party to check the other.

Nixon and Kissinger found their opening when skirmishes on the Chinese-Soviet border took a serious turn in March 1969. Soviet diplomats asked their American counterparts how Washington would respond if the USSR waged a nuclear attack on Chinese nuclear facilities or other sites. The Americans were against it.

Kissinger would later write that "a Soviet attack on China could not be ignored by us. It would upset the global balance of power; it would create around the world an impression of approaching Soviet dominance."[32] It's not clear why Kissinger thought the United States should exert political and diplomatic capital to prevent a conflict likely crippling, or worse, two adversarial powers.

In fact, the Chinese were surprised the Americans didn't see the benefit in it. According to a memo Kissinger later sent Nixon: "Mao even went so far as to suggest that we might like to see the Russians bogged down in an attack on China; after wearing themselves out for a couple of years, we would then 'poke a finger' in Moscow's back. I rejoined that we believe that a war between the two

Communist giants was likely to be uncontrollable and have unfortu-
nate consequences for everyone. We therefore wished to prevent such
a conflict, not take advantage of it."[33]

Mao understood what it seems Kissinger did not: Setting your
enemies against each other to advance your own position is the
essence of power politics. The White House, however, resolved to
deter Moscow by leaking Soviet plans to US media and, Kissinger
wrote, "deploring reports of a Soviet plan to make a preemptive military strike against Communist China."[34]

As a result of Moscow's aggression, Beijing started putting out
feelers about thawing relations with the Americans.[35] Since Nixon
had campaigned on making diplomatic overtures to Beijing, the
Chinese knew the Americans were open to it.

With the Soviets cornering the Chinese, the White House was
starting off in a strong position. Even a casual assessment showed
that Washington held the much stronger position—China was
massive but impoverished and backward, and the American empire
spanned two oceans. Further, by hinting to Moscow it might retal-
iate if it dropped the bomb on China, the Nixon White House had
flexed its muscle. But the Americans squandered the advantage by
courting the Chinese like a starry-eyed lover.

In Poland, for instance, US diplomats were under Kissinger's
instructions "to approach Chinese diplomats at the next social function and express the desire for dialogue." When the US ambassador
and his aide saw two PRC diplomats at a fashion show in Warsaw,
the Chinese fled the studio and the Americans gave hopeful chase,
shouting after them, "President Nixon said he wanted to resume his
talk with Chinese."[36]

In the summer of 1971, Nixon did what he said in his 1967 article
American presidents shouldn't do, lest they "serve to confirm to its
rulers in their present course." In June, he ended the trade embargo

on the PRC.[37] And in August, the administration withdrew its objections to seating China at the United Nations, where it took a permanent seat at the Security Council alongside the United States, France, the United Kingdom, and the Soviet Union.

What the White House got in return for its munificence was a trip to Beijing. Worse, after all that chasing, the Americans had lost focus. The supposed goal had been to leverage China against Russia and thereby strengthen America's position. But as it turned out, Nixon and his aide were unclear about what they wanted except to engage China, with the hope that their diplomatic efforts would boost the reelection campaign. But the grand geopolitical maneuver for which the two are typically credited—strengthening China to weaken Russia and thereby advantage America—is more popular legend than reality, because neither the president nor his aide really understood what they meant when they talked about balance of power.[38]

Here's Nixon speaking with *Time* magazine a little more than a month before his 1972 trip: "I think it will be a safer world and a better world if we have a strong, healthy United States, Europe, Soviet Union, China, Japan, each balancing the other, not playing one against the other, an even balance."[39]

What did he mean? After all, the plan was supposedly to do just that and play the Soviets and China against one another. As Kissinger would tell Nixon a week before going to Beijing, "We have to play this balance of power game totally unemotionally. Right now, we need the Chinese to correct the Russians and to discipline the Russians."[40]

That's what "playing the China card" was supposed to mean—building up Beijing to keep Moscow in check. In this context, balance of power clearly means playing one side against the other.

But Kissinger himself was confused about what he meant, in part because he'd misread his own historical model. The purpose of the

Congress of Vienna was not to build an international order, as he and Nixon had envisioned with their own idea of a concert system including Moscow and Beijing. Rather, the European agreements formalized what had already been decided on the battlefields of Europe—the Continent had fought itself to a stalemate and no one wanted to fight again, at that particular moment.

Balance of power was not *invented*, as Kissinger claimed, by the Europeans or by anyone else; rather, it is a state of nature that manifests itself in political and military affairs whenever more or less equally matched powers decide against risking life, land, and legacy unless there is no other choice. A balance of power can also be imposed by one party setting its rivals against each other to enhance its own standing. Sometimes this was what Kissinger meant by balance of power, but when it came time to deal with the Chinese, he also meant submitting to a concert system that would check every power, including America's.

For instance, here the former Harvard professor writes that the balance of power is "an informal commitment by each to pursue its interests with restraint."[41] But balancing yourself means weakening yourself, which benefits your rivals. And no one willingly commits to restraint unless they mean to surrender.

Nixon and Kissinger's China policy is a rarity in the history of statecraft. For in the cold, clear math of geopolitics, by attempting to forge a balance of power arrangement including the country they represented as well as its Chinese and Soviet adversaries, they were hobbling America. In this context, balance of power meant surrender.

And that in a nutshell is the true basis of the US-China relationship: For half a century, Washington has been building up Beijing at the expense of American peace and prosperity. It's an unthinkable equation to anyone who loves their country—unless they are getting rich in the exchange. What started as a US strategic mistake of the first order became an American conspiracy of corruption, making the profiteers and their enablers traitors.

Nixon wasn't disloyal to his country, nor was Kissinger, not at that point. They imagined they were playing a Cold War version of grand strategy, but they'd missed the fundamental point about balance of power. Instead of leveraging China against the USSR to force them into a stalemate to the advantage of the United States, Nixon and Kissinger meant to *persuade* US rivals *by example* that seeking dominance in the nuclear age would upset the tenuous global order. The only path forward was for all to commit *to pursuing their interests with restraint.*

Kissinger's European finesse flattered his boss's self-image. But what informed their China policy wasn't steely-eyed nineteenth-century realism but the perspective on global affairs they'd inherited from the missionaries and their progeny. In their efforts to persuade foreigners of their own best interests, it was inevitable that Nixon and Kissinger, and countless US officials to follow, would lose sight of their own country's priorities and make their fellow Americans vulnerable to foreign nations that had their own ideas about how to run their own affairs.

In May 1971, Zhou sent word that he welcomed Kissinger to come to China to prepare the way for Nixon to meet with Mao for "direct conversations." Kissinger characterized it as the "most important communication that has come to an American president since the end of World War II."[42] And in retrospect that is clearly true, for the Americans had set themselves up for a defeat that would shape the course of the next half century.

KISSINGER'S REALISM

China needed things. To stay afloat, the communist regime needed money, weapons, and technology. After war with Japan, civil war, the revolution, Mao's glorious schemes, and the famines and purges that followed, China was virtually in ruins. And when Zhou reached out to Kissinger, the country was in the midst of another violent upheaval, the Cultural Revolution.

Launched in 1966, the Cultural Revolution was Mao's gambit to revitalize the Party's revolutionary fervor. Facing internal challenges to his power while contesting the Soviets—a spent force, in his opinion—for leadership of the communist movement, Mao unleashed fanatical militias comprising high school and college students known as the Red Guards. They destroyed artifacts and desecrated memorials of China's pre-communist past to illustrate that there was no history before the Party. Time began with Mao and the revolution.

The Red Guards hunted counterrevolutionaries—that is, intellectuals, former landowners, and religious leaders—and punished and imprisoned party officials who'd crossed Mao, including the father of the future paramount leader of China, Xi Jinping. As many as two million people were killed during the decade-long Cultural Revolution, ending only with Mao's death.[43] Zhou wanted to explain the Cultural Revolution to Kissinger during the secret trip. But the American envoy showed no interest. He believed it was an internal Chinese affair.[44]

Kissinger was disdainful of human rights. According to one biographer, he believed that "an emphasis on realism and national interests—even though it might seem callous in its execution—was not a rejection of moral values. Rather, he saw it as the best way to pursue the stable world order that he believed was the ultimate moral imperative, especially in a nuclear age." Men like him, "with true responsibility for peace, unlike those on the sidelines, cannot afford pure idealism. They must have the courage to deal with ambiguities and accommodations, to realize that great goals can be achieved only in imperfect steps."[45]

Nixon and Kissinger had tangible goals, like getting out of Vietnam. By backing Hanoi, Beijing had helped kill more than forty-seven thousand Americans by the time of Kissinger's trip. He might have told Zhou that the extent of future ties with the United States was conditioned on the PRC's stopping all military support for its Vietnamese partners. Instead, according to Kissinger aide Winston Lord, at "a maximum" the Americans hoped the Chinese would "slow down the provision of aid to North Vietnam somewhat."[46]

Still, Kissinger was keen to establish America's bona fides, so he gave the Chinese intelligence regarding Russian troop movements. If the opening was facilitated by China's fear of the Soviets, Kissinger's initial move had shown he would allay their anxieties for free. He violated what he would later come to regard as a guiding foreign policy principle: You never get paid for services already rendered.[47] Zhou pocketed the costly gift and gave his guest nothing in return. When it came time to discuss Vietnam, he urged Kissinger to withdraw troops immediately. North Vietnam was a CCP ally and Zhou had no mind to stop helping Hanoi kill Americans.[48]

Zhou wanted to talk about Taiwan. For the CCP, what it calls reunification is not only a vital interest but is also a means of redeeming history. The formal American position had long been that Taiwan's status was "undetermined," but Kissinger pledged the United States would not support an independent Taiwan.[49]

Kissinger was representing a superpower, not a satellite or a satrapy. There was no gun at his head, no coercion to synchronize his mission with his hosts' national priorities. And yet the US relationship with the CCP began with the American diplomat conceding everything, including American deaths in Vietnam, and getting nothing in return, except confirmation that the Chinese would receive the US president.

In light of Kissinger's performance, it is remarkable to read his assessment of the man who had wiped the floor with him. He was smitten with Zhou. "He spoke with an almost matter of fact clarity and eloquence," Kissinger wrote in his memo to Nixon about his meetings. "He was equally at home in philosophic sweeps, historical analysis, tactical probing, light repartee. His command of facts, and in particular his knowledge of American events, was remarkable." Zhou, wrote Kissinger, "ranks with DeGaulle as the most impressive foreign statesmen I have met."[50]

Kissinger wrote his boss that he and Zhou had "laid the ground-work for you and Mao to turn a page in history." Kissinger cautioned that the Chinese "will prove implacable foes if our relations turn sour. My assessment of these people is that they are deeply ideological, close to fanatic in the intensity of their beliefs." Dealing with them, wrote Kissinger, "will require reliability, precision, and finesse."[51]

It was a strange way to counsel treating with a ruling cadre known for its epic brutality. Washington's status as leader of the free world was earned by its victory over the Nazis in World War II and the Cold War struggle against communism. Its reputation as defender of Western Civilization was owing to the courage and resources it mustered to fight truly evil forces. By going to China, Nixon was legitimizing the twentieth century's most murderous dictatorship.

MEETING MAO

It wasn't certain that Mao would see Nixon. The seventy-nine-year-old chairman of the Chinese Communist Party had a bad heart and had just been hospitalized with pneumonia. But he'd had a new suit and shoes made especially for the occasion, so shortly after the

American delegation touched down February 21, 1972, Mao summoned the American president. Nixon alerted Kissinger, and Zhou picked them up in a black Chinese car and took them to Mao's compound.[52]

The aging Mao met them with a female aide and moved them into his study where they sat in a semicircle. The four men exchanged pleasantries through translators. The Americans were eager to ingratiate themselves with the living leader of the largest cult of personality in modern times.

"I have read the Chairman's poems and speeches, and I know he was a professional philosopher," said Nixon.[53]

"I used to assign the Chairman's collective writings to my classes at Harvard," said Kissinger. It was as if the Americans were bidding for Mao's favor. Nixon raised. "The Chairman's writings moved a nation and have changed the world," said the president.

The Chairman and the president joked about Kissinger's penchant for secrecy.

"He doesn't look like a secret agent," Nixon said of his foreign policy advisor. "He is the only man in captivity who could go to Paris twelve times and Peking once and no one knew it, except possibly a couple of pretty girls."

Zhou laughed to hear American locker-room talk.

"They didn't know it," said Kissinger. "I used it as a cover."

"Anyone who uses pretty girls as a cover must be the greatest diplomat of all time," said Nixon.

Kissinger had already acquired a reputation as a ladies' man. "Power," he famously said, "is the ultimate aphrodisiac." Even feminists loved him. "Henry's the only interesting person in the whole Nixon Administration," said feminist pioneer Gloria Steinem. "If this were the Kennedy Administration nobody would pay attention to him."[54]

Mao wanted to know more about the women. "So your girls are very often made use of?" he asked.

"His girls, not mine," Nixon replied. "It would get me into great trouble if I used girls as a cover."

The American president and his advisor spoke coarsely, like salesmen trying impress a yet more vulgar client. The Chairman liked hearing the leader of the free world talk about girls. He also wanted to avoid substantive issues, like Taiwan, Vietnam, and the Soviet Union.

"Those questions are not questions to be discussed in my place," said Mao. "They should be discussed with the premier. I discuss the philosophical questions."

He told Nixon he'd pulled for him to win the 1968 election. "I like rightists," said Mao. "People say you are rightists, that the Republican Party is to the right."

Nixon said, "I think the important thing to note is that in America, at least at this time, those on the right can do what those on the left talk about."

Nixon was referring to the idea that only a man with the credentials he had as a hard-line anti-communist could get away with visiting communist China. And a phrase to capture the historic event would soon enter the political lexicon—"Nixon to China." But drawing on reputational capital to cross expectations is a time-tested political tactic to boost approval ratings with new constituencies. Nixon and Kissinger wanted the acclaim of the liberal establishment the president said he despised, approval that his aide openly sought.

Nixon tried to get Mao to discuss Taiwan and Vietnam again, as well as Japan, but Mao wouldn't have it. "All those troublesome problems I don't want to get into very much," the Chairman said. "I think your topic is better—philosophic questions."

Zhou complained about Dulles. Nixon pointed to Kissinger

and told Mao, "But they shook hands." Zhou liked this topic. He laughed again.

Mao was getting tired. He turned to Kissinger and asked him if he had anything more to say.

"We've had to learn a great deal," said Kissinger. "We thought all socialist-communist states were the same phenomenon. We didn't understand until the president came into office the different nature of revolution in China and the way revolution had developed in other socialist states."

Here Kissinger tacitly acknowledged not only the split dividing the Chinese and the Soviets, but the still-vital revolutionary élan that distinguished the former, whose pathological revision of society led to the deaths of millions. With their visit, the Americans signaled that they were eager to help the more radical of the two parties. After all, surely Kissinger understood that his hosts were playing the "America card" to leverage US power against the Soviets.

Mao turned to Zhou to check the time, but Nixon wasn't yet finished.

"Having read some of the Chairman's statements, I know he is one who sees when an opportunity comes, that you must seize the hour and seize the day," said Nixon. "The Chairman's life is well-known to all of us. He came from a very poor family to the top of the most populous nation in the world, a great nation. My background is not so well-known. I also came from a very poor family, and to the top of a very great nation. History has brought us together. The question is whether we, with different philosophies, but both with feet on the ground, and having come from the people, can make a breakthrough that will serve not just China and America, but the whole world in the years ahead. And that is why we are here."

Mao said he wasn't well. Nixon said that he looked good. Mao said that appearances were deceiving. But that's not true: No one is deceived against their will. The US officials wanted to believe, so they did. And they made the country they represented complicit in the CCP's effort to launder the reputation of a communist tyrant who'd killed Americans so that he came out looking like a statesman.

The interview was over. The men shook hands, took pictures, and Zhou led the Americans out of the residence and into history.

At least that's the standard account of Nixon's trip to China, that in the early winter of 1972 he and Kissinger and their Chinese inter-locutors had begun to write a new chapter in the chronicle of world affairs. But the evidence shows that the leader of the free world and his top foreign policy aide had traveled across the world to abase themselves before an aging tyrant.

Nixon's notes show that he had come to China prepared to aban-don Taiwan in exchange for help getting Americans out of Vietnam. In preparation for the trip, he ordered the Seventh Fleet out of the Taiwan Strait and the gradual withdrawal of US forces from Taiwan, where they had been stationed pursuant to the 1954 US-Taiwan Mutual Defense Treaty.[55]

But Zhou told Nixon what he'd told Kissinger: Beijing supported North Vietnam and would not be drawn into negotiations between Hanoi and Washington. Further, said Zhou, "if the war in Vietnam and the other two countries of Indochina does not stop...we will be forced to continue aid to their just struggles. We have only an obli-gation to sympathize with them and support them."[56]

In other words, Beijing was in fact negotiating the US withdrawal on Hanoi's behalf and under terms unfavorable to Washington: So long as American troops were on the ground in Vietnam, Cambodia, and Laos, the Chinese would help kill them. Rather than punish, or even pressure, China, Nixon paid them in US prestige and policy.

The Americans gave Mao and Zhou what they wanted and pledged that Washington would not support Taiwanese independence. This paved the way for the 1972 Shanghai Communiqué, what some scholars call "the original sin of U.S.-China relations."[57] According to Beijing's one-China "principle," Taiwan is part of China and will eventually be absorbed by it through peaceful or nonpeaceful means. Nixon withdrew some troops from Taiwan, but to his credit he did not accept PRC demands that the US end support for Taiwan. The United States formally acknowledged that "all Chinese on either side of the Taiwan Strait maintain there is but one China and that Taiwan is a part of China" and that the "United States Government does not challenge that position," and that it "reaffirms its interest in a peaceful settlement of the Taiwan question by the Chinese themselves."

The US press and foreign policy establishment celebrated "Nixon to China," but CCP leadership must have seen the president and Kissinger as desperate. Why travel so far to fail, unless the plan was to show deference to China?

But that was not how Nixon and his counselor understood it. "We have progressed farther and faster than anyone would have predicted, or the rest of the world realizes," Kissinger wrote Nixon after the trip. "For, in plain terms, we have now become tacit allies."[58]

That was a fantasy.

The Americans had misunderstood, or ignored, the character of communist China. They'd turned a blind eye to the Cultural Revolution and the serial campaign of mass murder that had led to it. China was impoverished because Mao's policies had ravaged the country, leaving tens of millions dead, including the so-called counterrevolutionaries—landowners and academics, among others—who knew how to make things work.

Mao's terror should have sent a clear sign to Nixon and Kissinger that their confidence in the new friendship they'd forged was foolhardy. How regimes treat their own people gives invaluably unambiguous information about how they will treat arrangements with foreigners. If Beijing was willing to murder its own people by the millions, there was little chance that cordial ties with such a regime would advance US interests. Nixon and Kissinger had not begun to induce change in China. Instead, they'd made America vulnerable to an ideological regime responsible for more deaths in modern times than Hitler and Stalin combined.

The opening to China is also the origin of globalism, nominally an order of international cooperation and relatively peaceful coexistence in which, like Kissinger's version of the Concert System, all are invited to satisfy their appetites, in moderation. At least that's the American perspective—the CCP never subscribed to Kissinger's ahistorical and denatured version of the balance of power. And as American elites further strengthened China, the prospect of Beijing volunteering to restrain itself became increasingly absurd, while Washington's ability to check the rival it had raised became ever more limited.

CHAPTER THREE

Maoist Chic

I admire the stand of China and the stand of Mao Zedong.[1]
—Malcolm X

RICHARD NIXON AND HENRY KISSINGER WERE RIDING A MASSIVE youth wave as Chinese Communism fueled the revolutionary ambitions of rising elites around the world. It was the golden age of global Maoism.

In France, Mao's permanent revolution was part of the Marxist mélange driving the May 1968 student protests purposed to revise French society. In Peru, Maoists dominated university faculty and student organizations and radicalized the country's indigenous population, seeding the Shining Path, a Maoist terror organization led by university professor Abimael Guzmán.[2] And Mao's forces were directly engaged in South Africa where the PLA trained anti-government militias, like the Azanian People's Liberation Army and the armed wing of Nelson Mandela's African National Congress.[3]

It's not surprising these societies were vulnerable to the millenarian promises of a pathological regime. With the French still processing guilt for having been conquered by and then collaborating with the Nazis, maybe Parisian youth had good reason for wanting to topple the idols of their parents' republic. Peru, like China itself, was a poor and miserable third world nation, and South African blacks were openly at war against the apartheid government.

But America? The United States was leader of the free world and the richest country in history, and yet Maoism nonetheless found fertile soil. The middle class was still decisively anti-communist, thanks in no small part to Henry Luce's publications, but the reaction to McCarthy had pushed the liberal consensus on China much further to the left. On campus, the Chairman was the cool alternative to the Soviet gerontocracy, appealing only to American radicals a generation or two older, chalky academics with pipes, patched tweeds, and sepia-tinted memories of John Reed. And for the middle-aged courtiers of the New York salon set, Mao was a foreign flavor that flattered their vanity by setting them apart from *Time* subscribers.[4]

The larger context of course was the war in Vietnam, political violence, and the civil rights movement. If the establishment had gotten all that wrong, and the best of the generation, JFK, RFK, and MLK Jr., had been gunned down in public, the experts were almost certainly wrong about China, too. And even if they were right that communism threatened the American way of life, didn't America deserve what it had coming after all the sins it had committed at home and abroad?

It was only fitting that the coup de grâce was destined to come from what African-American activists were describing as the leader of the nonwhite world—the Chinese Communist Party. And thus it was race—or more specifically white guilt—that gave Beijing an entry point into American society and culture. And in this moral climate, driven by a generation swamped in a lacerating orgy of self-pity and resentment, only the slightest push was required from Nixon and Kissinger to open China politically.

Starting in the mid-twentieth century, elite American cultural style became the terminal point of tastes and fashions transiting through white counterculture from their origin point in the African-American community. Today's elite aesthetic, from music and dance to marijuana and street fashion, would be unrecognizable without its source in black culture. Mao was hip thanks to African-American activists, especially the Black Panthers, the revolutionary darlings of the bicoastal elite.

After Kissinger's July 1971 trip, the Chinese invited Black Panthers founder, and its "Minister of Defense," Huey Newton, for a visit. His conviction on charges of voluntary manslaughter in the 1967 shooting death of an Oakland, California, policeman had been reversed, and after two retrials ended in hung juries, Newton was a free man. When he learned that Nixon was scheduled to go to China in February 1972, he was determined to get to Beijing before him.

Newton arrived in China in September 1971 with a delegation of other Black Panthers. The American media implored Nixon to pay it no mind. *The New York Times* wrote of Newton's trip: "The President's estimate—which we share—of the importance of his Peking visit is implied by the evident White House determination to think positively about Communist China and to ignore such potential sources of friction as the honors shown to Black Panther leader Huey Newton during his surprise Peking visit."[5]

Mao's regime had honored the White House's request not to host political rivals before Nixon's trip. But inviting the head of a group that preached armed insurrection against the US government was a provocation and a test, probing for American weakness. Where would the Americans draw a line to protect their honor? Nixon and Kissinger blinked.

Newton was welcomed with all the public fanfare due a revolutionary who'd struck deep in the heart of the imperialist enemy. He'd killed a cop and got away with it. When Zhou greeted him in Beijing, according to one saccharine account of their meeting, "Newton took Zhou's right hand between both his own hands. Zhou clasped Newton's wrist with his left hand, and the two men looked deeply into each other's eyes."[6]

For some, the ostensible coordination of black and CCP interests represented a joint front against imperialism. "It was practical for China's internationalist strategy to espouse deeply sensitive readings of racism in world affairs and history while advocating non-racial solutions," wrote one leftist scholar. "Black nationalism would be refashioned into a weapon of international class struggle."[7]

In plain language, Beijing believed that African-American activists were useful pawns in their war on America. In turn, black radicals saw the Maoists as their strategic depth, or foreign muscle. One 1960s radical, for instance, believed that the PRC's nuclear bomb was also "the Afro-American's bomb, because the Chinese people are blood brothers to the Afro-American and all those who fight against racism and imperialism."[8]

From one perspective, it seems that both sides had been overly optimistic in their assessments of each other's capabilities. After all, the United States still stands, never having devolved into the race war Mao had plotted.

However, even today the PRC exerts influence on domestic US politics through its rhetorical support—and, in some cases, financial backing—for minority causes. In the spring and summer of 2020, for instance, Beijing used the George Floyd riots as a platform to wage political warfare against the US government. Chinese officials and CCP social media influencers posted BLM slogans, like "I can't breathe," purportedly the last words spoken by George Floyd, who had heart issues and high levels of fentanyl in his system when he died.[9] With activists and the media framing the ex-convict's death as an instance of antiblack police brutality, Beijing saw it as an opportunity to pay back the Donald Trump administration for publicly criticizing its crackdown on Hong Kong's anti-Beijing activists.

Just days before Floyd's death, Secretary of State Mike Pompeo had condemned the Hong Kong national security law, which grants PRC authorities broad powers over Hong Kong and significantly curtails the city's autonomy, freedoms, and judicial independence promised under the principle of "one country, two systems."[10] Pompeo warned that it would be a "death knell" for Hong Kong's autonomy.[11] One PRC media outfit sarcastically called on the secretary of state to "stand with the angry people of Minneapolis, just like you did with people of Hong Kong."[12]

"Black lives matter, and their human rights should be guaranteed," said a spokesman from the PRC's Foreign Ministry.[13] Floyd's death reflected "the severity of racism and police violence in the US and the urgency to solve those problems," Another foreign ministry official tweeted, "I can't breathe."[14]

The pro-BLM messaging campaign was a familiar CCP tactic, part of its long-standing propaganda efforts to drive Americans against each other.

BURN, BABY, BURN

By the time of Kissinger's secret trip, there was a groundswell of support from almost every part of the US political spectrum—except from middle-class Americans white and black—who supported some sort of diplomatic engagement with communist China.

Interest in Mao and China had become a social marker signaling worldly sophistication that distinguished the coastal smart set from what they considered the ignorant and, in their estimation, racist, middle-class heartland. Andy Warhol, the tutelary genius of the downtown New York art world, was inspired by the cult leader. "I have been reading so much about China," he told a friend. "They're so nutty. They don't believe in creativity. The only picture they ever have is of Mao Zedong. It's great. It looks like a silkscreen."[15]

Warhol had read in *Time* magazine that Mao was the most famous person in the world, and his art dealer suggested he take him as a subject. After Nixon announced his trip to China, Warhol began painting Mao portraits, based on the image on the cover of his copy of *The Quotations of Chairman Mao*. Between 1972 and 1973, Warhol produced 199 *Mao* paintings in five series, as well as a series of ten screen-prints. For Warhol it was never about politics. "Since fashion is art now and Chinese is in fashion," he said of his *Mao* series, "I could make a lot of money."[16] Warhol made Mao capitalist iconography.

Of course, the Chinese didn't see it that way. As Kissinger told an art critic, "Mao is not an object to the Chinese people. He is a living Emperor. The Chinese care not that he murdered 75 million."[17] It's doubtful that the Chinese turned a blind eye to Mao's depredations—Kissinger was likely rationalizing the unpalatable truth that he and Nixon had legitimized the CCP, thereby joining causes with a movement led by black revolutionaries like Newton who made Mao chic.

"Radical Chic" was the title of Tom Wolfe's 1970 account of a much talked-about party at the home of Leonard Bernstein to raise money for the Black Panthers. The world-famous composer and conductor had invited the cream of elite Manhattan society, film-makers, Broadway directors, celebrity journalists, artists, actors, and heiresses to his Park Avenue apartment to be hustled by a street gang that printed and sold copies of *Quotations from Chairman Mao* to buy guns.[18] With "Radical Chic," Wolfe documented an early manifestation of what Chinese intellectuals would come to call *bai-zuo*, a derogatory term used to describe the guilt and self-pity of Western white liberals.

The Panthers, wrote Wolfe, assembled in the dining room "facing the whites in the living room. As a result, whenever anyone got up in the living room to speak, the audience was looking not only at the speaker but into the faces of a hard front line of Black Panthers in the dining room. Quite a tableau it was. It was at this point that a Park Avenue matron first articulated the great recurrent emotion of Radical Chic: 'These are no civil-rights Negroes wearing gray suits three sizes too big—these are real men!'"[19]

The Black Panthers were unabashedly Maoist. Huey Newton claimed that he'd immersed himself in the writings of the Chinese revolutionaries before he founded the movement. "My transformation was complete," he wrote, "when I read the four-volume *Selected Works of Mao Tse-tung* and learned more about the Chinese Revolution."[20]

Before Newton had taken Mao as his model, the Panthers were black nationalists who promoted self-sufficiency and self-defense, the pillars of black separatism. But with Newton's metamorphosis, the Panthers ditched sectarianism for the international class struggle by grafting themselves onto Maoist Third Worldism.

For Newton and his gang, Mao's revolution was different because it was colored. It wasn't like the liberal democracy of the first world, led by the United States and its allies, and the second world, comprising the Soviet Union and the Eastern bloc. Both these political forms were the products of European civilization. But unlike Marx, Engels, and Lenin, the fathers of communism, Mao wasn't white and he wasn't European. With Mao, wrote Black Panther ideologue Eldridge Cleaver, "something new was interjected into Marxism-Leninism and it ceased to be just a narrow, exclusively

European phenomenon."[21] "The Black Panther Party grew out of the Black Power movement," Newton wrote in his autobiography. "But this party transformed the ideology of Black Power into a socialist ideology...we have become not nationalists, like the Black Power movement in the past, but internationalists."[22]

The Panthers marketed themselves as part of a larger enterprise encompassing all the most wretched of the earth, from Oakland to Beijing, and Hanoi to Havana, all those cursed and oppressed by the imperialists. Finally black radicals had a center of gravity— a real state that had undergone a real revolution to which they could attach their own hopes and initiatives, and from which they hoped for political support and maybe other forms of aid, too.

The Panthers' emulation of the CCP extended even to arcane guidelines, like the "Eight Points of Attention, Three Main Rules of Discipline," essentially a guide to good manners written for Chinese peasants, which the Panthers adopted. Mao was not a philosopher. There was no intellectual content for the Panthers, or anyone, to absorb. He was a militant whose literary genius resided only in his ability to devise slogans simple enough to motivate millions to kill and die. But for criminals like Newton, revolutionary discipline rationalized their predatory violence.

Newton wasn't at the Bernsteins' party, but his comrades repeatedly cited his ten-point manifesto. "As our Minister of Defense, Huey P. Newton, says, 'Any unarmed people are slaves, or are slaves in the real meaning of the word'...We recognize that this country is the most oppressive country in the world, maybe in the history of the world. The pigs have the weapons and they are ready to use them on the people, and we recognize this as being very bad. They are ready to commit genocide against those who stand up against them, and we recognize this as being very bad."[23]

Newton and the Black Panthers connected white elites to the

larger trend in minority communities where Mao had become a major presence. "In Harlem in the late 1960s and early 1970s, it seemed as though everyone had a copy of...the 'little red book,'" wrote historians Robin D. G. Kelley and Betsy Esch, referring to *Quotations from Chairman Mao Tse-Tung.* "And it was not unheard of to see some young black radical strolling down the street dressed like a Chinese peasant—except for the Afro and sunglasses, of course."[24]

A Puerto Rican gang that originated in Chicago, the Young Lords, was allied with the Panthers and wrote their own ten-point manifesto. The Young Lords' NYC chapter made Mao's "little red book" mandatory reading for anyone who sought help kicking heroin in their drug treatment clinics.[25] And a group of young Bay Area Chinese-Americans adopted the language and style of the Black Panthers and named themselves the Red Guards after the cadres who'd murdered scores of Chinese to sanctify Mao's Cultural Revolution.[26]

But it was primarily African-American radicals who were attracted to Maoism, like Ron Karenga, the inventor of Kwanzaa. Despite the fact he led his own militia group in armed combat against the Black Panthers, he shared with them an affinity for the CCP. Malcolm X also looked up to Mao. "They used to have a saying that one doesn't have a Chinaman's chance," Malcolm said in 1964. "But they don't say that anymore. They used that expression back when China was weak. But now that Mao Zedong has been successful in making China a strong country, the Chinese have more chance than anybody else."[27]

By any means necessary was Malcolm's shorthand for a violent insurrection to topple the white power structure, a race war prophesied by numerous activists, white and black, including Newton's colleague, Cleaver. "In order to transform the American social order, we have to destroy the present structure of power in the United States, we have to overthrow the government...we say we will do this by any means necessary...and the only means possible is the violent overthrow of the oppressive ruling class." America, said Cleaver, "will be painted red. Dead bodies will litter the street."

Black radicals were talking specifically about killing people like the Bernsteins' guests, but that was not how the ruling class saw it. They believed that they shared an antagonist with the men in Che berets and dark shades—the white middle class or, in their view, the squares who voted for Nixon. They loathed the president and he hated them back, even as Kissinger wanted to woo them—these were the elites, after all.

Radical chic, Wolfe explained, was one of their "ways of certifying their superiority over the hated 'middle class.'"[28] They weren't just acting out their race guilt or buying indulgences from the revolutionary caste; they saw black militants as an instrument in their war against the Americans they held responsible for all the sins America had committed against the world, like Vietnam—or imperialism as Mao and the Black Panthers had it.

At the Bernsteins', wrote Wolfe, "the emotional momentum was building rapidly when Ray 'Masai' Hewitt, the Panthers' Minister of Education and member of the Central Committee, rose to speak." Wolfe continued:

Some of you here, he said, may have some feelings left for the Establishment, but we don't. We want to see it die. We're Maoist revolutionaries, and we have no choice but to fight to the finish. For about thirty minutes Masai Hewitt laid it on the line. He referred now and again to "that motherfucker Nixon" and to how the struggle would not be easy, and that if buildings were burned and other violence ensued, that was only part of the struggle that the power structure had forced the oppressed minorities

*into. Hewitt's words tended to provoke an all-or-nothing reaction.
A few who remembered the struggles of the Depression were profoundly moved, fired up with a kind of nostalgie de that old-time
religion. But more than one Park Avenue matron was thrown into
a Radical Chic confusion. The most memorable quote was: "He's a
magnificent man, but suppose some simple-minded schmucks take
all that business about burning down buildings seriously?"*[29]

With news of the Radical Chic soiree filling the society pages of
the New York press, the Nixon White House's advisor for urban
affairs, Daniel Patrick Moynihan, wrote the president that the
Black Panthers had become "culture heroes." Moynihan, later the
US ambassador to India and then US senator from New York, suggested that Nixon ignore the "provocations from groups such as the
Black Panthers."[30] Instead, the American president bestowed a kind
of legitimacy on their destructive project by making a pilgrimage to
their source of oracular wisdom.

MAO LIKE ME

The CCP's "endeavor to cultivate political alliance with the African
American left [has been] meticulous, targeted, and effective," one
researcher wrote about the relationship that each side used in its
conflict with America.[31] Black activists saw Mao's revolution as an
inspiration and hoped for support. For the Chinese, there were several
reasons to foster friendly relations with African-American activists:
to establish primacy over their Soviet rival; to obscure the regime's
own racial, or ethnic, fissures; and to exploit an American fault line
to foment violence and destabilize the capitalist juggernaut—or as
one African-American who was formerly a communist activist put
it, "to use the Negroes as the spearhead, or as expendables."[32]

But at first, the Chinese saw black intellectuals and activists as an instrument to break out of the isolation imposed by the United States after the revolution.[33] W. E. B. Du Bois, one of the twentieth century's most prominent African-American intellectuals, was among the first to visit postrevolutionary China.

Author of *The Souls of Black Folk*, the classic 1903 collection of essays and sketches, and cofounder of the National Association for the Advancement of Colored People (NAACP), Du Bois was a pan-Africanist committed to strengthening bonds between Africans who still lived on the continent and their cousins who had been sold into slavery. He'd been to China once before the revolution and traveled there again after, including a 1959 visit to celebrate his ninety-first birthday and give witness to the struggle for global justice.

Mao received him at his villa in Wuhan, and Zhou met him in Beijing.[34] Du Bois gave a lecture to more than a thousand university students, after which Zhou threw him a private birthday party.[35] Du Bois was impressed. He relayed the good news to his pan-African audience. "Come to China, Africa, and look around," he declared in a Beijing radio broadcast. "You know America and France and Britain to your sorrow. Now know the Soviet Union and its allied nations, but particularly know China. China is flesh of your flesh and blood of your blood. China is colored, and knows to what the colored skin in this modern world subjects its owner."[36]

This kind of description of revolutionary China would become boilerplate for African-American activists. They elided the particularity of Chinese civilization and instead categorized it simply as non-European, non-white. In that light, the revolution was a triumph for all non-white people: After centuries of subjugation, Mao had lifted the yoke of Western oppression and now the Chinese steered their own course.

Of course, the CCP encouraged blacks to see the revolution as a useful model, in part by recasting its domestic and foreign policies in the language, history, and symbolism of the African-American struggle. For Du Bois, his hosts had endured even more than blacks and for far longer. "As I read Chinese history in these last months and had it explained to me stripped of Anglo-Saxon lies, I know that no depths of Negro slavery in America have plumbed such abysses as the Chinese have seen for 2,000 years and more." The oppression "came not only from Tartars, Mongolians, British, French, Germans and Americans, but from the Chinese themselves: Mandarins and warlords, capitalists and murdering thieves like Chiang Kai-shek; Kuomintang socialists and intellectuals educated abroad."[37]

That was wholly CCP propaganda. The fact is that Du Bois knew nothing about Chinese history except what he was told by Party officials and minders. He can be excused for failing to comment on the massive famine brought about by Mao's collectivization plan, the Great Leap Forward, during his first trip. His biographer reasoned that like every prominent visitor to Mao's China, he was shepherded around in "ceremonial cocoons" and "knew absolutely nothing of the catastrophe inflicted upon the Chinese people by their omnipotent ruler."[38]

But he visited again in 1961, which gave him several years to learn how Mao's appropriation of land and crops to finance industrialization had starved tens of millions of Chinese to death. And thus, one of America's leading intellectuals took his place in the front of the long line of Americans, white and black, who lied about China and the threat it posed to the world.

After Du Bois's death in 1961, the CCP sought other African-American activists to advocate on its behalf and discovered Robert Williams, perhaps the most significant of the black radicals who swooned over Mao. Formerly the head of the Monroe, North

Carolina, chapter of the NAACP, Williams was an advocate of African-American armed defense, and wrote a book about it, *Negroes with Guns*. He fled the United States for Cuba in 1961 after he was charged with kidnapping a white couple during an armed confrontation with the Ku Klux Klan.[39]

It's hardly surprising that Mao, whose most famous slogan was "Power comes from the barrel of a gun," appealed to black activists accustomed to whites owning the monopoly of violence and using it against them, their families, and communities. But many were blinded to the fact that the regime they esteemed was also predatory. Others, however, cherished Mao's violence.

Williams's official contacts with the CCP began in the spring of 1963 when he wrote Mao and asked him to say something in advance of an upcoming African-American demonstration in Washington, DC, scheduled for August. This would become the famous March on Washington led by Martin Luther King Jr., whose nonviolent tactics were anathema to Williams.[40] Here Mao saw an opportunity to gain a step on the PRC's Soviet rival by burnishing his bona fides as the authentic standard-bearer of revolution, and also sow division inside America.

Given King's stature today, it seems strange that nowhere in Mao's open letter, "Statement Supporting the American Negroes in Their Just Struggle Against Racial Discrimination by U.S. Imperialism," does he mention King, one of the main leaders of the civil rights movement. Instead, Mao mirrored radical left US criticism of the White House and gave it further weight with the authority of an external revolutionary power.

The fascist atrocities of the U.S. imperialists against the Negro people have exposed the true nature of so-called American democracy and freedom and revealed the inner link between the reactionary policies pursued by the U.S. Government at home and its policies of aggression abroad.[41]

It was a broadside attacking US society and targeting specific American leadership.

The Kennedy Administration is insidiously using dual tactics. On the one hand, it continues to connive at and take part in discrimination against Negroes and their persecution, and it even sends troops to suppress them. On the other hand, in the attempt to numb the fighting will of the Negro people and deceive the masses of the country, the Kennedy Administration is parading as an advocate of "the defense of human rights" and "the protection of the civil rights of Negroes," calling upon the Negro people to exercise "restraint" and proposing the "civil rights legislation" to Congress. But more and more Negroes are seeing through these tactics of the Kennedy Administration.

By seeking to further divide the US along racial lines, Mao had shifted the focus of Beijing's interaction with African-American activists—the CCP was now actively seeking to use blacks to destabilize America with the goal of collapsing the imperialist enemy.

For Williams, Mao's statement was as significant as Abraham Lincoln's Emancipation Proclamation.[42] The Chinese invited him to visit in 1963 and 1964. Inspired by Mao, Williams amplified his disagreements with King's nonviolent tactics. In a 1964 article he called for a guerilla action, with "lightning campaigns conducted in highly sensitive urban communities with the paralysis reaching the small communities and spreading to the farm areas." There were other tactical measures he recommended: "During the hours of the day sporadic rioting takes place and massive sniping. Night brings all-out warfare, organized fighting and unlimited terror against the oppressor and his forces."[43]

In 1966 Williams and his wife decided to make China their home. On China National Day, commemorating Mao's October 1, 1949, proclamation of the People's Republic, Williams delivered a speech with the Chairman standing by his side. He praised the PRC's "great architect, liberator, helmsman, and universal leader and teacher, whose thought is transforming the whole world." According to Williams, it was Mao's "great thought . . . that lifted a starving, dehumanized China from the misery and mire of the dark ages to the benefits of the [twentieth] century in [seventeen] short years." Williams believed that the Cultural Revolution was "the greatest event in the history of mankind . . . A mass movement of the people, for the people and by the people determined to enhance and consolidate people's power."[44]

RACIST CHINA

Williams was inspired by what he described as a society free of racism and unified by the craving for universal social justice. Traveling Inner Mongolia, he was moved when students and workers sang to him in the streets. And at the National Minorities Institute in Beijing, according to one historian, "he asked to be photographed with sacred Tibetan texts as testament that the Chinese way would continue to tolerate, if not honor, religious traditions."[45]

That was untrue. "When Mao said he wanted to unite the people of China's various nationalities, what he meant was that he wanted to eliminate the identity of minority communities," Tibetologist and Indologist Maura Moynihan tells me. "He said that he was going to make China's minorities reincarnate as Red and expert Chinese citizens."[46]

By "Chinese," explains Moynihan, the CCP means Han, China's

ethnic majority. They make up 91 percent of the country and nearly 18 percent of the world's population with large communities in Taiwan, Hong Kong, and Macau, as well as Singapore, Malaysia, Indonesia, Thailand, Vietnam, and outside Asia in Canada, Australia, Europe, as well as the United States. The Party preaches national unity joining together the fifty-six officially recognized ethnic groups, but in practice Han identity dominates politically and culturally. From the Party's perspective, the Han majority drives modernization with a responsibility to drag ethnic minorities out of their past, rid them of their "backward" traditions and superstitions—that is, religion—and make them serve the Party's goals.

Resettling large Han populations in minority regions like Buddhist Tibet and Xinjiang, home of China's Uyghur minority, is a social and economic policy to dominate the minorities, as well as a security measure designed to keep in check potentially rebellious minority populations that resent being melded down to forge a stronger China.

The PRC's minority populations are one of the Party's most obvious vulnerabilities. Indeed, the CIA supported anti-PRC operations in Tibet, including clandestine programs, for nearly two decades after China annexed Tibet in 1951. The operations ended only when Nixon called them off before his 1972 trip to Beijing. Despite the difficulties in assimilating millions of people who don't want to lose their identity, or traditions, taking Tibet and Xianjing shored up China's western border by incorporating buffer zones separating the country from the other Asian giant, India.

Maura Moynihan lived in India for several years in her teens when Nixon named her father, Daniel Patrick Moynihan, ambassador in 1973. "I arrived in India at fifteen and was the new kid in class," she says. "And for the first time I met Tibetan refugees. They were scholarship students in my school."

This was when she began her advocacy on behalf of Tibetan independence. "But for seven decades the CCP has used Tibet as a torture lab and concentration camp. We know that about Xianjing because of cotton production there that's used by Western apparel manufacturing, so we were able to get more information about the camps. But it's much harder to get information out of Tibet." And it's because of that relative silence, she explains, that "Tibet is the best lens to observe how the CCP controls the narrative relayed to western elites—namely that China treats its minorities well."

Tibet is a sensitive issue for cultural and historical reasons as well. "At one time Tibet and China had a priest-patron relationship, dating back to Kublai Khan," says Moynihan. Starting in the thirteenth century, "Chinese rulers cultivated relations with Tibetan Buddhist leaders, especially the Dalai Lama, who acted as their religious teachers and spiritual guides and conferred their legitimacy on them."

In exchange for the Buddhist stamp of approval, the Chinese gave the Tibetans military and political support. But after the CCP took over, neither Mao nor any other communist leader had reason to petition the Buddhists for their blessings. Indeed, during a 1954 meeting in Beijing, Mao told the Dalai Lama that religion "has two great defects: It undermines the race, and secondly it retards the progress of the country." And Tibet, according to Mao, had "been poisoned by" religion.[47]

Mao's open contempt for Tibet and its world-famous spiritual tuition, along with the devastation his collectivization programs brought to the region, convinced the Dalai Lama that there was no chance of peaceful coexistence with the PRC. In 1959 Mao arranged to have him killed, but the Dalai Lama fled to India, where he denounced Mao and called for Tibetan independence.

Moynihan recalls a class trip to Kullu Valley on the India-China border. "I saw how militarized it was with PLA soldiers on one side

and Indian soldiers on the other and tons of Tibetan refugees building the Kangra highway. And I thought, Why doesn't the world
know about this, how the Tibetans are enslaved by the CCP?"

It's because Tibet is one of the most heavily monitored regions
in the world. "There's pervasive police presence and digital surveillance," says Moynihan. "Monasteries are closely watched, and
monks have to pledge loyalty to the Party. References to the Dalai
Lama are censored, and it's a crime to be caught with an image of
him. If you're found with a Buddhist text, it's a counterrevolutionary
thought crime."

Tibetans, says Moynihan, "are treated as badly as blacks ever
were." China, she explains, zeroes in on US race relations not
because of their sympathy toward minority populations, but to frac-
ture American society. "The CCP studies the society they want to
destroy," she says. "They find its weakness, whether it's class or race,
and then pour fuel on the fire, and keep stoking it. Their ultimate
goal is to ignite a civil war, and have an enemy destroy itself from
within."

The strange fact is that China itself is racist toward blacks. A 2013
Pentagon assessment "The Strategic Consequences of Chinese Racism" documents how CCP propaganda frames "international politics in terms of a 'racial balance of power,' and cast appeals to the
Third World along the lines of: now is the time for non-whites to
dominate international politics."[48] And yet, according to the report,
"the Chinese have a hierarchical representation of looking at other
groups, darker skin is lower class, and race matters. In this sense,
the racial stereotypes of the Africans commonly found within Chinese society suggest that this population is backward and dirty, and
prone to crime, particularly violent crime."[49]

With China's economic growth in the 1990s driving more African immigration, according to one research team, "the continued

presence of Africans in China is producing new racialized tensions exerted by the Han majority against the Black minority population. This Han racism is increasingly defining the lived experiences of the vulnerable Black migrant population in China."[50]

During the Covid-19 pandemic viral videos documented Chinese landlords kicking African migrants out of their apartments, barring them from stores, restaurants, and hospitals, and forcibly quarantining them. According to one study, "the Black community in China was again a target of multiple racial projects which sought to label their bodies as diseased and physical presence as a threat to the viability and safety of the Han majority."[51]

MAO HAD A DREAM

After the April 4, 1968, assassination of Martin Luther King, Mao wrote another open letter directed primarily to African-Americans. "At present, the world revolution has entered a great new era," he wrote. Categorizing King's murder as the match lit to burn down the American regime, Mao exhorted

> the workers, peasants, and revolutionary intellectuals of all countries and all who are willing to fight against U.S. imperialism to take action and extend strong support to the struggle of the black people in the United States! People of the whole world, unite still more closely and launch a sustained and vigorous offensive against our common enemy, U.S. imperialism, and its accomplices! It can be said with certainty that the complete collapse of colonialism, imperialism, and all systems of exploitation, and the complete emancipation of all the oppressed peoples and nations of the world are not far off.[52]

And African-Americans in particular should heed Mao's counsel, for "only by overthrowing the reactionary rule of the U.S.

monopoly capitalist class, and destroying the colonialist and imperialist system can the Black people in the United States win complete emancipation."[53]

As Mao had hoped, the streets ran with blood. Riots erupted in 110 US cities, including Baltimore, Newark, Chicago, Detroit, Kansas City, New York, Pittsburgh, and Cincinnati. Washington, DC, was perhaps hit hardest; more than ten thousand federal troops were deployed to quell the violence, including nearly two thousand soldiers tasked to defend the White House. After four days of rioting, the national capital was devastated, with thirteen dead and nine hundred businesses damaged at a cost of nearly $175 million in today's dollars.[54]

And yet, the pillars of the capitalist juggernaut still stood—it was African-American neighborhoods and businesses that paid the highest price for the violence. With the destruction of hundreds of businesses, thousands of jobs lost, and soaring insurance rates, many enterprises never reopened and the city's economy was left in ruins. Crime rates rose, pushing blacks as well as whites out the city for the suburbs, further depressing property values. It took some neighborhoods three decades to recover, and many still haven't to this day.

Naturally, the Black Panthers participated in the bloodshed. Two days after King's murder, Cleaver led a team of a dozen Black Panthers in an operation against the Oakland police for what he called a preemptive strike.[55] The shootout left one Black Panther, Bobby Hutton, dead. Hollywood leading man Marlon Brando gave the eulogy, staging once again the cultural elite's endorsement of radical causes.

After eruptions of violence throughout the 1960s and '70s, most Americans came to see that the murder of King, taken together with the assassinations of John Kennedy and his brother Bobby, was evidence that the only way forward was through nonviolent means.

The black insurrection Mao encouraged against America had failed, even though there would be other iterations of CCP-sponsored violence to come, including the George Floyd riots, virtually a parody of King's March on Washington.

Huey Newton, like Robert Williams, was the opposite of King, which was why the CCP found him useful. In turn, Newton must've recognized in Mao a fellow psychopath, and one who'd parlayed his madness into almost divine power. Newton wanted him to mediate with Nixon on his behalf. He'd brought to China the "People's Petition," asking "the peace-and-freedom-loving Chairman Mao Tse-Tung to be the chief negotiator to Mr. Nixon for the peace and freedom of the oppressed people of the world."[56] But Mao didn't see him; only Zhou did. The press asked him how Zhou would support the Black Panthers. Zhou, Newton replied, "said many things to me; but I will not comment on specifics." In other words, there was nothing on offer except the trip itself.

Newton stayed in China for ten days. "Everything I saw in China demonstrated that the People's Republic is a free and liberated territory with a socialist government," he wrote in his autobiography *Revolutionary Suicide*. "To see a classless society in operation is unforgettable."[57]

He reflected on what the trip meant for him. "What I experienced in China was the sensation of freedom," wrote Newton. "I felt absolutely free for the first time in my life—completely free among my fellow human beings. This experience of freedom had a profound effect on me, because it confirmed my belief that an oppressed people can be liberated if their leaders persevere in raising their consciousness and in struggling relentlessly against the oppressor."[58] And with this cliché formulation, Newton joined the list of prominent African-American activists who praised a totalitarian police state that silenced and slaughtered its own people.

According to Newton, the Chinese offered him political asylum. "But," he wrote, "I told them I had to return, that my struggle is in the United States of America."[59] Back home Newton killed again.

In 1974, he shot to death a seventeen-year-old black girl who called him by a childhood nickname he didn't like. The Panthers scared off eyewitnesses, and Huey was in the wind. He went to Cuba and returned to the Bay Area in 1977. He was shot to death on an Oakland street corner in 1989, the same year that the PRC put down a student protest in Beijing's Tiananmen Square. Thousands, maybe more, were killed, shot, or crushed under tank tracks. Instead of turning in revulsion from Beijing, Washington, encouraged by its corporate backers, stuck by its new partner. There was too much money at stake, money that the CCP would use in its war against America. Huey Newton had come to Beijing with his hand out too early.

CHAPTER FOUR

Trading in Blood

I see a world of open borders, open trade and,
most importantly, open minds.[1]

—George H. W. Bush

THE MAN WHO WOULD COME TO LEAD CHINA WAS HOSTING A
farewell luncheon in Beijing for the future president. But it was
only 1975, and neither Deng Xiaoping nor George H. W. Bush saw
what was in the future. With Mao's death the following year, Deng
would engage in an internal political battle that would decide not
only his political fate but his life. Bush at the time was the US envoy
to China, the second since the 1972 opening. Because the two countries did not yet have full diplomatic relations, Bush's title was not
ambassador but rather chief of the US liaison office to the People's
Republic of China.

Bush was hopeful for the future of the new relationship and had
appreciated his time in China. He and his wife, Barbara, rode bicy-
cles through the streets of the capital and took trips to the countryside. They were learning Mandarin.[2] But only a year after he arrived,

he wanted out. President Gerald Ford accommodated his request and named him CIA director.

With his guest's new job in mind, Deng leaned over his plate and, according to one CCP account, asked Bush, "Have you been spying on me all this time?" Deng smiled to see the American squirm. "Come on," said Bush, "no."[3]

The two men called each other friends. Deng knew that Bush's job as envoy was to report back to Washington, but by suggesting his role was to subvert China, the CCP official put him on the defensive. And now he saw that Bush spooked easily.

Nixon and Kissinger also thought Bush was soft. When Zhou Enlai had first reached out in 1971, Nixon asked for his foreign policy aide's opinion on potential envoys. He knew Kissinger wanted the mission but wanted to see him twist in the wind first.[4]

"How about Bush?" Nixon asked.

"Absolutely not," said Kissinger, "he is too soft and not sophisticated enough." Bush, he said, "would be too weak."

It was a peculiar assessment given that Bush, then US ambassador to the United Nations, was a decorated World War II pilot, but Kissinger would be proven right when it came to how Bush dealt with the Chinese. Bush would be most seriously tested by Beijing in 1989 when Deng sent tanks into the streets to kill student protestors. Deng blamed the United States for causing the unrest at Tiananmen Square and forcing China's hand. He said he was left with no choice but to order the PLA to open fire on students. According to Deng, it was the Americans who had put the US-China relationship in jeopardy and it was Bush's job to save it.

And Bush did save it, so to speak. He comforted the communists in order to keep China open for business—and that was just how Kissinger and the China lobby that he'd built around his China expertise and experience wanted it.

The massacre at Tiananmen Square marks a turning point in US relations with China. After the bloodshed—estimates suggest between 800 to 1,000 were killed on June 4, 1989—US policymakers could hardly claim to be naïve about the essential character of the Chinese Communist Party. There was no more ignoring the fact it was a totalitarian regime. By appeasing rather than confronting Beijing, the Americans showed they were cynical: There was too much money to be made in China to let Tiananmen disrupt the relationship. And thus the United States signaled that the CCP had leverage on the leader of the free world. Bush set the precedent for future presidents who, like him, would turn a blind eye to China's depredations against their own people as well as Americans.

The most generous assessment of the Bush era holds that Bush was boxed in by circumstance. He was a president, after all, and not a king who answers only to himself. He had to contend with the corporate establishment that lobbied hard not to punish China, and reckon with the historical moment. With the Soviet Union evidently in its death throes, Washington had little reason to risk turning China openly hostile. After all, this was the ostensible purpose of Nixon and Kissinger's 1972 opening to China—to weaken Moscow. And now Moscow was on the verge of collapse.

Also shaping Bush's decision was his party, the Republicans, proud to have initiated the opening. And there was the official policy of the United States, which was to preserve the ties with Beijing. And there was also foreign policy ideology, realism, holding that the US should prioritize its interests above humanitarian concerns. And like Kissinger, Bush saw himself as a realist, which meant staying firm even it meant countenancing the slaughter of innocents.

It's clear now that electing to maintain ties with China in the wake of Tiananmen did not serve America's best interests. If US lawmakers rightly outraged at the massacre at Tiananmen had managed to revoke China's trade status, Beijing might not have won a place in the World Trade Organization, which in turn led to the enrichment of the CCP at the expense of American prosperity and our national security.

And thus, to understand how central Tiananmen is to the history of the ensuing decades, it's worth asking: What if the US president hadn't prioritized ties with a communist regime at the expense of American honor and values? Maybe another president would have made a different choice.

REAGAN ROLLBACK

Ronald Reagan thought Nixon and Kissinger's reason for engaging China was specious. In a 1978 speech, the Republican candidate for president identified the contradiction at the core of what the Nixon-Kissinger wing of the GOP was advocating:

> *On the one hand, they say that Peking sees Moscow as the greatest threat to world peace today and that we must take advantage of this to make an alliance that will inhibit the Soviet Union from expanding its influence and provoking conflict. Yet, they also argue that unless the United States rushes to "normalize" its relations with Peking, the leadership there will suddenly drop us and embrace Moscow in a new alliance which would have ominous overtones for America's future security.*[5]

For Reagan, the confused urgency showed that what mattered most to them was engaging China, regardless of whether it would help defeat the Soviet Union. Reagan saw that behind all the talk about playing the Chinese against the Soviets, Nixon and Kissinger's opening had unbalanced America.

The big divide in foreign policy circles at the time was best illustrated in debates not over China but rather the Soviet Union. At the start of the Cold War, the United States employed a policy of containment, first sketched out by State Department official George Kennan. Under Nixon, Washington moved to détente which, according to Kissinger, was "the search for a more constructive relationship with the Soviet Union."[6] In practice, that meant more dialogue with Moscow, over arms reduction and other bilateral issues. But Reagan opted for a more aggressive posture, which pushed for confronting the USSR and reversing Soviet influence. This was known as "rollback." As Reagan famously told an aide when asked to explain his Cold War strategy: "We win, they lose."[7]

According to a 1983 White House directive, "the U.S. must rebuild the credibility of its commitment to resist Soviet encroachment on U.S. interests and those of its Allies and friends, and to support effectively those Third World states that are willing to resist Soviet pressures or oppose Soviet initiatives hostile to the United States, or are special targets of Soviet policy."[8] At the top of the list was Afghanistan, a Soviet satellite where insurgents were pounding away at Soviet forces. Reagan believed that the Chinese could help the Afghani rebels break the Red Army's will.

As former Reagan aide Michael Pillsbury recounts in his classic account of China's rise at America's expense, *The Hundred-Year Marathon: China's Secret Strategy to Replace America as the Global Superpower*, under Reagan the United States bought $2 billion worth of Chinese arms to give to the Afghani mujahideen. As a student of Chinese history, Pillsbury surmised that Beijing would be willing to use a third-party rival like America to undermine Moscow's global position. But, he writes, "Even I was taken aback at the ruthlessness of Beijing's ambition to bring down the Soviets."[9]

Maybe even more surprisingly, Pillsbury tells me, "As part of the Cold War against the Soviet Union, we began to sell weapons to

China. This is the main thing that happened with US-China relations under President Reagan."

Now a senior fellow at the Heritage Foundation, Pillsbury was a twenty-eight-year-old Pentagon analyst when he made the case for arming China. "It's almost unbelievable to people today," he says. "And at the time people wondered if we should really be selling weapons to China."

But Reagan, says Pillsbury, "was the greatest anti-communist president of all time, so he added a proviso: We're doing all this assuming that China remains independent from Russia, and moves toward a democratic system with a liberal trade policy. Reagan said, yes, let's arm China, let's transfer technology—almost 100 percent of anything the Chinese asked for we provided. But let's keep our eyes fully open just in case things go bad with China."

In fact, even as Reagan was selling arms to China, he was balancing Beijing with a $60 million arms deal with Taiwan. Shortly after the Carter administration officially recognized the PRC, severed relations with Taiwan, and withdrew all US troops, Congress passed the 1979 Taiwan Relations Act, which required the United States to continue to sell defensive arms to Taiwan. China was furious. Reagan said he was willing to gradually reduce arms sales over time—though he gave no specific end date—so long as the PRC maintained peaceful relations with Taiwan.[10] In 1982 Reagan's vice president, George H. W. Bush, went to Beijing to soothe his old friend Deng.[11]

In 1978 Deng had risen to the top of the Party after unseating Mao's handpicked successor. To many American China watchers, Deng seemed to be a transformative figure, the kind of reform-minded leader they'd hoped would follow Mao. In fact, his chief goal was just to keep the Party and himself alive.

"To save the regime and the Communist Party Deng was forced to adopt, or allow, limited market mechanisms into China's economy," says Miles Yu, top China advisor to Mike Pompeo, Trump's first term secretary of state.

Deng was concerned about repeating the catastrophe caused by Mao's forced collectivization programs, so he let farmers sell some of their crops independently. The larger output led to further reform measures in agriculture and later in other sectors. In Washington, some read this as a pivotal moment in US-China relations, since, on the surface at least, it looked as if the CCP was finally breaking loose of its anti-capitalist ideology—the communists wanted to make money.

"But the Party was still in control," says Yu. "This was just how Deng saved a screwed-up, communist regime. He ruled China by upholding what he called the four cardinal principles: the communist path; the dictatorship of the proletariat; CCP leadership; and Mao Zedong Thought and Marxism-Leninism. As long as he kept to those principles, he could afford to do something practical like let foreign companies invest in China and send students abroad to learn things that would help advance the Party. Deng's problem was when engagement with the West and ideas like democracy and human rights threatened the Party."

And that was why Reagan believed that promoting democracy and human rights were useful instruments to push back against the communist powers: He believed that fear of freedom was a vulnerability for regimes determined to keep their people enslaved.

"Reagan was very shrewd in conditioning our cooperation with China on benchmarks like moving toward a democratic system," says Pillsbury. "But the bureaucracy only heard the part about strengthening China through trade and investment."

THE CHINA TRADE

Deng described the reform process as "crossing the river by feeling the stones," says Clyde Prestowitz, who worked as a senior official in Reagan's Commerce Department. He was on the first US trade mission to China in 1982.

"The policy was to get American companies to invest in China and wean Beijing away from old Mao policies and create an environment more suitable to free trade," Prestowitz tells me. He says that at the time he could have hardly imagined that China would become one of world history's great economic success stories. "China was a very poor country. I never saw any place so poor."

And yet the economic reform process was already underway. "The leaders in Beijing fully grasped the significance of export-driven growth," Prestowitz wrote in his 2021 book *The World Turned Upside Down: America, China, and the Struggle for Global Leadership*. "They also understood the significance of introducing new technology through foreign investment. These special zones were able to offer tax and other incentives to attract foreign investors. For many industries, China's low wage level was also, of course, a major attraction."[12]

It's not as if the barons of US industry had just discovered inexpensive and efficient Chinese labor. "Chinese toil and entrepreneurial acumen powered the West," wrote one journalist describing the labor source instrumental in building the transcontinental railroad in the mid-nineteenth century.[13] The 1868 Burlingame Treaty between the United States and China was called the "cheap labor treaty" because it promised to import more Chinese workers to the US.[14] And that fomented racial strife on the east and west coasts as businessmen brought in Chinese workers to undercut white workers and break labor strikes.[15]

With the media helping to turn public sentiment against Chinese workers, Congress passed the Chinese Exclusion Act of 1882, the first significant law restricting immigration based on nationality or race. The next time US corporate giants would pit Chinese workers against their US counterparts to exploit cheap labor was in the name of free trade.

"When I came into the Reagan administration in 1981, the ruling doctrine of the time was free trade," says Prestowitz. That was fine when "the US government and other US investors owned more assets belonging to other countries than foreign countries held in America," he says. "The flow of profits to the US was bigger than the flow of dollars to foreign investors."

But that would soon change. At the end of Reagan's first term, the trade deficit with China was $6 billion. But by the time George H. W. Bush left the White House eight years later in 1993, the deficit would surge to $18 billion and growing.[16]

"When we run trade deficits," says Prestowitz, "more dollars go abroad than foreign money comes into the US. These foreigners buy apartments or farms or factories." In other words, they buy America.

For free trade evangelists, it doesn't matter who is buying up America, but for those who care about the welfare of their fellow citizens, their children's future, and their country's ability to defend itself from hostile foreign actors, then it matters: Americans should own America.

"But our establishment doesn't give a damn about Americans," says Prestowitz. "They convinced themselves that by doing business with China they were doing good, but it's Americans who paid the price. US officials thought it was their job to keep markets open. It wasn't until Trump that people started asking questions. But from the 1980s on, there was widespread belief that free trade would lead to liberalization and democratization. Reagan, Bush 41, Clinton, Bush 43, Obama, all believed that free trade is good and tariffs are bad."

That belief was based on a flawed understanding of some of the twentieth century's pivotal events: Academic economists were wary

of protectionist policies because they believed in a direct causal relationship that led from US tariffs to World War II.

With the first signs of the Great Depression starting to appear,
in 1930 Congress imposed steep tariffs on US trade partners under
the Smoot-Hawley Tariff Act to protect American jobs from foreign competition. "After the stock-market crash," says Prestowitz,
"it became a conviction among economists that Smoot-Hawley had
caused the depression, which in turn led to World War II."

Then politicians adopted doomsday talking points. For instance,
in a 1993 televised debate about the North America Free Trade
Agreement (NAFTA) between Al Gore and Ross Perot, Bill Clinton's vice president asserted that the tariffs were "one of the principal causes, many economists say the principal cause, of the Great
Depression in this country and around the world."[17]

But tariffs did not cause the depression, or World War II, says
Prestowitz. "The Smoot-Hawley tariffs helped the US economy."

Nonetheless, the idea took hold that tariffs are destabilizing and
lead to economic depression—which in this specific case led to the
rise of a genocidal tyrant, which led to a world war. If that's true, the
opposite must also be true: Free trade ensures world peace. Indeed it
was a guiding principle of America's postwar political establishment
that free trade liberalizes nondemocratic regimes.

Accordingly, in the war's aftermath, world leaders sought to create
an order designed to avoid a repeat of what they thought had led to
the rise of the Third Reich. In 1944, the Bretton Woods Conference
laid the foundation for international financial institutions like the
International Monetary Fund (IMF) and the World Bank. And in
1947, twenty-three countries, led by the United States, ratified the
General Agreement on Tariffs and Trade (GATT), a treaty aimed
at promoting international trade by reducing tariffs and other trade
barriers, and the WTO's precursor.

After World War II, says Prestowitz, "US economic policy became trade liberalization, and after WWII we took the lead in reducing tariffs. Guys like me who had been in business and knew something about trade knew there was a problem."

Among other things they knew was that many of the stewards of American prosperity, like the country's first Treasury secretary, Alexander Hamilton, believed that protecting domestic industry increased America's wealth and ensured its peace.[18] What a country makes and sells is an expression of its national character and the cornerstone of its national security. A people known primarily for growing bananas and coffee, for instance, is no match for one that makes airplanes and precision tools.

"But the economists, the guys who made trade policy until Donald Trump," says Prestowitz, "they all thought free trade was great and it would invariably lead every country to democracy, just like it had done with postwar Japan and Germany. They thought it didn't matter if our trading partners had a trade surplus with us."

It was companies from those same countries that most benefited from America's free-trade practices that started throttling US industries. "US companies were coming under predatory pressure from the Germans and the Japanese, and we were getting our brains beaten," says Alan Tonelson, a former research fellow at the US Business and Industry Council Educational Foundation who has written extensively on the US trade deficit with other countries, including China. "The auto industry was desperate to get into the Japanese market because there was such one-way trade going on. The Japanese were free to operate here. But you couldn't sell a Chrysler there. They just didn't want them, and they kept them out in myriad ways."

Author of the 2002 book *The Race to the Bottom: Why a Worldwide Worker Surplus and Uncontrolled Free Trade Are Sinking American Living Standards*, Tonelson explains how Reagan came under enormous pressure from the US auto industry, and an American public increasingly alarmed about Japanese trade policies, and imposed protective tariffs on four major U.S. industries—automobiles, textiles, steel, and machine tools. "He also threatened tariffs on semiconductors, which worked," Tonelson tells me. "But with Bush, US companies recognized that despite the Bush administration's endless promises, the Japanese were never going to open up their market."

Tariffs were out of the question. First, there was the ideological bias. "To their mind, tariffs led to WWII," says Tonelson. "The strongest opposition to tariffs during these Reagan years came from the media, university economists as well as the national security community. "They believed that the Cold War was not only continuing, but intensifying," he says, "so they were wary of doing anything that would antagonize major US security allies, like Japan and Germany, whose perceived strategic value became even greater."

US industries had to find some other way to expand profits. "They believed they had no alternative but to go to the Third World," says Tonelson. "And this was a watershed moment in US history because it's when US trade policy became US offshoring policy."

This explains why first Mexico and then China were so appealing to the US business community, even though the history of US-China trade relations showed that even if American goods got into Chinese markets, those markets were much smaller than what China's massive population appeared to promise.

US trade with China started right after the American revolution, with the 1784 arrival of the *Empress of China* in Canton (now Guangzhou). What the American traders wanted were Chinese goods that represented status and taste, especially porcelain, which we now know as china.[19] In exchange, the Chinese bought furs, sandalwood, and silver, but not enough of it, so the Americans joined their British cousins in the opium trade.

Among those who made great fortunes selling opium to the Chinese were John Jacob Astor, one of the most famous of America's early oligarchs; Warren Delano Jr., grandfather of the thirty-second president of the United States, Franklin Delano Roosevelt; and Robert Bennet Forbes, whose distant relatives include former US Secretary of State John Kerry, and Steve Forbes, editor-in-chief of *Forbes* magazine.[20]

American trade with China was profitable but, as one historian explains, it "did not generate enough income to come close to covering the costs of Chinese goods purchased in Canton." Thus, "from the very start of the United States' commercial relationship with China, there was a hefty trade deficit. In other words, America imported a far greater value of goods from China than it exported in return."[21]

A century later, US industry had a pretty good idea then that the market for their goods in China, and under a communist regime that had murdered its middle class, wasn't going to be big—not yet, anyway. But that wasn't really what they wanted from China.

"What companies really wanted," says Tonelson, "was to send their factories offshore. Not only would their production costs be much lower, and their profits would at least be maintained, they also found—and this is absolutely essential—that Chinese workers could be made just as productive as their US counterparts. After all, intelligence is evenly distributed all around the world, and these companies ultimately make the most possible money by making their workers more productive. They recognized that if they could make American workers incredibly productive, they could do the same with Chinese workers, especially when they didn't have to bother with inconveniences like labor unions or environmental regulations.

So they sent their factories to the third world and paid big bucks to secure passage of the trade policies that made exporting to the United States from very low-cost countries like China so profitable."

This was the business model that Henry Kissinger had carved out of his government career—opening doors for American companies that wanted to open shop in China. No one had made more of an impression on CCP leadership than the man who prepared the way for the opening. "Henry Kissinger knew the top people in China," says Prestowitz. "And US businessmen saw him as their American Godfather. He had all the connections. If you wanted to know the right people, Henry could get you to the right people."

In 1982 he opened Kissinger Associates with a $350,000 loan from Goldman Sachs, the Wall Street firm that would soon come to play a part almost as large as Kissinger's in propping up the communist regime.[22] He named Lawrence Eagleburger, his former aide at the State Department, the firm's president, and made Brent Scowcroft, Kissinger's former deputy on the NSC staff, head of the firm's Washington office.

Over the years Kissinger Associates' roster has included, among other top US officials, three secretaries of state, Kissinger, Eagleburger, and William Rogers; former Treasury Secretaries William Simon and Timothy Geithner; Energy Secretary Bill Richardson; Ambassador to China J. Stapleton Roy; and CIA director John Brennan. If they couldn't affect policies directly, they had friends in government who could.

By 1986, the firm had nearly thirty clients, including the biggest names in business: Chase Manhattan Bank, American Express, Coca-Cola, Atlantic Richfield, and American Grain.[23] They didn't need Kissinger's help in Washington where they already had lobbyists. They wanted his foreign connections.

"This is particularly true in China, where he is a popular figure and is viewed with particular respect," Heinz CEO Anthony J. F. O'Reilly told the press. "On China, basically, we were well on our way to establishing the baby-food presence there before Henry got involved. But once we decided to move, he had practical points to offer, such as on the relationship between Taiwan and Peking. He was helpful in seeing that we did not take steps that would not have been helpful in Peking."[24]

Kissinger advised US corporations that if they wanted to keep their position in China, they'd have to internalize the CCP's view and learn how to explain it to US officials from that perspective. The executives whose large and influential companies Kissinger represented understood that their access to China depended on whether they could and would lobby Washington on Beijing's behalf, like Kissinger himself.

TIANANMEN MASSACRE

As president, George H. W. Bush acknowledged that the US relationship with China was no longer keyed to the Soviet danger. In a visit to Beijing a month after his 1989 inauguration, Bush said:

> *Some have said in the world press: "The U.S. President is going to China because Gorbachev is going to China." That's crazy, that's wrong. I wanted to come because I agree with you on where the relationship stands, and that the prospects for our two countries to advance the relationship have never been greater. Support for this relationship has never been stronger in my country. So the China-U.S. relationship must stand on its own feet.*[25]

But what was the strategic purpose of the US-China relationship if the Soviet Union collapsed? If the rationale for the opening was to weaken Moscow, there was evidence the Soviets were wobbling, chiefly the fact that Mikhail Gorbachev was made prime minister to head off growing discontent. But the same was happening in China, where the Party saw that the opposition to its rule was gaining steam.

Throughout the mid-1980s, Chinese students and workers regularly gathered in Beijing and other large cities to protest. The Party's new relationship with the Americans had stirred hope for more change and reform than Deng had offered. They admired Reagan. They waved banners carrying slogans like LAW, NOT AUTHORITARIANISM and LONG LIVE DEMOCRACY. Their pro-American references would become even more explicit when they brought replicas of the Statue of Liberty to rallies.[26]

When the former CCP general secretary Hu Yaobang died in April 1989, students filled Tiananmen Square. They mourned a man who'd been forced out of his position two years earlier by colleagues alarmed by the popular acclaim he'd won as a reformer. The protestors demanded that his successor, Zhao Ziyang, fulfill the Party's promises to improve their lives. Zhao was conciliatory toward the students, even as Party elders imposed martial law in May. Deng replaced Zhao with former Shanghai mayor Jiang Zemin, and on June 3 they sent the PLA into the square to face down the students.

A State Department cable described how protestors chased away the first wave of lightly armed soldiers. US diplomats stationed in Beijing wondered if the action was intended "to prove that much stronger force will be necessary to regain control."[27]

The crackdown began that night. Some ten thousand troops ringed the square, according to another cable, and "a column of about 50 APCs [armored personnel carriers], tanks, and trucks entered Tiananmen from the east."[28] Protestors began shouting and "PLA troops in Tiananmen opened a barrage of rifle and machine gun fire." Another column of military vehicles entered and there was more gunfire. One woman told US embassy officials that she wit-nessed a tank running over eleven people.

The fighting lasted through the next day. Against overwhelming numbers of heavily armed troops, the civilians, thousands of them, stood their ground. Many swarmed military vehicles. They set APCs on fire, and went after troops with rocks, bottles, and Molotov cock-tails. Chinese civilians told American diplomats that as many as 10,000 people had been killed at Tiananmen.[29] US government esti-mates at the time varied from 500 to 2,600 with more than 10,000 wounded.[30]

On June 5 Bush announced that he was suspending arms sales and cutting off high-level meetings between US and PRC officials. Behind the scenes, Bush ordered the Pentagon to complete a prom-ised delivery of torpedoes, radar, and other military supplies, and later dispatched a secret envoy to visit Deng in Beijing.[31]

Liberal and conservative lawmakers were united in their demands to come down hard on Beijing.[32] But Bush urged restraint. "This is not the time for an emotional response," he said, "but for a reasoned, careful action that takes into account both our long-term interests and recognition of a complex internal situation in China."

Bush was in a bind. Like Nixon and Kissinger, he thought of himself as a foreign policy realist. And men like them, as Kissinger believed, cannot afford pure idealism. Nixon told Bush: "Don't disrupt the relationship. What's happened has been handled badly and is deplorable, but take a look at the long haul." According to Bush, Nixon didn't "think we should stop our trade [or do] some-thing symbolic, because we must have a good relationship in the long run."[33]

But for what purpose? With the Soviet Union collapsing the China card was irrelevant. In fact, the Chinese saw opposition move-ments in Ukraine, Georgia, and other Soviet republics disentangling themselves from the communist web and wondered if they, too, were destined for the dustbin of history.

Everyone agreed that China needed to change, and it was an article of faith for postwar US policymakers that the best way to encourage political liberalization was through economic reform. After all, free trade kept the West free and out of a third world war. From this perspective, the bloodshed at Tiananmen was just evidence China needed more time. Bush counseled patience. "The process of democratization of Communist societies will not be a smooth one," he said in his June 5 speech, "and we must react to setbacks in a way which stimulates rather than stifles progress toward open and representative systems."[34]

Prioritizing economic benefits through engagement had the not-incidental advantage of giving cover to US business elites pursuing their own economic interests with a totalitarian regime. Lawmakers were pushing for sanctions, but Bush said he "wanted to avoid cutting off the entire commercial relationship."[35] "I don't want to hurt the Chinese people," said the president. "I happen to believe that the commercial contacts have led, in essence, to this quest for more freedom. I think as people have commercial incentive, whether it's in China or in other totalitarian systems, the move to democracy becomes more inexorable."[36]

Meanwhile, Bush's predecessor struck a different chord. "You cannot massacre an idea," Reagan, now a private citizen, told a London audience shortly after Tiananmen. "You cannot run tanks over hope. You cannot riddle a people's yearning with bullets. Those heroic Chinese students who gave their lives have released the spirit of democracy and it cannot be called back. That spirit is loose upon the world this spring."[37]

In Reagan's view, human beings are more than simply the embodiment of enlightened self-interest. No man ever laid down his life for stock options. China had veered from Reagan's conditions—to meet benchmarks showing it was moving toward a democratic system—and his former vice president sent them a lifeline.

Bush tried to call Deng soon after Tiananmen but couldn't get through. He wrote him a letter "in a spirit of genuine friendship." He asked "for help in preserving this relationship that we both think is very important. I have tried very hard not to inject myself into China's internal affairs. I have tried very hard not to appear to be dictating in any way to China about how it should manage its internal crises. I am respectful of the differences in our two societies and in our two systems."[38]

He asked Deng if he would receive "a special emissary who could speak with total candor to you representing my heartfelt convictions on these matters. If you feel such an emissary would be helpful, please let me know and we will work cooperatively to see that his mission is kept in total confidence."

The trip was secret, like Kissinger's. Not even the US ambassador to China knew about it.

On July 2, Bush's emissary met with Deng and conveyed the president's regards: "He remembers with great affection his meeting with you in February."[39] Deng said that he trusted Bush and expressed regret "that the United States is too deeply involved" in China's domestic turmoil. "We have been feeling since the outset of these events more than two months ago that the various aspects of US foreign policy has actually cornered China," said Deng. "The crux of the matter," he added, is that the US "has impugned Chinese interests, has hurt Chinese dignity."[40]

He denounced the Voice of America for "rumor-mongering" and misreporting the number of casualties at Tiananmen. He complained that Congress had taken actions "against China on the basis of such rumors." He was referring to the sanctions that the House of Representatives passed unanimously, 418–0, at the end of June that banned or restricted arms sales, crime control equipment, and technology transfers.[41] These actions, said Deng, "are leading to the break up of the relationship."

It is up to the one who tied the knot to untie it, Deng said, citing a Chinese proverb. The burden was on Bush to show his friendship to the CCP, Deng told Bush's representative. "We will never allow any people to interfere in China's internal affairs."[42]

It was a remarkable display of brinksmanship. The Party had demonstrated its capacity for mass terror, a fact indelibly imprinted on the world's conscience by the now famous image of a lone protestor confronting a row of tanks. And yet Deng drew on the collective paranoid indignation of two generations of totalitarian murderers to accost America and its elected representatives for daring to notice the blood filling Beijing's gutters. And so according to Deng, if Bush didn't do something about congressional sanctions, history would show that he was responsible for the breakup, and maybe worse.

Bush's emissary took the message back to the president. And when Bush sent him back to Beijing in December, the White House was forced to reveal his identity—National Security Advisor Brent Scowcroft. Accompanying him on the trip was Deputy Secretary of State Lawrence Eagleburger. These were Kissinger's men.[43]

THE KISSINGER LOBBY

Scowcroft told Deng that he and Eagleburger were both "close associates of Henry Kissinger." Bush had hired them right out of Kissinger Associates. Kissinger said he didn't know beforehand of Bush's plans to send Scowcroft and Eagleburger, "and was flabbergasted when he found out," according to a biographer. "He realized that it would look as if he had been an unseen force behind the decision."[44]

But that is just how any Kissinger or any corporate leader would have wanted it to be seen, especially by CCP officials and prospective clients. The arrival of Kissinger's men in Beijing showed that he was able to project power even from outside government, a demonstration that could only make Party leadership more inclined to accommodate Kissinger's growing client list. It was a priceless advertisement for recruiting new business.

The China file had proven to be such a success for Kissinger that in December 1988 he'd started China Ventures, a limited partnership with plans to invest in joint projects with the communists. He lined up top American corporations like American Express, Heinz, and Coca-Cola, but then the massacre at Tiananmen spooked them. Or rather investors were haunted by the prospect of punitive US economic measures imposed on Beijing that would affect their own investments.

Accordingly, Kissinger used his prestige as *the* China expert to lobby against sanctions. He had a six-figure yearly contract as an ABC News analyst and wrote a regular column for the Los Angeles Times–Washington Post News Service. The day after PLA troops were sent into the square, ABC News broadcaster Peter Jennings asked him live on the evening news how the US should respond. "I wouldn't do any sanctions," said Kissinger.[45]

Defending China in *The Washington Post*, he wrote that the PRC "remains too important for America's national security to risk the relationship on the emotions of the moment."[46] We must act prudently, counseled Kissinger, for "the drama in Beijing is for Americans a test of our political maturity." No government in the world, he said, "would have tolerated having the main square of its capital occupied for eight weeks by tens of thousands of demonstrators."

It seems Kissinger hadn't disclosed to the network or the newspaper the conflict of interest raised by China Ventures. But the media knew about Kissinger Associates because it had widely reported the firm's work in China and its client list. That was why the press paid Kissinger—they leased his name to enhance their prestige. And he used their brands and reach to fill airtime and newsprint to help save the CCP from suffering any consequences for sending tanks against thousands of college students.

He and Nixon were disdainful of the human rights activists who wanted to come down hard on China. "Our foreign policy should not be a salve for our own offended sensibilities, a mechanism for making us feel noble and true," Nixon told one Republican senator. "Our foreign policy should be a tool for protecting our interests."[47]

What were American interests? Even with the Soviet Union on the verge of collapse, Nixon was concerned that the Soviets might entice China to side against America. Gorbachev, he feared, just might play the US card.[48] Nixon visited Beijing after Tiananmen and met with Deng and other leaders and assessed that "Sino-American relations are in the worst condition they have been in since before I went to China seventeen years ago." In a memo to congressional leaders, Nixon wrote:

Americans and Chinese see the tragic events of June 4 from totally different perspectives. The gap between us on that issue is totally unbridgeable. I pointed out to Chinese leaders that most Americans, including many friends of China, believe that the military crackdown was brutally excessive and totally unjustified. In response, every Chinese leader I talked to insisted that the suppression of the demonstrations was necessary and justified. They believe the American reaction was an unacceptable intrusion in their internal affairs. They believe the American media grossly exaggerated June's events.[49]

Here Nixon might have drawn on his own experience: In May 1970 Ohio National Guardsmen shot and killed four students at Kent State University demonstrating against the war in Vietnam. The shooting led to more protests across the country and widespread anger, much of it directed at the Nixon administration, which further galvanized opposition to the war. Americans were right to be angry about Kent State and to want justice. US policymakers should have taken it more seriously when CCP officials said slaughtering hundreds of their own wasn't a big deal because the American public would never see it that way. It was time for America to move on and move away from the PRC.

But it seems there was something else going on that prevented them from cutting off Beijing, something that had nothing to do with geopolitics or even trade. The Americans were embarrassed by what the Chinese had done. The Great Leap Forward and the Cultural Revolution were grislier than Tiananmen by many multitudes, but that was before the opening. Tiananmen left the US elites who'd embraced China as a partner dripping with gore. The establishment's new best friend was a mass murderer and didn't care who knew it. The Americans couldn't walk away from Beijing because they had to save the Party to spare themselves the guilt and shame for expecting anything more from a communist regime. Thus, instead of exerting maximum pressure on Beijing, or at the very least demanding concessions, Bush insulated the CCP from the wrath of the American public and its elected representatives.

Every year since 1980, Congress voted on whether to grant China most favored nation (MFN) trade status. With the 1990 vote, legislators sought to withdraw or heavily condition it on the PRC's human rights record.[50] Repealing MFN would have raised tariffs on Chinese goods by an average of 40 percent, a prospect that horrified both Beijing and their US corporate partners.[51]

Withdrawing MFN status from Beijing, said Bush spokesman Marlin Fitzwater, "would inflict severe costs on American business people, investors, and consumers," and impose "a multi-billion-dollar surcharge on American consumer imports."[52]

The efforts to preserve China's trade status were joined by Alexander Haig, Reagan's secretary of state and another one of Kissinger's men. "Haig wouldn't go to the bathroom without first raising his hand and asking Henry Kissinger's permission," wrote Nixon speechwriter William Safire.[53] Haig owed Kissinger his career in politics. The West Point graduate came to Nixon's White House having fought Chinese forces during the Korean War at the Battle of Chosin Reservoir, one of the conflict's turning points. Then he fought Beijing's allies in Vietnam, for which he was awarded the Distinguished Service Cross, the Army's second-highest medal honoring valor. In 1969, the Army detailed him to the National Security Council Staff, where he became Kissinger's deputy and then Nixon's chief of staff.[54] Now he'd become, like his mentor Kissinger, a China lobbyist.

Bush deputies encouraged businesses with a stake in China to join forces with the administration and pressure the Senate and the House to preserve the PRC's privileged trade status.[55] This group included, among others: retailers that sold Chinese-made goods, like toys, footwear, and apparel; firms with investments in China, including those with factories in China that were manufacturing goods to be exported back to the United States, like Nike; as well as exporters like Boeing fearful that Beijing would impose retaliatory sanctions.[56]

The lobbying effort was spearheaded by the US Chamber of Commerce, which helped organize the Business Coalition for US-China Trade that included 125 business groups. The US-China Business Council, representing more than three hundred member corporations, also played a crucial role. There were also organizations representing specific industries, like the National Association of Manufacturers, the American Toy Association, US Wheat Associates, the National Foreign Trade Council, the Northwest Regional China Council, and the American Soybean Association.[57]

By urging industry to pressure lawmakers to defend Beijing's MFN status, Bush won the fight but put Congress on the wrong side of the electorate. The House voted in 1991 and 1992 to link the annual extension of China's MFN status to human rights, economic, and proliferation policies. But Bush vetoed the legislation both times, and while the House voted in both cases to override the veto, the Senate did not have the votes to do so.[58]

After Tiananmen, public support for China plummeted. Favorable views toward China went from 72 percent in a 1989 poll conducted before Tiananmen to 39 percent in early 1990. A May 1990 survey revealed that 53 percent of respondents supported measures that would pressure China to democratize. Another 1990 poll showed that the public disapproved of Bush's handling of relations with China by a 5–2 margin.[59]

The public had turned not just against China but also against a political and corporate establishment that enriched itself by tying American honor to a communist party that fired on its own citizens. A fissure opened between the US ruling class and middle class on China that would only continue to grow.

BLOOD MONEY

In October, four months after the massacre, Haig visited Tiananmen Square to celebrate the fortieth anniversary of Mao's revolution. He sat at a rostrum alongside a Czech Politburo member, North Korea's minister of finance, and the vice chairman of the Sino-Soviet Friendship Association.[60] It was like the scene in *The Manchurian Candidate* where representatives from the worldwide communist front meet to brainwash American soldiers—except this soldier, who had reached the highest ranks of the US military and American politics, had joined the other side of his own accord.

His former boss Kissinger arrived in November. He'd traveled with Maurice Greenberg, chairman of the American International Group, the worldwide insurance and financial services corporation. "Henry's image and influence in China is such that just by the fact that you're with him there's a nice rub-off effect," said Greenberg.[61]

AIG was building a huge office complex in Shanghai, where the company started in 1917, and Greenberg wasn't bothered by Tiananmen at all. "He was openly sympathetic to the Chinese leaders," according to Prestowitz. Greenberg wanted to get back to AIG's roots in China and that meant courting "Party leaders and lobbying the hell out of Washington."[62]

Deng assured US corporate and political elites that Tiananmen "was just domestic politics, and it should in no way deter them from taking advantage of China's ultra-low wages by using it as a production location from which to export to world markets and to sell into the growing China market."[63]

For some US industrialists, Tiananmen had created big opportunities. Robert Galvin, the CEO and chairman of Motorola, told Prestowitz that after the massacre the Chinese were so desperate for investment and technology that they were willing to make major concessions. Previously, the CCP had required foreign firms to enter joint ventures with Chinese partners, but when Galvin offered to build Motorola factories in China on the condition that Motorola retain 100 percent ownership of the business, Beijing agreed.[64]

"We aren't a bunch of carrion birds coming to pick the carcass," Bush's older brother Prescott told the press after Tiananmen. "But there are big opportunities in China, and Americans can't afford to be shut out."[65]

Starting in 1978, while his sibling was CIA director, Prescott's company had put together more than thirty joint ventures in China. He made his first trip there shortly after his brother was sworn in as vice president in 1981. Traveling to China shortly before his brother's February 1989 presidential trip, he won a 30 percent stake in a multimillion-dollar golf club in Shanghai. During negotiations, he became friendly with Shanghai Mayor Jiang Zemin, the future CCP general secretary.[66]

Prescott was also earning a $250,000 consultant fee from a firm financing a deal to send Hughes Aircraft communications satellites worth $300 million to China. Congress's July 1989 sanctions bill banned such transfers but included a proviso that the president could waive sanctions if a deal was in the national security interests of the United States. Prescott's younger brother lifted the punitive measures in December 1989, and the White House explained that the job held by the president's brother had not influenced the president's decision.[67] In reality, Prescott Bush was just part of a larger matrix of corporate elites keen to get back to business after Tiananmen.

Bush lost his 1992 reelection bid to the forty-six-year-old governor of Arkansas who challenged his stance on China. It was wrong, Bill Clinton said in his first debate with the incumbent, "to do what this administration did when all those kids went out there carrying the Statue of Liberty in Tiananmen Square. Mr. Bush sent two people in secret to toast the Chinese leaders and basically tell them not to worry about it."

But Clinton would soon come to see China like Bush did. The Bush administration started the process to get China into the General Agreement on Trade and Tariffs, predecessor of the WTO, and handed it off to the Clinton White House. The WTO, said its US publicists, would serve American workers and guarantee every US company a chance to get into the growing Chinese market. Everyone from Main Street to Wall Street was going to get rich.

But anyone who understood Kissinger's role mediating between US and CCP elites knew the truth: If normalizing trade relations was going to get everyone into China, then no one would need to pay Henry Kissinger for access to China. And neither Kissinger nor any other China lobbyist was advocating for a policy that would make themselves redundant. After all, as Alan Tonelson explained, Washington didn't have a trade policy with China; it had an offshoring policy. The US-China relationship was designed to enrich the ruling class.

President Bush took a cut, too. Starting in the mid-'90s, companies like Atlantic Richfield, IMC Global, the Chubb Group, and the Carlyle Group paid him to go to China and give a speech to attract senior CCP officials. "Events like this help renew contacts," an Atlantic Richfield spokesman said. "It helped to raise our profile in the region." Bush opened doors. "If you're unknown in China and trying to get known, and you're trying to get a license there, having a former president at a reception might get people to come who might not come otherwise," a Chubb official told the press. "We get to rub shoulders with them and get to know them better."[68]

Corruption was built into the design of the US-China relationship. Even House members and senators who weren't drawing directly from China's coffers benefited. By ensuring China stayed open, they made oceans of cash available to donors who fed it back into their election campaigns, an endless cycle generated by Washington's need to preserve the status quo.

This geopolitical pay-to-play scheme became the centerpiece of what the forty-first president of the United States called the New World Order. Coined in reference to the US-led global coalition to push Saddam Hussein out of Kuwait in 1991, Bush's phrase was meant to describe a future in which global relations would be governed by the rule of law and international institutions would jointly keep the peace and punish transgressors. It was what Kissinger had envisioned with his conception of the concert system: globalism. But rather than a cooperative international order with the main powers balancing each other out, Americans got something else: With a ruling class profiting from relations with a totalitarian regime disdainful of human life, the US establishment became so numbed to cruelty that contempt for the middle class became part of its governing style.

Maybe it wouldn't have mattered who was president, whether it was Reagan or someone else who was incapable of persuading himself that appeasement was realism. The opening had created a momentum of its own, and only bad things could possibly follow from hitching US interests to a totalitarian regime.

And yet Nixon himself later had second thoughts about the foreign policy masterstroke he and Kissinger were credited for. Before his death in 1994, he acknowledged the US political establishment had "gone a bit overboard on selling the American public on the political benefits of increased trade" with China. On reflection, he admitted, "We may have created a Frankenstein."[69]

With this confession, Nixon laid the foundations for the work of a future president. Trump was right—America's problems with China began with the opening itself.

CHAPTER FIVE

Business with Friends

I can't think of one single reason why the Chinese leadership would be wanting to help us with investment opportunities.[1]

—Richard Blum, investor and husband of US Senator Dianne Feinstein

DIANNE FEINSTEIN WAS MORTIFIED: HER HUSBAND WAS ARGUING with the general secretary of the Chinese Communist Party. "Oh, my God," she thought, "what's going on here?"[2]

Feinstein had known Jiang Zemin since the early 1980s, when she was mayor of San Francisco and he was mayor of Shanghai. There was a sister-city agreement between the two Pacific Ocean financial centers that would benefit them both. Feinstein was married to Richard Blum, an investor, who also profited. Feinstein and Blum and Jiang were friends.[3] Jiang visited the couple and spent Thanksgiving with them.[4]

"China made friends first," she said. "And then they did business with their friends."[5]

By the mid-1980s, the mayor of Shanghai and the husband of San Francisco's Democratic mayor were in business together.

Blum was vice chairman and director of Shanghai Pacific Partners, which entered into a joint venture with a Chinese government bank called Shanghai Investment and Trust Company. Together they built a $30 million high-scale retail-residential complex just outside Jiang's city.[6]

And now Jiang had the top spot in the party. He'd been promoted right before Tiananmen Square and was complicit in the massacre. Blum told the press in 1989 that because of the bloody crackdown on dissent he had suspended further joint-venture deals with the bank.[7] But when asked in a 2012 interview if he'd pulled out of his investments in China after Tiananmen, he admitted he hadn't. "You couldn't blame the whole Chinese nation, or even the key officials, for what happened at Tiananmen Square," said Blum. "There were some that were responsible for it. Some of it didn't want it around. Some of it didn't want it to happen. To blame the whole Chinese nation for Tiananmen Square is a bit racist."[8]

He'd lied that he'd withdrawn his investments, and over the following three decades lying about the nature of his investments and the rationale behind his wife's policies became a habit for them. They had to keep changing their story to maintain their image according to the spirit of the moment. What they were doing was so bad they needed to seem to themselves beyond reproach.

During the early phase of the US-China partnership, from the opening through Tiananmen, its main political advocates were Republicans, like the living monument to US-China relations, Henry Kissinger. There were radicals like the Black Panthers and their white liberal fellow travelers who pushed Mao's cause. But with the Democratic mayor, then senator, and her husband lending support from the more moderate precincts of the liberal establishment, it was a sign that the political class as a whole was increasingly getting comfortable with the Chinese Communist Party.

Few US elites wanted to think bad things about Jiang. They didn't want to believe he had anything to do with Tiananmen, and they plugged their ears when they heard about the industry he pioneered, "medical tourism"—cutting open the bodies of political dissidents, pulling out their organs, and selling them off to CCP elites and foreigners. They couldn't afford to question Jiang's decency or probity since he was the one who gave them access to China.

He flattered the Americans and even played the clown for them to show he was harmless. He crooned for Feinstein and danced with her. He was publicly smitten with the mayor of the city where, he said, he had "left his heart." When Richard Nixon visited Beijing in 1989, Jiang recited Lincoln's Gettysburg Address, in English. Nixon was inspired to get out of his chair and join in.[9]

In turn, the Americans trusted Jiang, especially when he soothed their concerns about their own self-image. For instance, he told Feinstein soon after Tiananmen that "China had no local police." She said that Jiang told her, "It was just the PLA. And no local police that had crowd control. So, hence the tanks." Feinstein admitted it was bad, "but," she said, "that's the past. One learns from the past. You don't repeat it. I think China has learned a lesson."[10]

It was about a year after Tiananmen, as Blum recalled, that Jiang wanted to see him and his wife for dinner. "New job, but same old Jiang Zemin," said the new party leader, greeting Blum and Feinstein in Beijing. The evening started well enough. They sat for their meal and then, according to Blum, Jiang started speaking about Tibet. It was, said Blum, "the standard propaganda about Tibet." Then, Blum told an interviewer, "I kind of blew my fuse."[11]

Tibet was important to Blum. He founded the American Himalayan Foundation to help Tibetans. He knew the Dalai Lama and liked to be described as a mediator between him and Beijing, though it is not clear why the Tibetan holy man would need anyone to mediate if the CCP and People's Liberation Army stopped hounding Tibetans.[12] Perhaps Blum was just exaggerating his role.

Blum told Jiang that he'd met a Tibetan nun imprisoned and tortured by Chinese authorities. She gave Blum two cloth bracelets she'd made in prison, "for mental protection against the Chinese," she said. Blum was wearing one at dinner. "Jiang Zemin, you see this bracelet?" said Blum. "It was given to me by a Tibetan nun. She's twenty-seven years old. She could've been your daughter, she could've been my daughter. I want to tell you what happened to her."[13]

As he recounted the nun's story to the CCP's general secretary, Blum got so mad that his hand was shaking. "I couldn't stop it," he remembered. His wife, he said, "was not particularly pleased, to put it mildly." The evening ended, said Blum, "on less than a wonderful upbeat."[14]

Some months later, Jiang's son was visiting the United States and invited Blum to dinner. Jiang Mianheng had gone to Drexel University in Philadelphia, then worked for Hewlett-Packard before he returned to China when his father became general secretary. Mianheng asked Blum if he was going to see Jiang on his next trip to China. "I'm not sure your father wants to see me," Blum said. The son had heard about their argument over Tibet and told him not to worry about it. "We have an old Chinese proverb that says, until you've had a real argument, you can't truly be friends."

When he met with Jiang in Beijing, Blum remembered, "I walk in to see the old man, he greets me like I'm his long-lost son." They talked about the Chinese economy and then Jiang said what his son had said, "You can't really be good friends unless you've had a real argument." That impressed Blum. Jiang, he said, "had that kind of openness."

Blum admired Jiang for brushing off his impassioned protest on behalf of a stranger. He wanted to see if Jiang had forgiven him for making a scene, and Jiang made it easy for him. Why wouldn't he? He knew that if Blum cared so much about the suffering of others, he wouldn't have dined a year after Tiananmen with the man who took control of the CCP after the massacre.

For Beijing, histrionics like Blum's were part of the cost of doing business with the Americans. Let them scream about human rights so they can unburden themselves of their guilty consciences. We will show we don't begrudge them their enlightened scruples. And then we'll all get back to work.

With Jiang as general secretary, China entered a crucial period in its relationship with the US, the post-Tiananmen phase. They'd embarrassed their American friends by spilling so much blood in public, and they needed a path into the WTO.

Accession to the world's trade body would: give China greater access to global markets due to reduced tariffs and trade barriers; increase foreign direct investment and facilitate the transfer of advanced technology; create millions of jobs, especially in urban areas, leading to mass migration from rural to urban regions; and grant China a seat at the table to shape global trade rules. In short, the WTO would unleash Beijing on the world by supercharging a totalitarian regime's political, diplomatic, and economic influence in global affairs.

But WTO bylaws stipulated that before accession, the US would first have to grant China's permanent normal trade relations (PNTR). Feinstein's historic role was to use her influence, first as a local California politician and then as a US senator, to get China across the finish line. It would benefit her as well as her husband the investor. And thus, the marriage of Feinstein and Blum stood for the larger coupling of corporate and political US interests.

The Feinstein-Blum-Jiang nexus also marked the start of a new phase of the US business community's relationship with China.

Up until the 1980s, American corporate interest in China was primarily in trade—more accurately, it was to access to China's cheap pool of educable labor to replace the American workforce. As one of the first major investors in China, Blum added another piece to the US-China partnership: with finance, the US ruling class began to capitalize China directly. Offshoring manufacturing to China dragged a third world backwater out of poverty, but with financiers like Blum and the Wall Street giants who followed him capitalizing China's state-owned enterprises, the party became fabulously rich as Americans staked their own wealth to the future of communism.

CHINATOWN

Feinstein was appointed mayor of San Francisco in 1978 after the previous mayor was assassinated. She first visited China in June 1979, months after the Carter administration opened full diplomatic ties with the PRC. Her goal was to establish her city as a major port for China trade, making it America's gateway to the Pacific. "There is a real opportunity for increased trade with China," she told the press before her trip.[15] "We have the potential to revive the port's health as a center of commerce."

The same year, the PRC opened a consulate in San Francisco, and Feinstein wanted to bind the city more closely yet with a partnership with China's major port city, Shanghai. "It was sort of a race between Los Angeles and San Francisco to establish a Sister City relationship with Shanghai and of course San Francisco won," she recalled in a 2005 speech, "and it was the first such Sister City relationship between an American city and a Chinese city."[16]

The two cities launched exchanges, mostly cultural and educational in nature since commercial enterprise was limited throughout her term as mayor during the 1980s.[17] The numbers would grow in the '90s as China became wealthier thanks to the United States—a period that coincided with Feinstein's move to Washington as a US senator, Jiang's ascent, and the push to get China into the WTO. Today California is the top US destination for PRC foreign direct investment. Between 2000 and 2016, for instance, California outpaced every other US state by attracting about $26 billion, twice what New York reaps, and roughly one-quarter of all Chinese investment in the United States.[18]

Given its central role in the history of China and America dating back to the middle of the nineteenth century, it was almost inevitable San Francisco would play a key role in the Party's plan to shape receptive and hospitable local communities across the country.

Chinese immigrants had first arrived in San Francisco in the late 1840s as part of a larger migrant wave stirred by the Gold Rush. By the early 1850s, an estimated twenty-five thousand Chinese, mostly men, had come to the United States and worked in mining or jobs supporting the gold economy—running laundries, shops, and kitchens—and this gave rise to an economically self-contained San Francisco district that came to be known as Chinatown.[19]

It was perhaps because of the crucial role that Chinese had played in creating California, and in particular building the Transcontinental Railroad—by 1868 the Central Pacific railroad employed some twelve thousand Chinese workers, more than 80 percent of its entire workforce—that conflict with other groups was inevitable.[20] In 1877, an anti-Chinese riot led by angry white workers, many of them Irish immigrants, raged for three days in Chinatown, killing four Chinese and destroying more than $100,000 worth of Chinese-owned property. Five years later the 1882 Chinese Exclusion Act capped Chinese immigration and froze the growth of Chinatown.

The legislation was repealed sixty-one years later after the bombing of Pearl Harbor and US entry into World War II when Washington saw China's Nationalist government as an ally against Japan.

The Immigration and Nationality Act of 1965 pushed the doors open for more Chinese immigration, and Chinatown grew again.

The district had historically been pro-Nationalist, but the communists' 1949 victory altered Chinatown's political and social dynamic. Some of the new migrants were at odds with their Chinese-American neighbors and became a conduit for radical causes that influenced Bay Area politics, a milieu that eventually produced the Black Panthers. Naturally, this made San Francisco a prime target for propaganda, espionage, and subterfuge—the remit of what the CCP calls United Front work.

The United Front originally referred to a broad communist alliance that Mao credited as the key to the CCP's victory over Chiang Kai-shek's Nationalist forces. Every Chinese leader since then has emphasized United Front work as crucial for advancing the Party's goals by rallying, and cultivating, allies to defeat a common enemy—and since the fall of the Soviet Union that's been the United States alone.[21] The CCP's United Front Work Department (UFWD) uses a network of organizations and individuals that operate in parallel to China's diplomatic and intelligence apparatus to neutralize opposition and shape the political environment at home and abroad.[22]

The cultivation of radical African-American activists is one example of United Front work, the sister cities program is another. It's a crucial part of the UFWD's foreign operations designed to influence and leverage overseas Chinese communities, like San Francisco's large Chinese-American community. These are seen as potential propaganda bases where Beijing finds natural allies who can help China project power.[23] Alternately, if those communities support rival ideologies, like Taiwanese independence, or prodemocracy movements, they're perceived as threats to be stamped out.

"San Francisco is a key place where China leverages so much influence," says Nathan Picarsic, a fellow at the Foundation for

Defense of Democracies, a Washington, DC, think tank. "As the biggest Chinatown in America, the overseas population there has both in terms of numbers and in terms of influence an outsized say relative to what other Chinatowns or overseas populations have. And because California is the top US state for investment, there's the influence that San Francisco's Chinatown has through commercial and trading relationships. So, it's highly prioritized within their system."

Silicon Valley adds another dimension to the significance of the Bay Area. "It's the hub for the technology China wants to access from the United States," says Picarsic. "It's an entry point into the broader U.S. markets."

It's also an access point where the CCP has sought to influence local and state officials, like Feinstein. With Tiananmen Square staining China's international reputation, the CCP redoubled its United Front outreach to co-opt foreign elites and shape foreign relations through its subnational strategy.

"The subnational strategy flows down from the logic of the United Front," says Picarsic. "They want things that are outside of China to do China's bidding, and 'subnational' refers to the United Front's efforts to use political assets below the national level to influence Washington or circumvent it."

The CCP sees America's federal system as a gap in our defenses. "The Chinese can just go and sign a deal with state and local government to have access to invest," says Picarsic. "And they can get states and local governments to advocate on their behalf at the federal government level. So, if a Chinese company is investing in Arkansas, they can get the governor of Arkansas to go and tell the federal government, 'Hey, take it easy on these guys because they're putting money into my state.' China understands the value of co-opting those actors within our system."

United Front work doesn't neatly fit into traditional espionage or lobbying categories. As one former senior US intelligence official who worked across several administrations tells me: "It's different, because most adversarial countries, like Russia, try to infiltrate and influence by targeting top-level US officials. But the Chinese go bottom up."

China's ability to target from the bottom up and deploy massive resources to compromise US officials at state and local levels is partly a function of the country's massive size. Smaller countries with fewer resources and a finite number of operatives can only afford to go after big fish. But China's resources are virtually limitless, with thousands of people—not just professional intelligence operatives but also businessmen, students, and others—to throw at a problem.

"China can influence at the congressional member level," says the former US intelligence official, "especially where they have members of Congress that have businesses in their districts that have big deals with China, and they leverage those businesses to put pressure on Congress to do things China wants. For example, John Deere has huge money in China. It's a nexus for their Asian franchise, selling tractors and farm equipment, so they exert influence in the local, state, and national races in the districts around the John Deere headquarters in Illinois."

Beijing can even afford to target congressional staff. "They'll pay for congressional staff to visit China and try to identify people that could be of potential assistance and bring them around early to being a supporter of China," says the former intelligence officer. "Maybe they get them in a compromising position so they have to be a supporter of China."

After sex, the easiest way to compromise targets is through money, which gives the CCP an instrument the Soviets never had. "We never had that commercial interest with the Soviet Union at the level we have with China," says the former intelligence official. "China is embedded in our economy."

And that was the CCP's intention from the start—to get US elites to believe that China's financial success meant theirs, too. And often it did, even if it cost America.

THE SENATOR AND THE INVESTOR

The Americans' theory of postwar development held that trade, investment, and economic reform inexorably led to political liberalization. By force-feeding China goods and money, the United States would make it too costly for the communists not to participate in their own destruction and give way to genuine liberals. But Mao himself had seen this coming. He warned that the West would use concepts like democracy and human rights to drive the PRC into the US-led order. He called it the theory of "peaceful evolution."[24]

Mao thought the Americans were naïve, but he hadn't foreseen that as the Cold War was winding down, the US ruling class would become cynical, too, affecting national security as well as the country's moral fabric. Why would corporate elites care if the PRC liberalized, especially if it meant that China's workforce would come to expect a standard of living as high as the US middle class they'd betrayed? From that perspective, Tiananmen was something like a proof-of-concept spectacle: If the regime was willing to gun down students, it wouldn't have any problems keeping labor in line.

With trade, CCP overseers showed their US partners they could keep production lines running and with finance Party elites could also guarantee outcomes for select American investors. "The Party handpicks the winners," says Brian Costello, a California-based entrepreneur and tech investor. "Investing in China isn't about navigating free-market competition or dealing with typical market uncertainties. It's about aligning with the Chinese Communist

Party's predetermined champions. American investors are chosen to profit in China, and not randomly—they're carefully selected based on their potential to transfer critical technology or their ability to influence US policies in Beijing's favor. This creates a manipulated environment where chosen companies and people reap artificially high returns."

As one US intelligence report warns:

> *The PRC may view the U.S. business community as an especially important vector to influence local, state, and national leaders, given that companies are key constituents of and often contributors to politicians at all levels. The PRC may use market access, investments, or economic dependency as leverage, and overtly press U.S. business leaders, particularly those with commercial interests in China, to lobby Washington for policies Beijing favors.*[25]

In other words, Costello explains, "When the Chinese permit Americans to invest in China's preselected corporate winners, it is essentially bribery on a grand scale, transforming the U.S. corporate elite into active agents of Beijing's geopolitical agenda."

Perhaps that explains the remarkable confluence between Feinstein's policy positions on China and Blum's financial success in China. Indeed, as Blum's associates told the press, he began doing business in China when his wife was mayor in the 1980s.[26]

Feinstein's willingness to downplay Tiananmen and relay Jiang's laughable excuse that there were no police in the capital of a police state for the government to call on, leaving Beijing no option but to call out the PLA against unarmed civilians, indicated early on her inclination to downplay China's human rights abuses in favor of continued engagement. And that policy profited US corporate elites, like her husband.

After Feinstein's unsuccessful 1990 run for governor, she won a special Senate election in 1992 and moved to Washington, where she served two of the largest Chinese diasporas in the United States—the San Francisco/Oakland/San Jose area and the greater Los Angeles area. She quickly emerged as a key advocate for maintaining normal trade relations with China, arguing that isolating Beijing would be counterproductive. She started as one of the wealthiest senators, and with her trade policy positions synched to Blum's blossoming investment in the Chinese market, her bank account would balloon over the course of her political career.[27]

As his wife started her senate term, Blum's China portfolio included the $30 million residential and retail high-rise on the outskirts of Shanghai he'd helped build as vice chairman and director of Shanghai Pacific Partners, one of the first joint ventures between San Francisco and Chinese investors. In 1989, Blum had also acquired a 6 percent stake in Northwest Airlines, then the only US carrier with nonstop flights to China, which positioned him to benefit from expanding US-China commerce.[28]

In May 1993, Feinstein declared her strong support for continued trading with China while her husband was planning to deploy more capital there. His firm, Richard C. Blum & Associates, entered a joint venture to found Newbridge Capital, an emerging markets private equity fund that sought opportunities in China. Blum was planning to bundle $2 to $3 million of his own money with $150 million from other investors to invest in China's state-owned enterprises that sold bicycles, cement, and telecommunications equipment. In August of the same year, Jiang invited him and Feinstein to Beijing to meet with top Chinese leaders.[29]

In 1994, when some in Congress sought to rescind China's trade status over human rights abuses, Feinstein warned that sanctions would "inflame Beijing's insecurities."[30] The same year, she told the media that Blum's economic interest in China was "news to me." She was skirting the truth when she said, "All I know is presently he doesn't have any investment in China."[31]

Despite the high regard Jiang might have had for his two American friends, there's evidence he didn't entirely trust them—or at least wanted to make sure he was dealing with honest brokers. Just as Feinstein was embarking on her Senate career, China's ministry of state security wanted a spy to keep tabs on her.

Russell Lowe was a longtime Bay Area political activist who promoted pro-Beijing causes before he came on as Feinstein's office director.[32] Lowe would work for her for twenty years—during which time she was briefed on America's most closely guarded secrets as a member of the Senate Intelligence Committee. Feinstein said that he had "no access to sensitive information," but the FBI was concerned he was reporting back to handlers at the PRC's San Francisco consulate.[33]

The intelligence official says he wasn't surprised when he heard the news that the CCP had spent two decades spying on a US official who couldn't have been closer to the top leadership in Beijing. "I didn't find it amazing that they had penetrated her office. These are relationships that are cultivated over years and California politicians, largely Democrats now, are very susceptible to Chinese influence. They want the money for elections. And liberals are naturally sympathetic to the Communist Party."

In 1995, Feinstein gained a seat on the Senate Foreign Relations Committee, further elevating her role in China policy. She used her floor time to defend Beijing's progress. She insisted that "China is changing" under Western influence and that lecturing Beijing on human rights from afar would not work. "It's one thing to talk about human rights here," she said, but "pounding the desk here isn't going to make China change. China is changing. And it's the Western influence in China that's helping the change."[34]

In a June 1996 hearing on China's MFN status, she objected to how her colleagues singled out Beijing. Feinstein asked why China was subjected to criticism while no one said anything about Russia's invasion of Chechnya or the war in Liberia. "What is absolutely wrong about American foreign policy," she said, "is its hypocrisy."[35]

She and her husband denied that his business in China profited from her China advocacy. "He is in San Francisco running his business, I am in Washington being a United States senator and they are two separate things," Feinstein told a reporter. "I don't know how I can prove it to people like you. Maybe I get divorced. Maybe that is what you want."[36]

It's true they were in two different US cities, but they met often in the Chinese capital. Between 1995 and 1997, they visited together three times.[37] On their January 1996 trip, Blum and Feinstein went to another dinner with Jiang. They dined in the room where Mao died. "We were told that we were the first foreigners to see his bedroom and the swimming pool," said Feinstein. She said her "husband has never discussed business with Jiang Zemin, never would, never has."[38]

And yet that same year, Blum's China investments accelerated. Through Newbridge Capital, he helped orchestrate investments in Chinese state-run companies. In 1996, Newbridge acquired a 24 percent stake in a Chinese state-owned steel manufacturer for $23 million. The deal was facilitated by a former Chinese official from the state investment firm China International Trust Investment Corporation (CITIC). Newbridge also invested $14 million for a 24 percent stake in a Chinese food and beverage company run by another ex-CITIC executive.[39]

In a 1996 editorial published four months after their visit to Mao's sanctuary, Feinstein argued Beijing's case.[40] "Tying most-favored-nation to improvement in human rights is ineffective at best and counterproductive at worst," she wrote. "Revoking the trade status would be seen by China as the United States promulgating a complete break in Sino-American relations, putting in grave danger U.S. strategic interests in Asia."

China's human rights abuses were evidence it wasn't a normal country. But according to Feinstein it was nonetheless a matter of US national security to ignore Beijing's bloody hands and integrate it into the global system.

"Just 30 years ago," Feinstein wrote, "China was engaged in the massive upheaval of the Cultural Revolution and Great Leap Forward, during which 20 million Chinese were either killed or imprisoned. Human rights were at their lowest point. Since then, the positive changes in China have been dramatic. Chinese society continues to open up with looser ideological controls, freer access to outside sources of information and increased media reporting. More people in China vote for their leadership on the local level than do Americans."[41]

It takes a special kind of contempt for your own country to make the case for China by telling Americans that they're less civic-minded than the subjects of a third-world tyranny. This was Huey Newton speaking: The People's Republic of China is freer than America. The Oakland Maoist praised China to make the United States look bad, and the senator from California leveled differences between America and the PRC to run cover for a communist regime.

As Feinstein became increasingly strident in her support of Beijing, scrutiny of her husband's China investments intensified. In March 1997, news broke that a managing director of Blum's Newbridge Capital, Peter Kwok, had consulting ties to a subsidiary of

China Ocean Shipping Company (COSCO), a state-owned shipping giant.[42] At the time, COSCO's pending lease to run the Long Beach Naval Shipyard terminal had stirred controversy in Washington over national security issues. When *The Wall Street Journal* reported Blum's indirect link to COSCO (through Kwok), Blum and Feinstein vehemently denied any wrongdoing or influence peddling. Blum said he had "never even heard of" the Long Beach project until reading about it in the news, and characterized his connection to COSCO as "trivial," contending that Kwok's COSCO role predated Newbridge. Feinstein likewise asserted she had "nothing to do with" the port deal's approval and that any business ties between her husband's associates and COSCO were irrelevant to her work.[43]

With mounting evidence that Blum did indeed invest in Chinese enterprises, Feinstein changed her message. Now she claimed there was no conflict of interest between her work and her husband's. Blum, she claimed, had never sought to exploit her access to Jiang to increase his opportunities in China, and his business there had no effect on her foreign policy or trade positions regarding China. "We have built a firewall," she said about her political career and his investments in 1997.[44] "That firewall has stood us in good stead."

Blum also sought to allay conflict-of-interest concerns by announcing in 1997 that he would donate any personal profits from his Chinese investments to a Tibetan refugee charity. According to Blum, it was to "remove any perception that I...benefit from or influence my wife's position on China."[45]

As Blum laundered his business dealings with the regime by donating to a charity that helped its victims, Feinstein bizarrely amplified her pro-CCP apologetics. During Jiang's US visit in the fall, she called for a joint US-China human rights commission to examine the "evolution of human rights in both countries." She compared Tiananmen to the 1970 killing of four students during an anti–Vietnam War protest at Kent State and called for a commission of comparative human rights to study "the success and failures [of] both Tiananmen Square and Kent State."[46] But the Americans she was trying to persuade knew how the two incidents differed. The CCP sent the People's Liberation Army into Tiananmen Square to put down the protestors, but no political body ordered the troops from the Ohio National Guard to shoot unarmed Americans.

As part of a 1997 Justice Department investigation into Chinese money going to US political campaigns, the FBI warned Feinstein that Beijing was trying to push campaign funds her way.[47] She told the press that she had "no reason to believe" that China had in fact contributed to her campaign. "None whatsoever." She had a point: Why would the Chinese donate to her campaign when they were already in business with her husband?[48] At this point, Newbridge Capital was managing billions, with a presence in Beijing and Shanghai, and stakes in multiple Chinese ventures.

Still, Feinstein was mad. "If there is credible evidence," she said, "tell me what it is. Enable me to protect myself. That's the job of the FBI." According to her, none of the FBI agents "told me where or when or how or what to look for." Someone must have told her where to look, since she returned $12,000 from donors with connections to a CCP-affiliated bank.[49]

In 1999, Feinstein took a leading role in rallying support for China's permanent normal trade relations status, arguing that granting China PNTR would integrate it into the global system and benefit US businesses. That same year, Blum appeared to adjust his investments: Feinstein's office stated that Blum had divested his last direct holdings in mainland China by 1999.

In truth, Blum's firm was still deeply involved in China-related business via intermediaries. From 1998 to 2000, Newbridge Capital invested nearly $400 million into East Asia, including companies with profits tied to China's booming market. For example, Newbridge invested in Hong Kong–based Kerry Properties, which was building high-rises in mainland China, and tech startups aiming to expand China's internet infrastructure.[50] Thus, Blum's venture funds were positioned to profit from China's growth—at the same time that Feinstein lobbied to lock in PNTR with Beijing.

When news that Blum's business was still intertwined with China's market went public, he claimed he had earmarked some of these China-related assets for charitable donation and had sold others by August 2000. Feinstein denied any conflict, asserting that her vote in September to pass the PNTR legislation was based solely on US interests.[51]

Still, she drew fire, including from her Republican Senate opponent that year, who accused Feinstein of profiting indirectly from policies she enacted.[52] She insisted that all required financial disclosures were made and that her advocacy of US-China trade was long-standing and principled.[53] She won reelection in 2000.

In 2001, the PRC formally joined the WTO, which, she argued, would gradually pull China toward international norms. Most of her colleagues made the same case. But what set her apart was that her spouse was in a position to exploit the liberalization of China's financial sector.

In 2002, Newbridge Capital entered talks to acquire a major stake in Shenzhen Development Bank, one of the first Chinese banks available for foreign investment. In 2004, after two years of regulatory wrangling, Newbridge completed the acquisition, paying $145 million for an 18 percent stake.[54] As the largest shareholder, Newbridge became the first foreign firm to gain effective control of a Chinese bank—a coup for Newbridge and its investors.[55] In 2009,

Newbridge sold its Shenzhen stake to Ping An Insurance, a Chinese financial services company, for $1.68 billion, netting Newbridge a 900 percent return on investment.[56]

"That windfall is by no means normal in a regular market environment," says tech investor Brian Costello. "But in the context of a communist party rigging the game to benefit its American friends, it is par for the course. And some of the big Wall Street firms made considerably more."

In 2003, Newbridge partnered with state-owned China Netcom to rescue Asia Global Crossing's undersea cable network. Newbridge took a 24.5 percent stake in the new Asia Netcom venture while China Netcom held 51 percent.[57] The deal gave Newbridge a role in a major Chinese telecom infrastructure asset.

By 2003, Newbridge was a $1.2 billion firm, with an asset base continuing to expand through new funds and co-investments.[58] Within five years, it grew to oversee around $50 billion in assets under management as it opened offices in Beijing and Shanghai.[59] Newbridge professionals placed in the country's key markets allowed Newbridge to source deals and navigate regulatory relationships within China.[60]

In the same timeframe, as U.S.-China frictions grew over jobs, product safety, and espionage, Feinstein counseled against confrontational legislation, warning that isolating China could backfire. In 2007, the Senate introduced a bill that would have sanctioned China for currency manipulation—lawmakers believed that China was deliberately undervaluing its currency by as much as 40 percent to give Chinese companies an unfair advantage in international trade.[61] Feinstein preferred diplomatic engagement. "There was originally this kind of anti-communist view of China," she said. "That's changing. China is a socialist country, but one that is increasingly becoming capitalistic."[62]

But it was using capital to undermine the United States, sometimes in coordination with her husband's investments.

In 2005, for instance, a Chinese company named Lenovo announced that Newbridge was one of three US firms that had staked its purchase of IBM's personal computer business. The sale raised security concerns, and indeed in 2010 US officials found that "a large amount of Lenovo laptops were sold to the US military that had a chip encrypted on the motherboard that would record all the data that was being inputted into that laptop and send it back to China," according to 2010 court testimony from a US official who managed computer operations centers for the US Marines in Iraq. "That was a huge security breach. We don't have any idea how much data they got, but we had to take all those systems off the network."[63]

In 2007, another firm Blum invested in acquired a company named Aeroflex that violated US export control regulations by shipping off chips to China that were used in PRC satellites.[64]

Feinstein consistently rejected any implication of impropriety, stressing that her record on China was the same long before her husband stood to benefit. Nonetheless, the pattern was clear by 2010: Feinstein's advocacy for closer US-China economic ties paralleled Richard Blum's expanding investments in China, as both halves of the couple rode the wave of US-China normalization to new heights.

At the time of her death in September 2023, her net worth was estimated to be between $69.4 million and $110 million, including a blind trust valued between $5 million and $25 million, several large bank accounts, a multimillion-dollar condo in Hawaii, a mansion in Washington, DC, a private jet, and a $37.5 million stake in Carlton Hotel Properties.[65] Blum was worth at least $1 billion at the time of his death in 2022.[66]

They were the perfect China Class power couple, admired and envied by an echelon of worldly US elites delirious with the prospect of becoming fabulously wealthy—thanks to a totalitarian police state powered by slave labor. They hid their shame and justified their betrayal with the lie that became their legacy: Relations with China would benefit all Americans.

CHAPTER SIX

The Greatest Theft

We can't continue to allow China to rape our country.[1]

—Donald Trump

B Y THE MID-1990S, EVERY MAJOR POLITICAL PROBLEM THAT THE
United States had suffered in the 1970s had been resolved, to
America's advantage. Inflation was low and unemployment had
declined throughout the decade, reaching historic lows in 1999 at
4 percent. Gas was cheap. The Soviet Union was gone. The Japanese economy was no longer the looming threat it seemed during
the 1980s. Wall Street was in an upswing after the 1987 crash, and
the champagne was flowing in the suddenly fashionable Tribeca and
Soho neighborhoods where venture capitalists dined with internet
dreamers long before anyone saw the dot-com boom for the bubble
it was. America was invulnerable.

So when Bill Clinton made it a priority to get China into the
World Trade Organization, few of the wise men of Washington
believed that it would backfire. But Trump did.

For more than a decade at that point, he'd been warning of trade imbalances. The problem at the time was Japan, then China later. Trump said about US trade with Tokyo: "It's not free trade. If you ever to go to Japan right now and try to sell something, forget about it," he told Oprah Winfrey. "Just forget about it. It's almost impossible."[2] Maybe it seems strange that a corporate style setter in a yellow power tie who filled the tabloids with news of his romantic liaisons read the signs right, but by the time Clinton was readying to normalize trade relations with Beijing permanently, Trump was among the few business elites who took a stand against it.

"I'm a good businessman and I can be amazingly unsentimental when I need to be," he wrote in his 2000 book *The America We Deserve*. "I also recognize that when it comes down to it, we can't do much to change a major nation's internal policies. Maybe I should do what regular politicians do—overlook principles, ignore human rights and hope for the best."[3]

But, he wrote, he couldn't "shrug off the mistreatment of China's citizens by their own government. My reason is simple: These oppressive policies make it clear that China's current government has contempt for our way of life. It fears freedom because it knows its survival depends on oppression. It does not respect individual rights. It is still, at heart, a collectivist society. As such, it is a destabilizing force."[4] For Trump, how Beijing treated its own people showed how it would treat others, especially Americans.

Many US lawmakers agreed, like Senators Daniel Patrick Moynihan of New York and George Mitchell of Maine, as well as California Congresswoman Nancy Pelosi, all Democrats. They opposed US engagement with China for several reasons, especially human rights. But the pro–US worker position, America First, was most powerfully advocated by Missouri congressman Richard Gephardt.

In 1988 the Democrat legislator ran for president with a message of economic nationalism and argued that the American worker was hurting from foreign competition. He'd seen two Chrysler plants in his district shut down in the early 1980s because of Japanese competition.[5] He pushed for sanctions, like the ones Trump later imposed on China, to punish "free-riders" on the global trading system.[6] Gephardt said that the system was rigged by political and business elites with support from the intellectual classes, and described that cohort much the same way Trump would come to define the Swamp.[7] The establishment, said Gephardt, was "a loose term for academics, editorial writers and some who have a vested economic interest in not changing some of these problems, who believe you have to accommodate decline."[8]

Gephardt said the China debate was about "principle and value and belief."[9] Consequently Gephardt, like Trump, was called racist for defending Americans.[10] "The [trade] debate is often smothered at the outset by the issue of race," said Gephardt. Fighting Japan's unfair trade practices before he turned to China's, he found that "Americans who criticize Japanese trade practices are often labeled as racist Japan bashers."[11]

He talked about China's use of prisoners in the manufacturing sector: "We can't compete with slave labor." He called China's political system "free-market Stalinism."[12] He opposed most favored nation (MFN) trade status for China, reasoning "that unlimited access to the U.S. market comes with certain responsibilities." And market access, he said "is a privilege, not a right. I believe that the communist government in Beijing has forfeited that privilege. It is time we revoke China's most-favored-nation status." According to Gephardt, it was "time for a new policy of firm engagement that finally advances our national interests and ideals."[13]

Kissinger disagreed. He had been on the other side of the China issue for more than two decades. He'd supported trade with the

PRC from the start. "Our interest in trade with China," he told Mao in February 1972, "is not commercial. It is to establish a relationship that is necessary for the political relations we both have."[14]

And in a joint US-PRC statement at the conclusion of the trip: "Both sides view bilateral trade as another area from which mutual benefit can be derived, and agreed that economic relations based on equality and mutual benefit are in the interest of the people of the two countries. They agree to facilitate the progressive development of trade between their two countries."[15] Indeed, during the trip Nixon personally approved the sale of ten Boeing planes to Beijing.[16]

Maybe Bill Clinton meant it when he criticized George H. W. Bush on the 1992 campaign trail for coddling dictators but he would come to countenance repeated blows to American honor in order to coddle his donors.

In the first presidential debate a month before the election, Clinton said it was wrong "to do what this administration did when all those kids went out there carrying the Statue of Liberty in Tiananmen Square. Mr. Bush sent two people in secret to toast the Chinese leaders and basically tell them not to worry about it."[17] Clinton said it was only thanks to Congress that "China has finally agreed to stop sending us products made with prison labor. Not because we coddled them, but because the administration was pushed into doing something about it. And recently the Chinese have announced they are going to lower some barriers to our products, which they ought to do since they have a $15 billion trade surplus with the United States under Mr. Bush."

The trade deficit would more than double under Clinton, reaching $39.5 billion at the end of his first term and more than doubling again to nearly $84 billion at the end his second.[18]

Clinton said he would be firm with China. "I would say if you want to continue as most-favored-nation status for your government owned industries as well as your private ones, observe human rights in the future. Open your society. Recognize the legitimacy of those kids that were carrying the Statue of Liberty. If we can stand up for our economics, we ought to be able to preserve the democratic interests of the people of China. And over the long run they will be more reliable partners."

Clinton's tough talk on China was designed to win support from labor unions and soothe senior Democrats like Mitchell, who'd sponsored legislation to prevent Bush from granting China most favored nation status in 1991 and 1992 unless Beijing met specific benchmarks on human rights.[19] Bush vetoed the legislation both times, but Clinton assured Democratic lawmakers that wouldn't happen on his watch.

In 1993, Mitchell pushed similar legislation while business leaned hard in the other direction. Hundreds of companies and dozens of trade associations signed a letter to Clinton demanding he not condition MFN status on meeting human rights benchmarks. Signatories like the accounting firm Arthur Andersen, Phillips Petroleum, and AT&T had significant investments in China, and many were large Democratic National Committee donors.[20]

Clinton told Mitchell there was no need to bother with a bill: He told him he'd renew China's privileged trade status for another year but would issue an executive order stipulating that subsequent approval would require Beijing to meet mandatory obligations, like ending the export of prison-labor products to the United States.[21] But the CCP continued to flood the US with goods made by prisoners, including political dissidents and ethnic minorities. Nonetheless, when China's MFN status came up in 1994, Clinton revoked the executive order, and announced he was delinking human rights from trade.

According to Clinton, severing trade status from human rights in fact gave him the "best opportunity to lay the basis for long-term sustainable progress in human rights."[22] How? Because by not isolating China the United States could "engage the Chinese with not only economic contacts but with cultural, educational and other contacts, and with a continuing aggressive effort in human rights."

It was double-talk. Clinton had more than enough to pressure the communist regime—if you want access to the world's biggest market, you have to change. Instead, delinking trade from human rights signaled another key moment in the US-China relationship—more evidence, along with the 1972 opening itself and then Tiananmen, that the United States was willing to squander leverage on the CCP and forfeit American honor in exchange for gilded fantasies.

This was the moment when the Democratic and Republican establishment fell fully into alignment on China. They were all Kissinger's children, and together with the corporate establishment, the media and cultural elites, they were the core of America's China Class.

After Clinton delinked trade from human rights, Kissinger wrote an opinion article, with Jimmy Carter's secretary of state Cyrus Vance, congratulating the president for making the right decision. "Americans," they wrote, "need to consider the unique aspects of China's national experience. It is a great power that cannot be told what to do about its government and economy any more than we would tolerate their dictating these matters to us."[23]

But as Kissinger had made plain in the wake of the Tiananmen massacre, the Chinese did have their say in internal US matters. The PRC had lobbied US policymakers through none other than Henry Kissinger, who used the media and his corporate clients to make Beijing's case.

While Americans strongly believe in the universal appeal of human rights, the Chinese consider our demands interference in their domestic affairs, especially when the U.S. goals are publicly and loudly proclaimed. Preaching at the Chinese about our values in public was bound to exacerbate relations without substantially advancing our human rights objectives.[24]

Kissinger wanted from Clinton what he got from Bush before him—to stay on the path he'd cut first as a statesman and then as a consultant. The Bush administration could have shut the door on China after Tiananmen. Instead the forty-first president and Kissinger's men rebuilt relations with China, and turned everything over to Clinton. By delinking trade from human rights to grant China MFN, the new president gave Kissinger's policy preferences bipartisan legislative authority.

Clinton's mission was to get China into the WTO. It would be done in steps. He'd passed his first test by staring down congressional opposition from his own party to delink trade from human rights. Next was to guide negotiations with the Europeans to form the WTO, and most crucially to upgrade China's MFN status on a permanent basis, what was later described as permanent normal trade relations (PNTR).

What Clinton couldn't have foreseen was that CCP aggression would make it considerably more difficult for him to get Beijing into world trade's governing body. His success would enrich and unleash the most murderous regime in modern times.

CHINAGATE

In September 1996 news broke that the DNC had returned a $250,000 donation from a shell company headed by a foreign national after questions arose about its legality.[25] After Clinton's

1996 victory, there were further reports of large contributions to Democratic candidates, including the president, that had been bundled by Asian businesses and individuals, as well as Chinese intelligence officers and assets.

Why would Beijing throw money at Clinton and his allies since he was on China's side to start with? He'd delinked trade from human rights, and there was little chance he'd change his China policy at that point. But WTO entry was so important to Beijing that the CCP wouldn't want to take chances: With US corporate giants pushing Clinton on one side, Chinese intelligence would push from the other to make sure Clinton did the right thing.

A February 1997 *Washington Post* story reported that the FBI believed Chinese agents had coordinated contributions to the DNC through the PRC's US embassy.[26] The plan was first discussed in early 1995 and called for Chinese officials to channel more than $2 million into US campaigns.[27] Nonetheless, the White House continued to frame what would become known as Chinagate as a matter of improper campaign fundraising. In reality, it was a broad intelligence operation that involved several channels, the most significant of which led directly from PRC intelligence agents and assets to the White House.

The leading players were: Mochtar Riady and James Riady, John Huang, Johnny Chung, Liu Chaoying, and PLA General Ji Shengde.

Mochtar Riady was a Chinese immigrant raised in Indonesia and owner of the Lippo Group, an Indonesian multinational company with diverse business interests, including real estate and financial services. In 1980, he met John Huang, a Taiwanese national who'd moved to the United States in 1969.[28] The two were attending a financial seminar in Little Rock in 1980, where first-term Governor Bill Clinton was a featured speaker. In the early 1980s, Riady bought a minority interest in an Arkansas-based bank and sent his son James to Little Rock to learn the business. The younger Riady was introduced to Clinton, for like DNC bosses, China saw Clinton as a man on the go. It appears that the Riadys had approached the future US president as a target of the CCP's subnational program.

According to US intelligence sources, the Riadys had long-standing ties to Chinese intelligence. Their relationship with CCP spy services was based on mutual assistance—Beijing arranged international business opportunities for the Riadys and demanded kickbacks and other forms of help, apparently including compromising senior US officials.[29]

After Clinton's 1992 victory, Huang was named to a senior-level post at the Commerce Department, where he had access to classified intelligence. He was briefed dozens of times by CIA officers on US intelligence activities in Asia and viewed hundreds of pieces of raw intelligence that revealed sources and methods, the US intelligence community's crown jewels. Often after the briefings, Huang surreptitiously visited an office across the street from the Commerce building that was maintained by Lippo associates. There he received faxes and packages and made phone calls that wouldn't show up on Commerce Department records.[30]

In September 1995, Huang was moved to a DNC fundraising post, a move Clinton coordinated with James Riady, who was present at the Oval Office meeting when Clinton approved the transfer. In another Oval Office meeting with Clinton in 1996, Riady lobbied for good trade relations with China. That same year, the Lippo Group and associates raised $1 million for Democrats.[31] Huang himself raised $3.4 million, half of which the DNC was compelled to return when it could not determine where it came from.[32] Decades after the scandal, Chinese state media would celebrate Huang as the "man who helped Clinton become president."[33]

Then there was Johnny Chung, a California businessman born in

Taiwan who became a conduit for PLA money directed to the Clinton campaign. Between 1994 and 1996, Chung made forty-nine visits to the White House. According to Chung, Hillary Clinton aides charged him for bringing clients to events at the White House—which, said Chung, "is like a subway: You have to put in coins to open the gates."[34]

Chung was on a Commerce Department trade mission to China when he met with a woman who was a colonel in the PLA, Liu Chaoying, also an executive at a state-owned aerospace company. Liu's father was a PLA admiral, Liu Huaqing, known as the "father of the modern Chinese Navy," and at the time the vice chairman of China's Central Military Commission. Her elder brother, Liu Zhuoming, was a vice admiral in the PLA Navy.[35]

Famous for her fur coats and designer shoes, Liu Chaoying connected Chung to the head of Chinese military intelligence, General Ji Shengde. According to Chung, Ji told him, "We really like your president. We hope he will be reelected. I will give you $300,000. You can give it to your president and the Democratic party."

In 1998, Chung pled guilty to campaign finance and related bank fraud charges. He was sentenced in December 1998 to probation and three thousand hours of community service.[36]

John Huang pled guilty to campaign finance charges in 1999. He was sentenced to one year of probation and ordered to pay a $10,000 fine and serve five hundred hours of community service.[37]

In 2001, James Riady pled guilty to a felony charge of conspiring to defraud the United States by unlawfully reimbursing campaign donors with foreign corporate funds in violation of federal election law. He paid a $8.6 million fine.[38]

Dozens of others were charged, including Charlie Trie, who owned a restaurant in Little Rock where he'd often served his friend then-Governor Bill Clinton. No one went to prison.

Naturally the PRC Chinese denied its involvement, and Washington, DC, China experts feared the scandal would make it harder to defend the communist regime. According to a China analyst at the Brookings Institution, Nicholas Lardy, "critics of China would point to any evidence of an influence-buying plan by Beijing to argue that it cannot be trusted on other subjects."[39]

But of course China had been buying influence since at least the mid-1980s, when Kissinger began bringing US corporate elites to Beijing to secure business deals conditioned on their agreeing to lobby for China in Washington. The evidence that China paid for political favors was clear to anyone who cared to look. Indeed, by the time news of Chinagate broke in 1996, Senator Dianne Feinstein's long friendship with Jiang and her husband Richard Blum's investment success in China had plainly illustrated the dynamic.

And yet even today Chinagate is not properly understood as part of a broader offensive against the United States. In line with its United Front work, Beijing aimed to penetrate the American political system by buying access, grooming friendly policymakers, and obtaining strategic information about America's most sensitive US institutions—including our nuclear weapons labs.

By 1995, US intelligence officials had figured out the Chinese had been stealing secrets from major nuclear weapons laboratories since the mid-1980s. The officials compared China's haul to the secrets the infamous 1940s Soviet spy ring stole from Los Alamos, claiming it was "as bad as the Rosenbergs." But the breach wasn't made public until 1999—after all, the espionage conflicted with Clinton's China policy. Had Clinton made it public, it might have derailed PNTR and subsequently China's accession to the WTO. According to one US official, "it undercut the Administration's efforts to have a strategic partnership with the Chinese."[40]

The administration feared Chinagate would do the same, so aides obscured the facts: In reality, the problem wasn't ambiguous campaign finance laws, but that the Chinese were pushing money to Democrats to win favor with the president's party. Rather than put some room between the White House and Beijing, the Clinton team stood firm: "We believe there's no basis for any change in our policy toward China," a Clinton spokesman said at the time, "which is one of engagement."[41]

White House officials denied that Clinton or his aides knowingly participated in any wrongdoing. Suggestions that the president sanctioned improper contributions were "flat-out wrong," a Clinton press aide said in early 1997.[42] In time the Clintons would solve the problem of apparent impropriety—or outright criminality—when they set up the Clinton Foundation, which was proud to take PRC money. For instance, Alibaba Group, a Chinese e-commerce company, donated between $500,000 to $1 million.[43] Rilin Enterprises, a company owned by a billionaire PRC official, pledged $2 million to the Clinton Foundation in 2013.[44]

Clinton dismissed the Chinagate scandal entirely. "I do not know whether it is true or not," he said of Chinese intelligence's fundraising drive for the Democrats. "Therefore, since I don't know, it can't...and shouldn't affect the larger long-term strategic interests of the American people in our foreign policy."[45]

LIGHTHIZER

From the perspective of a former US official who'd served as Reagan's deputy US trade representative and had spent the 1990s warning about the dangers of engaging China, Chinagate was no mystery: "The money," wrote Robert Lighthizer, "was meant to influence the decision on whether China should be permitted to join the World Trade Organization." For China, he wrote in a 1997 *New York Times* article, "accession to the W.T.O. is critically important not only to enhance its prestige but also because membership would offer assurance to investors that China is part of the trading community and give it protection from countries taking unilateral action against it."[46]

China's industrial strategy, he wrote in his 1997 article, "is based on its 'right' to become an export powerhouse. Viewed in that light, it is not an exaggeration to say that if China is allowed to join the W.T.O. on the lenient terms that it has long been demanding, virtually no manufacturing job in this country will be safe." That is, Beijing's plan was to make America poor and hollow out its industrial base to leave it incapable of defending itself.

China's "leaders view economics the same way they view defense, foreign policy or human rights," Lighthizer wrote in a subsequent article. "It is a means of expanding the power of the state and maintaining control of its population." And that, he explained, left "no room for reasonable doubt that the Chinese are intent on becoming the dominant power in Asia, wholly without regard for the legitimate security concerns of the United States."[47]

Lighthizer, along with Trump and Gephardt, was one of the few figures during the Clinton years who argued against the conventional wisdom that trading with China would change the nature of the communist regime or help American workers. In 2011, as Trump contemplated a third-party run for the presidency, Lighthizer wrote an article defending Trump from Republican criticism of his protectionist policies.

"At the beginning of this nation, Alexander Hamilton and his followers were staunch conservatives who helped found American capitalism—and avowed protectionists," wrote Lighthizer.[48] "Can anyone really think that getting tough with China is a 'liberal' idea?"

Was it a conservative idea, Lighthizer asked, to "allow a foreign adversary to use currency manipulation, subsidies, theft of intellectual property and dozens of other forms of state-sponsored, government-organized unfair trade to run up a more than $270 billion trade surplus with us and to take U.S. jobs?"

All free trade with China had accomplished, Lighthizer concluded, was "strengthening our adversaries and creating a world where countries who abuse the system—such as China—are on the road to economic and military dominance."

Trump would name Lighthizer US trade representative in his first term, and he became one of the stars of the administration's China policy. I spoke with him in Palm Beach where he lives not far from Mar-a-Lago.

"China is the most significant geopolitical rival the US ever had," he told me, "and infinitely more capable than the Soviet Union."

The United States had repeatedly forfeited its advantage over the course of several administrations, most notably Bush the elder's. "The Chinese learned from Tiananmen," says Lighthizer. "Six months after it and they went back to business as usual."

Like Trump, Lighthizer believes that every US president since Nixon was bad on China. But Clinton, he says, was the worst: "Clinton gave us the UN trade agreements that created the WTO. And then he did PNTR, which led the way for China to enter the WTO the next year. It was a decade of doubling down on dung. And we paid the price for it. PNTR was the worst economic decision the US ever made, and even I wouldn't have predicted it would be this bad."

I asked what he'd understood about China at the time that almost everyone else got wrong.

"In the first place, the Chinese were never going to open their markets. They were always going to be mercantilist. And by the way, so were the Japanese. And so was America. People would say, 'No, a great way to build your economy is through free trade.' But everybody built their economy on protectionism. There's no great economy in the world that was built on free trade. None."

It was business elites, academic economists, and the editorial boards of major American newspapers that advanced the idea that with free trade, says Lighthizer, "they could sell a lot of stuff to China. And then the dream changed—they'd move manufacturing to China and export to the United States."

He says he never believed that trade would make China more democratic and more open. "I always laughed when they said China would become like a larger version of Switzerland if we just trade with them. Thomas Friedman argued that people who trade don't go to war and that trade makes people democratic and peaceful," says Lighthizer, referring to the *New York Times* foreign affairs columnist. "There's nothing in world history to support that position."

Another academic conceit Lighthizer dismisses is that there's nothing wrong with a trade deficit. The surging imbalance China has long enjoyed with the United States, he says, "is a transfer of American wealth."

Lighthizer puts it in the simplest terms. "If you have a trade surplus with the US, you are accumulating dollars. And what can you do with dollars? Ultimately, you have to end up buying stuff in America, equity, debt, or property. You end up buying stuff in the US currency, so the dollars end up going back to the country where they come from. Maybe they say, what we'll do is we'll trade with Europe with those dollars. And then the question is, what does Europe do with these dollars? They have to buy equity, debt, or property in the United States. So when you run a trillion-dollar trade deficit, what you're really doing is you're trading the wealth of the country. And if you're trading it for something that will make your country stronger and better over the long term, then it's not a bad trade. If you're trading it for consumer goods or the like, then it's not a good trade and that's what we're doing."

He's still sickened that Washington let the trade deficit with China get so large. "It was just outrageous," he says. "It comes from the incorrect notion that economists have that trade deficits don't matter. So here's how their logic goes: The first part, which I agree with, they say, 'Well, if you have a trade surplus with Mexico and a trade deficit with Germany, it evens out.' And I don't disagree with that, although there still are questions of content of trade, and in the case of China do you want to transfer wealth to China? But setting those aside, as a general matter, if you have a surplus in one country and a deficit with another country, it kind of evens out. And it's also true that if you have a deficit in one year and a surplus the next year, that will also kind of even out."

But to some economists, says Lighthizer, debt doesn't matter at all. "So I'd say to the economist, 'If debt doesn't matter, why don't you have a $25 million house? Why are you living in a crappy little house? All you have to do is take on debt, right?' Of course debt matters. It's ridiculous."

But then, says Lighthizer, economists will take it even a step further. "They say, 'No, a trade deficit is really a good thing because it shows that people want to invest in America.' And what do they mean by that? By that, they mean that the dollars have to come back to America. But what's happening is not that there's some guy with a Euro who wakes up and says, 'I want to invest in America.' No, it's a guy with a dollar who says, 'I have to buy US assets'—because ultimately that's all you can do with the dollar. So, do trade deficits matter? No, they don't matter at all if you don't care who owns your country. But you and I, we care that Americans own the country. And it's a hell of a lot better than China."

THE CHINA CLASS DEBUTS

"I would like to play some flute," said Jiang Zemin. He turned to his host and said, "I know you play very good sax."[49]

President Clinton was throwing a dinner party for the Chinese leader at the White House in October 1997. It was the event of the season. Kissinger was there, so was his former aide Alexander Haig. Secretary of State Madeleine Albright brought an actor as her date— Patrick Stewart, then newly famous for the lead role in the 1990s reboot of *Star Trek*.[50] And for sure this, too, was a strange new world, where the American elite and senior CCP officials toasted each other over glasses of Pinot Noir and Chardonnay.[51]

Jiang in his prepared remarks urged the assembled elites from the United States and China to "respond to the will of the people and continue our march forward towards the establishment and development of a constructive strategic partnership between our two countries."[52]

There was a protest across the street from the White House with a handful of US lawmakers including Moynihan, New Jersey congressman Chris Smith, and Pelosi. Clinton, she said, "accused President Bush of coddling dictators. Now he's flacking for them."[53]

A handful of celebrities attended the rally, like Richard Gere. The actor had put his career at risk with his pro-Tibet activism and found that Hollywood was so desperate for access to China's enormous market it would willingly toss overboard one of its top box-office draws. "I want to dedicate this evening to all the people who are not here and have no representation," said Gere. "The 1.2 billion Chinese, and for the 6 million Tibetans who have no representation."

The protest was virtually ignored by the press despite the fact, or because of it, that most of the media's biggest names were inside the White House, including: *New York Times* publisher Arthur

Sulzberger Jr., *Wall Street Journal* publisher Peter Kann, *Washington Post* chairman Katharine Graham, CNN president Tom Johnson, CBS anchor Dan Rather, his NBC counterpart Tom Brokaw, and ABC's Diane Sawyer.[54]

Hollywood executive Harvey Weinstein joked with a reporter that he didn't know Chinese. "But I'm willing to learn," said the longtime Clinton fundraiser.[55] In 2000, Weinstein's Miramax Films would buy distribution rights to *Crouching Tiger, Hidden Dragon*, shot partly in China. It was a spectacular hit, adding romance, and a watercolorist's eye, to the classic Hong Kong–style martial arts genre, and captivated a global audience. Weinstein followed up with another martial arts picture, *Hero*, featuring action star Jet Li and directed by Zhang Yimou, who would later go on to direct Beijing's 2008 Olympics.

Hero tells the story of a nameless warrior whose mission is to assassinate the first emperor of China, Qin Shi Huang (246–210 BCE), but who ultimately chooses not to, realizing that unity under a strong ruler is the greater good. It's an extraordinarily beautiful account of love and sacrifice, courage and loss, and a thinly disguised rationalization of the PRC's current-day campaigns to break and assimilate its minority populations and political dissidents for the greater, communist, good. On that view, the suffering and death of, among others, the student protestors at Tiananmen, bourgeois counterrevolutionaries, Tibetans, and others glorifies the Chinese Communist Party. Given the film's unquestionable artistry, taken together with the scale of Beijing's depredations relative to the favorable opinion China still enjoys among global elites, *Hero* is a historic achievement in the annals of cinematic totalitarian propaganda, on par with, if not surpassing, Leni Riefenstahl's magisterial 1935 tribute to the Third Reich, *Triumph of the Will*. So, while Weinstein, now a convicted sex offender, never learned

Chinese, he helped translate the Party's murderous idiom for audiences worldwide.

Other Hollywood titans were at the Clinton White House that fall evening, led by Disney CEO Michael Eisner. Big Tech was represented by, among others, Steven Jobs, founder of Apple, which would later offshore the bulk of its manufacturing to China, as did many of the CEOs from the other multinationals assembled that night, including Boeing, Motorola, Xerox, Atlantic Richfield, United Technologies, PepsiCo, Time Warner, Mobil, Procter & Gamble, Cargill, Bell Atlantic, and General Electric.[56]

"I feel like I'm Forrest Gump eavesdropping on a moment in history," said director Steven Spielberg. And it was. It was the precise moment that the US ruling class acknowledged as one—from media and politics to business and entertainment—that their wealth, power, and prestige was staked to the US-China relationship. America's China Class was celebrating its debut.

American workers knew what was in the offing; they'd seen it before.

"This whole thing sounds real familiar like what they said about NAFTA," a steel union spokesman said of increasing trade benefits to China. "They said all this [NAFTA] is really going to create jobs in the United States. It's not happened. It's not going to happen in China."[57]

"We learned a hard lesson with NAFTA, and every trade agreement that has come down the pike since then," said the head of a textile union. "When big business says there's going to be a market open in China, we remember the same message about Mexico. There was going to be a middle class created in Mexico. We know that in China right now there is no middle class that is going to be able to purchase our goods."[58]

Others who'd spent time in China knew that the millenarian

promises of a new age built on free trade with a communist party would inevitably come up empty.

"There was always a fundamental problem with letting China into the WTO," lawyer and journalist Hans Mahncke tells me. "WTO law requires that traders have access to independent courts or tribunals to review decisions made by customs authorities. In the US, you have a trade court. And China has that, too. But obviously it's not free. If you're a foreign student in China, you know this. If you've traveled frequently to China for work, you know this. There are no free courts in China and there won't be for as long as the Communist Party is in charge. And this fundamental incompatibility between WTO law and the nature of China's legal system was never addressed in any way. To me, that was the most fundamental thing. I was making this point as far back as 2000—but who was I? Just some kid."

Mahncke was enchanted by China when he first visited as a child in 1979 and was lured back decades later to teach law when China entered the WTO. With a PhD specializing in WTO law, he was a prized guest.

"What's often overlooked is that by the end of the Cultural Revolution in 1976, China's legal profession and legal academia had been virtually erased—lawyers and scholars were sent to farms, labor camps, or worse. This left a massive vacuum and a deep hunger for legal knowledge, which is precisely why Western legal experts were brought in."

The Chinese brought over Mahncke and other Westerners, he explains "because they wanted to know how to litigate WTO disputes between countries, which are adjudicated in Geneva. They wanted to know how to handle a case if, say, the US made a claim against them. They had no experience in this kind of law whatsoever and that's what they wanted to know from us, the tricks."

Among other things, the Chinese wanted to know how to get around prohibitions against state-owned enterprises. Under the WTO bylaws, a state-owned enterprise (SOE) is not supposed to benefit from the relaxed tariffs and other privileges granted by the body: Industry subsidized by government money isn't free and fair trade.

"But every single Chinese company is, in effect, state-controlled," says Mahncke. "First, many companies have CCP minders. In important firms, the Party owns the golden share and therefore the decisive board vote. Further, all Chinese companies are helped by the state. If a company is supposed to put up certain numbers, then those numbers will be reached by hook or by crook. Sure, a Chinese company can go bankrupt and if no one wants to bail you out, then the company is finished. But," he explains, "if the CCP has a stake in the business's success, the party will not allow it to go bankrupt. And by the way, it's not just the CCP, it's also the PLA. The military's role in the economy is huge."

Neither institution had any misgivings about hiding the facts from Western powers thirsting for China's cheap labor.

"The WTO is extremely finicky in terms of how things are calculated, like for instance the cost of manufacturing," says Mahncke. "They get into huge detail on these issues to see what's subsidized. But with China this is a completely useless enterprise. If there's an issue, if someone complains that a Chinese company is being subsidized, the Party will tell the bank to issue a false ledger. Often they don't even have to do that. And that's what started bugging me quite early. I could just see, okay, they want to learn about the rules, but then they're going to go there and start playing with those rules. And so very early I wondered, am I teaching to foster understanding and cooperation, or to empower a hostile actor?"

Mahncke explains that disputes between a trader and a country are litigated in a local court, but disputes between countries go to

Geneva. "There's a legal judgment at the end of the process but the only enforcement mechanism is through reciprocity," he says. "That means you punish them the same way they're punishing you. So, let's say the US wins a case against China and then it can impose duties on some Chinese good that's subsidized. But many times the claim won't be enforced because of some diplomatic consideration or some other trade-off."

For instance, the United States may want to avoid trouble with a prominent company that also donates significant money to political campaigns, like Walmart, for example. Historically, Walmart has been responsible for importing a significant portion of Chinese goods into the United States. Between 2001 and 2013, Walmart accounted for approximately 11.2 percent of total US goods imported from China.[59] While the chain giant has been diversifying its sourcing strategies of late, 2023 data shows that Walmart is still heavily dependent on Chinese manufacturing—60 percent of its imports came from China.[60]

The last thing a company so reliant on Chinese exports wants is duties imposed on the Chinese goods on its shelves. And a company that size has the resources to make the problem disappear. Walmart's political action committee contributed approximately $1.16 million to federal candidates during the 2023-2024 election cycle. Of this amount, 42.63 percent went to Democrats, while 56.72 percent supported Republicans.[61] A report by United for Respect indicates that since January 1, 2023, Walmart and the Walton family have invested more than $32 million in political activities, favoring Republicans over Democrats by more than five to one.[62] US workers and perhaps even US policymakers may want to punish China for its trade practices, but they're no match for megaretailers like Walmart and its team of lobbyists.

The point of trade with China, says Mahncke, "was always

primarily about getting cheap stuff out of China. Maybe US companies initially thought they could get into China but as long as they could sell their stuff in the US with their company name on it, that's what they really wanted."

Mahncke says that calling it offshoring is too generous. "All they do is give the Chinese a sketch of something they want to make. It can be a very complex sketch, with specific standards defined in these manuals that are encoded into a computer-aided design program. So the guy over there in China just feeds it into their machine and then they start spitting out the metal sheets and the right size and shape and the screws and this and that. And then they assemble it. And with the industries that I'm aware of, like agricultural machinery, we're talking a quarter of the cost. Then they send it over for cheap and sell it to Americans at a big margin."

And the Chinese make their own products with those same manuals. "When you set up shop in China," he explains, "you have to be in a joint venture and you have to hand over your intellectual property. I've always wondered, what's the point of being there? To me, there's very little point in being there because you can't get your money out. But I think the real lure of China was making cheap products there and selling them for a premium in the U.S. That model is what kept the whole system going."

HOME FREE CCP

With Clinton putting China in the clear, offshoring became even more popular for US companies, as shown by China's growing trade surplus with the United States. And underlying those numbers is a stark and typically unremarked fact: The US trade deficit with China is not with China alone but also represents an imbalance with US and other multinational corporations that offshored their manufacturing to China.

The revenues earned by the parties involved, China and their US or other foreign partners, typically depend on the level of Chinese content in the products the foreign companies send from China. "The Chinese suppliers get that share of the revenue their parts, components, assemblies etc. represent," says economist Alan Tonelson. "Or they may have agreed to some other revenue-sharing formula. In any case, that revenue earned by the Chinese is taxed by the PRC government and used to support military spending and other priorities of Beijing's. And the Chinese content of these exports has gone up substantially over the last several years. So how do their US corporate partners fare? If they're not suffering too much theft of their intellectual property or allowing their technology to be extorted by their Chinese partners—or if they're avoiding harassment under Xi Jinping's rule—chances are they're doing just fine."

Regardless, as Tonelson explains, "the soaring US trade deficit, especially since the early 1990s, has been jet-fueled by US companies sending export-oriented manufacturing to low-cost countries, especially China. The main objective was not to serve these new so-called emerging markets, as they kept telling Congress and even presidents and certainly reporters, but to sell back to the US."

Within a decade of PNTR, more than half of the US-China trade gap would come from offshored production by multinational firms, with US companies in the lead. American and other foreign firms accounted for 55 percent of China's exports in 2010 and 68 percent of its trade surplus. In 2011, foreign producers made 52.4 percent of China's exports and represented over 84 percent of its trade surplus.[63]

The US-China trade gap is concentrated in certain sectors, with electronics and computers at the top of the list. By 2011, US imports from China in this sector would yield a deficit of about $136 billion, by far the biggest industry deficit.[64] In 2011 the US trade deficit in textiles, apparel, and leather with China would reach about $46.4

billion.[65] That same year, the machinery and industrial equipment sector saw a nearly $20 billion trade deficit with China.[66]

As China's own companies grew, the foreign share of exports would shrink, for instance, to about 28.6 percent of exports in 2023.[67] But that also reflects the PRC's success in stripping US and other foreign companies of their intellectual property in order to make the same products but under their own name.

That the US trade deficit with China represents how US and other multinationals joined forces with the communist regime to enrich themselves starkly underscores the plain fact: Regardless of what the US political and corporate establishment said about China's entry being good for all Americans, it was designed to leave the US middle class out in the cold.

A week before Congress introduced the May 15 legislation that would grant China PNTR, Clinton summoned past US leaders to the White House to show support for the bill, including former Presidents Jimmy Carter and Gerald Ford as well as Kissinger.[68]

"The agreement is, of course, in our economic interest," said Kissinger, "since it grants China what has been approved by the Congress every year for 20 years."[69] But, he added, "we are here together not for economic reasons. We are here because cooperative relations with China are in the American national interest. Every President, for 30 years, has come to that conclusion. And a rejection of this agreement would be a vote for an adversarial relationship with the most populous nation of China, with the longest uninterrupted history of self-government."

Vice President Al Gore, also the Democratic candidate for the 2000 presidential race, chimed in. "By making China live by the same global trading rules that other nations follow, we will strengthen the forces of reform across the board in China," Gore told the White House audience. "We will create a powerful new pressure on China to establish the rule of law, which is the foundation not just of a free and open economy, but also of the kind of political reforms that we're working to promote."

His GOP rival, Texas Governor George W. Bush, also supported the bill. "Passage of this legislation will mean a stronger American economy, as well as more opportunity for liberty and freedom in China," said Bush.[70]

"Granting permanent normal trade relations to China is all about opening their markets to U.S. goods and investment," said Delaware senator Joe Biden. Plus, it would show the communist regime that we were honest brokers. But "denying China permanent normal trade status," Biden added, "could have the opposite effect. It will convince China's leaders that we want to keep them weak and backward; and that we hope to contain them through our economic coercion."[71]

The PNTR vote signaled that Beijing was home free and that there was no indignity that Washington and its corporate allies wouldn't suffer to sustain an ugly fantasy. The political class had brushed aside multiple Chinese intelligence operations, one targeting the president and another US nuclear labs, while the corporate establishment gladly turned over its intellectual property to the PRC's state-owned enterprises. They were all accomplices to what Trump called "the greatest theft in the history of the world."[72]

CHAPTER SEVEN

Paper Tigers

We need to urge China to become a responsible stakeholder.[1]
—Robert Zoellick

THE STORY OF THE GEORGE W. BUSH PRESIDENCY AND CHINA IS typically told as a tale of comparative flight paths. It starts shortly after his inauguration.

People's Liberation Army pilots liked dogging the Americans. In the early spring of 2001, one PLA flyer got close enough to US aircraft to hold out a piece of paper showing his email address. Washington complained that the reckless bravado endangered US crews. Beijing countered by falsely accusing the Americans of flying in Chinese airspace. On April 1, 2001, that same Chinese pilot came within ten feet of a US Navy EP-3 spy plane, fell back, and then made another run closing to five feet. On what would be his last approach, he was sucked in by the American plane's propellers and his fighter jet was sliced in half.[2]

The American aircraft was depressurized and began to drop out of the sky. The crew thought they were done for. The pilot regained control of his plane and landed on Hainan Island at China's southernmost point. Bush's defense secretary, Donald Rumsfeld, told the president it was an act of aggression.

"I said I did not favor an apology or suspending our reconnaissance flights," Rumsfeld wrote in his 2011 memoir, *Known and Unknown*. "The Chinese knew they were in the wrong. Capitulating to their threats and feigned outrage could embolden China's military and political leaders to commit still more provocative acts. I did not believe that America would benefit from being seen as a weak supplicant. Moreover, I thought that there should be some kind of clear penalty for China's dangerous behavior."[3]

Henry Kissinger took the other side. "Obviously there is a point where it becomes a test of wills and I think that should be avoided by both sides," he said.[4] The PRC, he said, wasn't trying to "challenge" America; rather, the collision was an accident.

The Chinese held the US flight crew for ten days and released them after the US ambassador to China sent a letter expressing regret for the death of the Chinese pilot and for failing to get clearance to land.[5] Bush supporters in the press saluted the president for what they described as a show of strength.[6]

Rumsfeld disagreed. Shortly before the plane was brought down, he'd presented the president with a blueprint for what he described as a cold war with China. After Beijing had brought down a US plane, he thought it was a bad idea for America "to humble itself" before China, but he knew what he was up against. "American companies were investing many billions of dollars in China," he wrote in his memoir. "There were significant economic interests in maintaining good relations with the PRC by offering an apology and moving on."[7]

Within six months, the September 11 attacks would eclipse the Hainan Island episode and dictate US foreign policy for almost two decades. It wasn't until Donald Trump that any senior US official took China as seriously as Rumsfeld did.

Bush's eight years are often seen as the lost years of America's China policy. Just as US policymakers were formulating plans to counter the PRC, Washington had no choice but to divert its attention to fight what it labeled the global war on terrorism (GWOT). But that's only partly accurate. The Bush administration saw clearly the effects of engaging China for thirty years—despite promises of holding China to account, the Americans kept rewarding them.

It was under Bush that China's accession to the WTO was made official, two months after the historic attacks, on November 11. "I believe that as this century unfolds and people look back on this day, they will conclude that in admitting China to the WTO we took a decisive step in shaping a global economic and commercial system," said senior Bush aide Robert Zoellick, who piloted China policy during Bush's first term.[8]

Zoellick's prediction may yet come true, disastrously binding America to China until the world's oldest democracy is absorbed by a communist police state. But even at present, it's clear that China's entry was a historic event no less momentous than 9/11, and as destructive.

MINORITY REPORT

Like Mao, Jiang Zemin liked rightists. After Dianne Feinstein, most of his friends in US politics were Republicans, like Nixon, Kissinger, and the new president's father. "Bush Sr. came over to China many, many times and had many meetings with me," the communist party chairman said shortly after the January 2001 inauguration. "We believe Bush Sr. will definitely push Bush Jr. to bring U.S.-China relations to a new level."[9]

Soon the younger Bush's brother was in business with Jiang's son.

Neil Bush admitted he knew nothing about the semiconductor business, but in 2002 Jiang Mianheng gave the American blueblood a five-year consulting contract worth $2 million plus bonuses.[10] As Prescott Bush had piggybacked on George H. W. Bush's name, Neil represented the second generation of Bush siblings to draw on the prestige of the White House to profit from China.

The newly elected president had said on the campaign trail that Clinton was wrong to call "China a strategic partner"—"but neither," Bush said, "is it our enemy." Rather, China was a "strategic competitor."[11] The clumsy phrase illustrated US policymakers' inability to come to terms with the issue—and after all, how do you describe the threat that you raised against yourself? Stronger, clearer language might have brought forth a plan of action, but by hedging words, the Americans continued to drift.

During Bush's trip to Shanghai a month after the 9/11 attacks, Jiang vowed that China would stand by the United States in its war on terror.[12] In exchange, the White House legitimized Beijing's detention of China's Muslim Uyghur minority by designating the East Turkistan Islamic Movement (ETIM) a terrorist organization.[13]

"I'm immersed in work about the Uyghurs and I'd never heard of that group before the global war on terror," says Uyghur activist Nury Turkel. He's a naturalized US citizen who heads the Washington, DC–based Uyghur Human Rights Project, and is the author of *No Escape: The True Story of China's Genocide of the Uyghurs.*

Turkel was born in a detention center in Xinjiang, an autonomous region in northwestern China that borders the Tibet Autonomous Region to the south, and among other states, Russia, Pakistan, Afghanistan, and India. Xinjiang is home to more than 11 million Turkic Muslims, of which Uyghurs are the largest group. With the 1949 revolution, the CCP began moving Han Chinese into Xinjiang, just as they'd later do with Tibet, to change the region's ethnic and racial composition and surround the regional Uyghur majority with loyal regime clients. Though a few armed Uyghur separatist movements skirmished with PRC authorities, they typically over-stated their influence and ability to fight the PLA.

Turkel says that before the war on terror, Beijing never used terror-ism as part of its Uyghur narrative. "Right before 9/11 CCP officials held a press conference saying Xinjiang is safe and that prospective investors should feel safe and confident putting their money into the region," he says. "But after 9/11 Beijing claimed that China is also a victim of global terror."

The PRC sold its case by pointing to the December 2001 capture of twenty-two Uyghurs in Pakistan who were categorized as terror-ists.[14] "They were political refugees," says Turkel. "They had noth-ing to do with any terror group, never mind ETIM. They had fled China and were in Afghanistan, and when the US invaded, they crossed the border into Pakistan where they were grabbed by bounty hunters who turned them over to US forces at $5000 a head." Paki-stan is a long-standing Chinese ally and, as Turkel explains, "Paki-stan helped the Chinese in this case, too. The Uyghurs were sent to Guantánamo, where Chinese officials interrogated them, but mem-bers of Congress had no access to them."

In January 2002, the CCP published a white paper asserting that that ETIM "is supported and directed by [Osama] bin Laden. Since the formation of the 'East Turkistan Islamic Movement,' bin Laden has schemed with the heads of the Central and West Asian terrorist organizations many times to help the 'East Turkistan' terrorist forces in Xinjiang launch a 'holy war,' with the aim of setting up a theo-cratic 'Islam state' in Xinjiang."[15]

Key terms like "holy war" and "Islamic state" and claims the group was affiliated with the mastermind of the 9/11 attacks were employed to win American favor and show that China was fighting the same ideology that took thousands of lives in US cities that autumn morning. As a result, the State Department designated ETIM a foreign terrorist organization.[16]

Turkel acknowledges that there are some bad actors within the Uyghur community, but Beijing characterizes the entire population as a source of global terror. "Foreign governments, NGOs, and Western reporters have no access to the CCP's files, so nothing is independently verified. It's all based on what the Chinese say. Here in the US, we have instruments to uncover the truth, like Freedom of Information Act requests. There's no such thing in China. Whatever the CCP says becomes a fact. And some in the West just repeat what they say."

By reinforcing Beijing's caricature of the Uyghurs, the United States and other Western powers gave legitimacy to Beijing's collective punishment and preemptive policing of the entire population. In Xinjiang, says Turkel, "the CCP has brought to life *Minority Report.*"

The CCP's "Strike Hard Campaign Against Violent Terrorism" is a real-life version of the surveillance program employed in the 2002 Tom Cruise science-fiction thriller to identify suspects before they commit a crime. According to a Human Rights Watch report,[17] CCP authorities collect DNA samples, fingerprints, iris scans, and blood types of all residents in the region ages twelve to sixty-five and require voice samples for passport applications. The data is entered into centralized, searchable databases that generate lists of targets for detention. A mobile app aggregates data and flags those deemed potentially threatening. Phones are searched for communications apps like WhatsApp and Telegram and monitored.

The political goal of China's security regime in Xinjiang is, as CCP officials exhort their colleagues, to break the Uyghurs, "break their roots, break their connections, and break their origins."[18] And break their faith in anything that transcends the materialist ideology with which the party has supplanted conceptions of supernatural divinity. "You're supposed to worship CCP leadership," says Turkel. "But if you believe in God, you don't believe in Mao Zedong Thought or Xi Jinping Thought. For the party, religion is supposed to be in line with communist ideology, but what kind of religion can be in line with communism?"

Since 2017, as many as a million Uyghurs have been held in hundreds of facilities in Xinjiang, including "political education" camps and prisons.[19] The Party makes an example of the harder cases, with torture, forced abortions, sterilization, and execution.[20] Many of these prisons and labor camps are managed by the Xinjiang Production and Construction Corps, a Chinese state-owned enterprise described as a "quasigovernmental paramilitary organization," which has its own police and army reserves. It's also believed to be the largest cotton producer in all China.[21] Thus, the detention centers are crucial nodes in China's supply chains, where detainees are forced to make goods destined for American shopping centers.

China's textile industry is the world's largest, and Xinjiang is China's cotton heartland, producing about 85 percent of China's cotton and roughly 20 percent of the world's supply.[22] Few finished goods are exported directly from Xinjiang to the United States. Instead, Xinjiang materials are sent to factories in eastern China or neighboring countries, like Vietnam or Bangladesh, where they're sewn or stitched, and so forth, into apparel, footwear, or other textile products sold to the US.[23] The supply lines themselves are so tightly interwoven that even after US lawmakers passed the Uyghur Forced Labor Prevention Act in December 2021, famous US companies like Nike, Adidas, New Balance, and others that ostensibly wanted to sever their links to Xinjiang slave labor couldn't. A 2023 congressional report shows that Nike, for instance, was still "sourcing garments made not only from cotton from the Uyghur Region but also viscose, lyocell, polyester, leather, and linen from the region."[24]

Trading with China was supposed to pressure the communist regime to liberalize. "Economic freedom creates habits of liberty," Bush said, "and habits of liberty create expectations of democracy."[25] But the exact opposite happened. Free trade had given Beijing a financial incentive to institutionalize slave labor and reward American corruption in the bargain.

HUGGING PANDAS

Months into the war on terror, Kissinger was still rattled by the response of Rumsfeld and others to China's downing of the US plane the year before. "Those who believe that confrontation with China can be a national strategy," he told a Shanghai audience in April 2002, "do not understand the dynamics of the current and foreseeable international system."[26]

This was the system he had given birth to by balancing American interests against China's. In this framework, the WTO couldn't be anything other than an instrument designed to increase the weaker and poorer power at the expense of the stronger and wealthier one. And Kissinger marveled at its success, how American manufacturers and investors had made China richer than anyone could've imagined. "If anybody had told us that this was possible," he said, "it would have been considered a fantasy."[27]

Thus, the role of Kissinger and the other custodians of the relationship was to restrain the Americans. "We have extraordinary opportunities," he said in Shanghai. "We must not squander them in needless disputes."[28]

The WTO and the Bush administration's freedom agenda for the Middle East issued from the same part of the American elite's psyche; but the belief, held with a quasi-evangelical faith, that securing

American peace and prosperity requires us to induce foreigners to act like Americans, is a symptom of narcissism. Bush officials, for instance, believed that the root cause of 9/11 was the lack of democracy in the Middle East, and once despotic regimes like Saddam Hussein's were toppled, the nascent liberal energies of the Arab masses would inexorably transform their society from tyranny to representative government, like ours. In the same way, trade would eventually compel a communist party that pushed slave-made products into global markets to adopt liberal norms, like ours.

But trade policy, like war, is a blunt instrument. Success means advancing the interests of your side. The GWOT and WTO showed that US policymakers instead saw trade and war as means to shape outcomes among foreigners whose priorities Washington bureaucrats could not begin to fathom.

The new international order engendered by Kissinger's concept of the balance of power was a specifically American project designed at a particular historical moment, and yet US elites spoke of it like it was part of God's creation. "Globalization is akin to a force of nature," Robert Zoellick told a Beijing audience in 2002. "It can sweep aside antiquated and dysfunctional customs, institutions and ways of thinking. It is not something that can be stopped by a leader, or by a nation, without incurring unacceptable costs."[29]

Zoellick was US trade representative for Bush's first term and was seen as having his eyes on even bigger and more influential jobs. "So he adopted the doctrine of free trade," says the former Reagan Commerce Department official Clyde Prestowitz. "He was politically ambitious and what he really wanted was to be secretary of state or secretary of the Treasury."

Zoellick had worked in the George H. W. Bush administration at both State and Treasury, where he was involved in negotiations over NAFTA and creating the WTO. After a brief tour through academia and Washington, DC, think tanks, he joined Goldman Sachs in 1997.

By the time Zoellick came aboard, Goldman Sachs had become Wall Street's China whisperer, thanks largely to CEO Henry Paulson, whom Bush made Treasury secretary in 2006. Paulson's assiduous cultivation of top Chinese officials led to enormous public offerings of Chinese state-owned enterprises on US exchanges, which enriched the party and the firm. Zoellick was head of international affairs, Goldman's "global ambassador and networker-in-chief," with a strategic role in the firm's expansion of financial markets business and investment in China.[30]

Zoellick told the Beijing audience, "There will be no more important relationship than ours in this century. Neither of our countries will achieve what it wants, and needs, if we allow our differences to overshadow our common goals."[31]

It was because he sounded just like Kissinger that Beijing loved Zoellick. "If Henry Kissinger was an unavoidable name in US-China relations in the 20th century," China's state media gushed at the time, "only Zoellick can be compared to him in the 21st century."[32] He appears to be the first US official stuck with the label "panda-hugger," a derogatory term in US policy circles characterizing officials giddily advocating engagement and cooperation no matter what China does. Having in fact really hugged a panda during a visit to China, Zoellick earned Chinese-state media's praise as the "chief" panda-hugger.[33]

China, of course, didn't see the WTO as a deal that made everyone winners, which became evident when the PRC began dumping goods in the United States to undercut domestic manufacturers. The Americans wanted their government to protect them. In 2002, for instance, a New Jersey manufacturer wanted relief when China was dumping parts for mechanized scooters, and the US International

Trade Commission (USITC) agreed. The recommended remedy was quotas limiting the number of those imported Chinese parts for three years, but Bush vetoed the action.[34]

"In determining not to provide import relief, I considered its overall costs to the US economy," he wrote in a memo to Zoellick. "The facts of this case indicate that imposing the USITC's recommended quota would not likely benefit the domestic producing industry and instead would cause imports to shift from China to other offshore sources."[35]

The rationale was this: If the White House protected domestic manufacturers getting wiped out by cheap Chinese imports, it would unravel the WTO. And that couldn't be allowed to happen since, after all, globalization was akin to a force of nature. Eventually, industry stopped bringing cases and the trade deficit with China exploded, nearly doubling from $83 billion to $162 billion between the end of Bush's first year and the end of his first term.[36]

TOTALITARIAN WARFARE

For Beijing the WTO was another instrument in its arsenal to bring the Americans to their knees.

China was no match for the United States in conventional military terms. Sure, they'd won a propaganda victory by bringing down another US spy plane and forcing an apology from the Americans, as they'd been doing since Mao's day. But the US had repeatedly demonstrated its overwhelming military power, and the Chinese took notice. PLA military strategists studied Operation Desert Storm, the George H. W. Bush administration's 1991 war to drive Saddam Hussein out of Kuwait, and were awed by the military, economic, political, and diplomatic power required to land half a million troops in the desert and vanquish a foe after a ground operation lasting only a hundred hours.

But some of the Chinese army's top military minds were convinced the United States had reached the apex of its strength. There would be no more wars like the Gulf War. And the Chinese assessed that the Americans didn't know how to wage the campaigns that would mark the future. But the CCP did. As a revolutionary regime, political warfare was its specialty.

In 1999 two PLA colonels, Qiao Liang and Wang Xiangsui, published a book titled *Unrestricted Warfare*, which laid out how to make war using nonmilitary as well as military means—anything was on the table to defeat America

The Chinese were faced with "an incredible war machine," says retired Air Force General Robert Spalding, a former B-2 stealth bomber pilot. With Operation Desert Storm "the Chinese saw precision-targeted bombs going down the ventilator shafts and into the windows of Iraqi military targets." Accordingly, says Spalding, the military strategists were tasked "with developing a doctrine for dealing with a very powerful United States."

The crucial lesson they learned was to avoid direct military conflict with America. Rather, use everything else as a field of confrontation. Unrestricted warfare, says Spalding, uses "all means, including armed force or nonarmed force, military and nonmilitary, and lethal and nonlethal means to compel the enemy to accept one's interest."

It's a totalitarian doctrine designed by a totalitarian regime with massive surveillance powers and determined to shape every aspect of public and private life. Therefore, unrestricted warfare makes no distinction between military and nonmilitary personnel. Every citizen is a soldier fighting for the national interest, from diplomats and scientists to computer hackers and journalists. The only rule in unrestricted warfare," says Spalding, "is that there are no rules."

Spalding served as military attaché in the US embassy in Beijing at the beginning of Trump's first term and later moved to the White

House, where he was senior director for strategic planning. *Unrestricted Warfare*, he says, is the "main blueprint for China's efforts to unseat America as the world's economic, political, and ideological leader." Fluent in Mandarin, he deciphered the difficult, dense, and often meandering text for his book-length study of China's totalitarian military strategy, *War Without Rules: China's Playbook for Global Domination*.

Studying CCP political warfare, says Spalding, required him to "understand a new context for warfare that really had more to do with emotions and psychology and controlling political narratives. I had to educate myself to see these patterns, because it's a completely different way of thinking, and our brains are not encoded to understand political warfare to the level that the Chinese Communist Party and the People's Liberation Army are."

When Spalding briefed senior US military officials, he found they were incapable of grasping political warfare strategy and had no interest in adapting to it. "The response was, 'This is not our fight, we don't even know how to do this.' As a constitutional republic, we don't think of war in those terms. The Department of Defense is entirely unsuited for political warfare, because it's just not in our tradition."

That leaves PLA military planners with a strategic advantage. Spalding marvels that even in 1999 the PLA colonels assessed that Osama bin Laden was the kind of nonstate actor capable of waging this new kind of war. Indeed, the Al Qaeda leader shared Mao's low opinion of the United States and used the same phrase to characterize their view. The Chinese tyrant said that "the United States is nothing but a paper tiger."[37] And according to Bin Laden his cadres "were shocked by the low morale of the American soldier and they realized that the American soldier was just a paper tiger."[38]

The Bush administration's inability to win in Afghanistan and

Iraq showed that the two PLA men had rightly assessed that the United States could not duplicate the overwhelming success of Desert Storm. The US armed forces weren't any less capable a decade later when George W. Bush made war against the same adversary his father's generals had overrun easily. But the context had changed; even the media ecosystem was different.

Desert Storm was the first war carried live on cable TV, but by 2003 the Arab satellite network Al Jazeera had risen to challenge CNN. Airing bin Laden's videos and promoting religious authorities who called for Muslims around the world to kill Americans in the Middle East, the proudly anti-US network shaped both the military and media environment against US forces.

But it was the political landscape that had changed most dramatically. The first Bush's war was a sign that the Cold War era had come to an end and a new world order was taking shape. For the younger Bush, no matter how many allies he drew into the Middle East, his efforts were in conflict with the spirit of the age. From a global perspective, American rage and grief were justifiable responses to 9/11, but like everyone else around the world the Americans, too, would have to acclimate themselves to the unavoidable phenomenon of global terrorism, which was finally just an effect of the dark side of globalism. Making war against the most violent of the holdouts who resisted the flattening effects of globalism that were destined to make the world a large cooperative enterprise made America no better than the enemies of globalism.

But it's precisely because US leadership exposed America to globalism—to China—that the world has become a dangerous place for Americans, much more so than it was even during the Cold War, a half-century-long nuclear standoff.

"The Soviet Union is so much less a threat than the Chinese Communist Party because we never let the Soviets in," says Spalding.

"We have completely allowed the Chinese Communist Party full access to all aspects of our institutions and society."

Globalization provided an array of new weapons to anyone who knew how to use them, from bin Laden to Beijing. The internet was a worldwide platform for nonstop information warfare. International bodies like the World Health Organization and United Nations Human Rights Council were soft targets for the CCP to influence and infiltrate or instruments to turn against American interests. And this was how Beijing saw the WTO, which was how China made war against America even while America was fighting the global war on terror.

DUMPING WAR

"China was systematically dumping goods into the United States to weaken our industries and wipe out jobs," says former Commerce Department official Nazak Nikakhtar. "China was starting to take the record in terms of dumping into the United States, more than any other country."

Nikakhtar helped set up the department's China/Non-Market Economy Office during the George W. Bush administration and then returned to Commerce as under secretary for industry and security and assistant secretary for the International Trade Administration during Trump's first term. "Nobody thought that a poor developing country like China would ever race ahead of the United States," she tells me. "The thinking in the US government was that if China wanted to tap the supply chains on chemicals and wood products and all the low-value commodity items, fine, let China have it. Because there was this notion in the US that it was the high-technology items, the innovation that's going to make all the money. So who cares who produces the cheap manufactured goods? But it obviously didn't stop with the cheap goods, and China started gradually chipping away at our high-value industries and we ceded them to China, we just let them have it."

Nikakhtar and her colleagues documented what the Chinese government was doing. "From 2002 through 2007, when I was in the US government, we were consistently failing trade audits of Chinese companies. We found over and over again that the Chinese companies falsified their books and records so they could continue dumping into the United States to such an extent that it was wiping out American industries. And so we were watching all this happen and we knew that this wasn't going in the right direction. But the rest of the US government and the United States clung on to the hope that the Chinese would reform and become market-oriented."

American manufacturers saw the disaster unfolding in real time. "By 2000 the Chinese had done a lot to destroy the textile industry and other industries in this country," says Dan DiMicco, the former CEO of Nucor Corporation, America's largest steel manufacturer, and the cofounder and current vice-chair of the Coalition for a Prosperous America. "Typically, once the Chinese decide to make an industry strategic as part of their overall strategy to further their goal of dominance, they build massive overcapacity literally overnight. For me the real wake-up call came with what China did to us in the steel industry."

At the start of Bush's first term, China had no more steelmaking capacity than the United States but would soon overtake everyone. "In 2010 the Chinese had a total capacity to make 150 million tons of steel," says DiMicco. "Japan and a few of the other European countries were much larger producers. But we were right up there."

DiMicco was part of the first Trump administration's transition team. He says he and the president first became acquainted in the early 2000s when the steel executive was on broadcast media promoting a book that defined the problems facing US manufacturing. DiMicco remembers the talk in the industry at the time. "Our customers are saying, hey, we're losing our customers. And if we lose our customers, you, Nucor, are going to lose yours. So they're destroying not just the steel industry but also forcing Caterpillar tractors and automobile companies to move their supply chains to China. Despite the fact that we built steel mills and efficient state-of-the-art stuff. The right kind of steel mills for today's world. China was building a big integrated blast furnace with coal-fired power plants, and all the stuff that would have made it much more costly for them to compete with us. But their government subsidized their steel industry and they dumped to destroy us."

From 2000 to 2010, says DiMicco, "China was up over a billion tons of steelmaking capacity. It's peaking today at 1.3 to 1.4 billion tons. You have to understand, the whole world has a demand for only 2.3 billion tons." China laid waste to the US steel industry and US manufacturing. Companies that depended on steel and hadn't offshored their manufacturing were wiped out.

"Our manufacturing has gone from 23 percent of GDP in 2000 to 10 percent today," says DiMicco. China today is like 55 percent of global manufacturing. We are 11 percent. That's not the way it was. That's the way it is today. It was all part of their strategy. They've done it in every major manufacturing sector that they've decided to dominate."

Back in Washington, Zoellick recognized that the picture didn't look so rosy anymore. In 2005, Bush appointed him deputy secretary of state, and in September he gave another big speech on China, this time in New York. The tone was notably different than the 2002 talk in Beijing.

"The U.S. business community, which in the 1990s saw China as a land of opportunity, now has a more mixed assessment," said Zoellick. "Smaller companies worry about Chinese competition, rampant piracy, counterfeiting, and currency manipulation. Even larger U.S. businesses—once the backbone of support for economic engagement—are concerned that mercantilist Chinese policies will try to direct controlled markets instead of opening competitive markets. American workers wonder if they can compete."[39]

Zoellick enumerated the ways that China had benefited by joining the international system and said it was time for the CCP to live up to America's best hopes for it. "It is time to take our policy beyond opening doors to China's membership into the international system," said Zoellick. "We need to urge China to become a responsible stakeholder in that system."

What he meant was, China wasn't playing by the rules and it was time for China to play fair because it promised it would. Zoellick was saying what everyone knew to be true but had no ability to affect. So he repeated the phrase *responsible stakeholder* several times throughout the course of his talk. "We now need to encourage China to become a responsible stakeholder in the international system," he said, sounding like a phonograph needle stuck in a groove. "As a responsible stakeholder, China would be more than just a member—it would work with us to sustain the international system that has enabled its success."[40]

The phrase *responsible stakeholder* stuck, not least because its pleading urgency highlighted the administration's weak position. The US side had leverage—it could implement WTO mechanisms to hold China accountable; it could even raise the ante and threaten to break the trade body over China's head. But Beijing knew nothing of the sort would ever happen because the US political class's corporate partners wouldn't allow it—there was too much money at stake. Experience showed that all the Americans would do was talk.

"Zoellick wanted the Chinese to be responsible stakeholders because he wanted them to be like America and part of our system," says Prestowitz. "But China didn't want to be part of our system. They just wanted to use it against us. Zoellick wanted to hug China but China wouldn't hug him back."

In spite of China's open war on US domestic manufacturing, Washington continued to urge it to act like a responsible stakeholder even after it became clear that engagement and cooperation with Beijing had simply degraded America by making it complicit in China's criminality and depravity.

"We knew that the Chinese were lying about their labor books and records, but we just thought it was to drive down their anti-dumping rates," says Nikakhtar. "We didn't have the vocabulary back then to recognize this was an indication they were using forced labor."

It wasn't just the Uyghurs and political dissidents the PLA was pressing into service. "China was getting poor people from the countryside into work," she says. "These factory workers were essentially being held hostage in the factories and dormitories. They had no collective bargaining rights, for wages, or just to have humane conditions. They worked unreasonable hours, working on chemicals with no masks, no protective gear or shoes. If one of them got physically harmed so they couldn't work anymore, they were disposable because there's so many of them in the countryside. We knew this in the US government. Why we didn't flag the forced labor conditions back then is surprising. The US government wasn't identifying it as forced labor back then."

The Americans didn't even know how to protect themselves, their companies, their interests, and their market shares. "I saw company after company give up its intellectual property," says Nikakhtar. "China wanted their IP and they said, 'All right, I'll give it to them, and we're going to set up this joint venture and China's going to help me make some off my innovations, manufacture my products cheaply in China, and export to the US.' I'd warn the US companies: 'Don't you understand that China is just going to steal your IP?' They said, 'No, we have clauses in our contract and we can litigate this.' I'd question them further. 'Litigate where? Litigate in China's courts? You're not going to win. And then what? International arbitration? The Chinese companies will bankrupt you through a prolonged litigation process. How much money do you have to do this? And if you're giving up your IP voluntarily, you're not going to win your international arbitration case.' But companies just thought, 'I'll give up my IP now and I'll worry about the consequences later.'"

The result, says DiMicco, is that "all these companies like Boeing, Caterpillar, GM, Ford, etc., that heavily invested in China and got all kinds of sweetheart deals, all they did in the end was give the Chinese a chance to steal every bit of technology they ever had to build up their own national champions."

The Chinese had not only US technology but also the US dollars amassed from the trade imbalance. They invested in infrastructure, which quickly transformed a peasant society into something that looked like a growing middle class with middle-class wants. Finally, the Chinese market that US companies had so long dreamed of was starting to take shape. But the American companies that had created it had almost no access to sell in it.

"Now some of the Chinese are going into work in factories, and they are starting to need things," says Nikakhtar. "They don't have a lot of money, but they have money to buy things, clothing and whatever else. And then the people who go into the city centers to work. So now you need cars." But not American-made cars.

"It's CCP pride," says Nikakhtar. "The Chinese government says we don't want you to use foreign products. We want you to use Chinese products because we never want to be foreign reliant."

It was the same with virtually everything—Chinese-made goods for China. And when the Americans were permitted to sell into the Chinese markets, it was Chinese parts assembled in China. And then Beijing started making more advanced items, also based on US technology.

"With auto technology that they'd stolen from US IP, they can make armored vehicles," says Nikakhtar. "And with airplane technology, they can make military aircraft. With US semiconductor technology, the Chinese raced ahead in hypersonic technology. America had a joint semiconductor venture in China and transferred American technology to the Chinese military."

Within less than two decades, the US went from offshoring manufacturing of cheap goods to forfeiting IP that helped build the Chinese military. And that was only part of the toll.

"The problem isn't just that we gave away our manufacturing plants," says DiMicco. "Our supply chains have disappeared. We have no foundries in this country anymore. We couldn't make a large forging of steel if our life depended upon it. We have no lead smelters in this country anymore. We are dependent for just about everything on foreigners." That includes munitions.

"If we have to go to war with China or Russia or Iran or anyone, if our goods are coming in from overseas—steel, primary metals, aluminum, etc.—how are we sure they're going to get across the Pacific and Atlantic Oceans safely? We don't have a shipbuilding industry anymore. Submarines, aircraft carriers, are all dependent on our relations with foreigners." Especially our number one adversary, China.

It was investments in American infrastructure that gave the US

the advantage in the Cold War. "Science and technology, our manufacturing base, the US National Highway System, all of these things
led to our economic growth," says Spalding. "And that economic
growth is ultimately what defeated the Soviet Union. The Chinese
Communist Party took that model and flipped it on its head. During
the Cold War, we owned the supply chain. Now, China dominates
our supply chain."

Washington saw what was happening but did nothing to stop it.
It wasn't because America was committed to fighting the global war
on terror, but rather because US elites had committed their careers
to globalism.

"It was the era of globalization," says Nikakhtar. "We became so
infatuated with globalization, with making money, that we con-
ceded that we were going to lose manufacturing, but we clung to
the hope that we would retain innovation. But how do you innovate
without the actual capability to manufacture the goods that you're
innovating?"

THE NEW ECONOMY

According to the apostles of globalization, it didn't matter that
America had exported manufacturing jobs to China because there
were much better jobs in the offing. One of the WTO's chief selling points was not only that it would open new markets for American businesses, but it would also create high-wage jobs for American
workers in the new tech and service economy.[41]

Sure, a forty-eight-year-old at the steel plant might've run out
of time to make the jump from blue- to white-collar work, but his
kids surely would, so long as they had the right training to meet the
demands of the new internet-driven knowledge economy. But by the
middle of the George W. Bush years, it was obvious that Americans
had already been shut out of millions of those jobs, too.

It had started decades before when the federal government, academia, and big tech joined forces to depress the natural market price for U.S. knowledge workers. Their instrument was a 1985 National Science Foundation memo arguing that the supply of US scientists and engineers would soon dry up and the soon-to-be-booming tech industry needed more workers with science, technology, engineering, and mathematics (STEM) degrees.[42] The good news was that there was a huge pool of smart and ambitious STEM students all across the world—if only Washington would revise its immigration laws to gild their path to America.

In fact, there was no shortage of American STEM students. The memo was part of an effort to justify importing cheaper, foreign labor and drive down the costs for the emerging tech industry. Since the surplus of cheap labor discouraged American students with a higher standard of living from entering STEM fields, US graduate programs filled up with foreign students, whose tuitions are typically funded by their governments. The bulk of the new students, and workers, were from Asia, with India and China at the top of the list.

To pave their way, the Immigration Act of 1990 created the H-1B visa program, which allows US employers to temporarily hire foreign workers in specialized occupations. These occupations often include IT, engineering, finance, medicine, and academia. The program for a three-year visa and another three-year extension, with provisions allowing the visa holder to apply for a green card, was capped at 65,000 when the bill was passed. From 1998 to 2000, the heyday of the dot-com boom, the cap was raised to 115,000; and from 2001 to 2003 it went up to 195,000. There were more H-1B denials under Trump, but under Biden the cap settled at 85,000. There are no limits on H-1B employees for colleges and universities, nonprofit research organizations, or government research institutions. Taken together, estimates show, there are at least 500,000 H-1B workers residing in

America at any given time. Over three decades, that means millions of jobs that should have been given to Americans since 1990 went instead to foreign workers.

"The H-1B was designed from the very beginning to provide low-cost, white-collar labor to tech," says Mark Krikorian, executive director of the Center for Immigration Studies. "It was not to import people with talent that we don't have—considering that the computer industry was invented here to begin with. It was to reduce the bargaining power of American workers by bringing in foreigners either to replace them or to just blow up the labor supply so that the wages didn't go up. Wages for tech workers have not gone up. If there were a shortage, they should be going up. Employers would be bidding for people's services. And in fact, wages in the tech industry have basically been flat for years."

Contrary to the belief that H-1B visa holders are all genius-level talents, says Eric Ruark, an executive at NumbersUSA, a nonprofit focused on immigrant reform, "they're not the best and brightest. It's not like these are the best in their field. In most cases, they're entry-level computer science grads, coders, or programmers. They're capable, but they're not more capable than Americans they're displacing. And we know that because we've seen countless examples of where Americans have had to train their replacements."

The legislation was written to allow employers to hire guest workers without having to demonstrate that there's not an available worker already in the United States. "There are no requirements for any H-1B employer to demonstrate that they tried to recruit domestically," says Ruark. "If you are an H-1B employer, all you have to do is attest that you aren't displacing American workers—but you don't have to prove it. And no one's checking. In effect, there is zero oversight. And that's the way it was designed: So the companies aren't breaking the law by not hiring US workers."

Many of the tech and service jobs that were supposed to come with WTO never materialized for the same reason that corporate and political elites had pushed for China's accession to the WTO—because they wanted to cut labor costs. And that drove down middle-class wages. The game had been rigged against Americans but that wasn't really part of the original design. At first, American Cold War leadership just wanted to fix what World War II had broken and, through free trade, avoid another great war.

America's WWII victory led to an enormous expansion of wealth around the world—raising former adversaries like Japan and Germany out of postwar penury to restore their middle classes and also creating a middle class where one never existed before, like China. Peasants who survived Mao's purges gave rise to a generation of factory workers and after them lawyers and accountants. Individuals made money as the CCP got rich, and finally the Chinese found something they wanted to buy from America—investment vehicles, like stocks, bonds, and real estate. There was so much demand that Wall Street created new instruments to meet the need with structured finance that turned illiquid assets into tradable securities like, most famously, mortgage-backed securities.

For Americans, China's most significant export isn't toys or consumer electronics or anything like that—rather, it's capital. With foreign money from around the world pouring into Wall Street, money became easy to borrow, with mortgage and car loans cheaper than ever before. The bounty Americans enjoyed numbed many to how much offshoring and the loss of good middle-class jobs had—and would—hurt the country. For that was the original sin: exporting our ability to make real things not only swelled the trade deficit and invited foreigners to buy our country, it also left us holding little, except paper vulnerable to political winds. America was on its way to becoming a paper tiger.

It suited the logic of the age that Bush named as his new Treasury secretary a man who'd bent Wall Street rules to save the Chinese Communist Party from bankruptcy. Only later did it become clear that the failure of US leadership to rally resources, as the CCP's war against the homeland continued, intensified and prepared the battleground for an all-out confrontation between Americans and the China Class.

CHAPTER EIGHT

Masters of the Universe

I saw myself as a custodian for this
profoundly important relationship.[1]

—Henry Paulson

To help make the case for China's entry into the WTO,
Wall Street giant Goldman Sachs circulated a study to US lawmakers projecting that WTO accession would boost China's GDP
growth and increase US exports to China by at least two-thirds by
2005.[2] The reality was different.

By the time Bush named Goldman Sachs CEO Henry Paulson
his Treasury secretary in July 2006, America's manufacturing heartland in the South and Midwest was reeling from the effects of the
WTO, a phenomenon that came to be known as China Shock. Yet
the president and his new cabinet member agreed that "protectionist
measures were unhealthy."[3]

Paulson had joined Goldman Sachs in 1974, after a brief stint in
the Nixon administration. He wrote of the president who opened
China: "I grasped the brilliance of his moves, triangulating our

strategic interests to throw the Soviet Union off balance."[4] Paulson would traverse a similar path.

Two months into his job as Treasury secretary, he was in China meeting with an up-and-coming CCP official who would soon become China's next leader—Xi Jinping. He escorted Paulson on a walk by the same lakeside spot where Zhou Enlai had walked with Nixon during the famous 1972 trip. Xi told the new Treasury secretary that retracing those historic footsteps underscored the importance of what the American was trying to do for US-China relations. "Xi's words," wrote Paulson, "drove home the important responsibility that President Bush had given me. I saw myself as a custodian for this profoundly important relationship, and I dearly wanted to improve the way it was managed."[5]

Nixon and Kissinger had opened China up for America, but Paulson opened it up for Wall Street. As Clyde Prestowitz explains: "Paulson showed the Chinese how to tap global capital markets, especially US markets like the New York Stock Exchange, to turn CCP enterprises into major world corporations still under state control." It marked a new phase in US-China relations and a decisive moment in world history. "Without Paulson stepping in like that," according to Prestowitz, "the Party would have gone broke. He helped save the Party and made it rich."

And thus, Paulson's decades-long partnership with Beijing, first as an investment banker then as a member of Bush's cabinet, did as much damage to the United States as any other China Class elite, save Kissinger himself.

CHINA'S BANKER

In 1990, Paulson was named to cohead Goldman's investment banking division, where he took the lead role on Asia. Bank executives debated the relative merits of the so-called Asian Tigers—Hong

Kong, Singapore, South Korea, and Taiwan—and China. "I simply did the math in my head," Paulson wrote, "as successful as all those countries were, together they had about one-third the population of China."[6]

Paulson estimates that between 1990 and the time he left Goldman in 2006, he made about seventy trips to China.[7] What seems to have got his attention was the virtually primitive nature of the country's infrastructure. China's communications, transportation, energy, and banking sectors were all run by decrepit state-owned enterprises, and Paulson saw opportunity in communism.

His idea was to merge the state-owned enterprises serving the country's various regions and provinces into one big company and take it public. "He told the Chinese, 'We can get you on the New York Stock Exchange, and show you how to tap global capital markets, especially US markets,'" Prestowitz says. "He made it possible for CCP enterprises to turn themselves into major world corporations still under Chinese state control."

Paulson helped the Chinese Communist Party get access to the US financial system. And Beijing in turn gave him access. When Paulson left to join the Bush administration, he reportedly held a substantial personal stake in the Industrial and Commercial Bank of China after Goldman invested $2.58 billion of internal funds mixing client, employee, and corporate cash in January 2006. When Goldman sold its last ICBC holdings in 2013, gross proceeds from the sales came to $10.1 billion, nearly four times its original stake.[8] As the CCP demonstrated with Richard Blum and Dianne Feinstein, it chooses winners to make its friends rich.

"Goldman made out like bandits," says Prestowitz. "Paulson, too. The entire US establishment, Democrats and Republicans, played this game without adhering to the rules. They all made out like bandits. Everyone did, except the US public."

Paulson scored a historic win in 1997 when he repackaged several regional Chinese phone services as China Mobile and took it public. It became the first major Chinese state-owned enterprise with its shares listed on the New York Stock Exchange. The initial public offering (IPO) earned the CCP $4.04 billion and hundreds of millions for Goldman Sachs underwriting it.[9]

According to Paulson, the China Mobile IPO "was meant to be a showcase and the cornerstone of the next ambitious phase of reform, the restructuring of the giant state-owned enterprises that dominated Chinese commercial life."[10]

But reform was out of the question. After all, the Chinese companies weren't even really privatizing, as Paulson acknowledged. The CCP, he wrote, "chose to maintain control of companies whose shares they sold in a wide range of industries, keeping them under the Party, which handpicked company leaders."[11] Unfortunately, US investors didn't know that. Paulson and Goldman Sachs, Prestowitz explains, "kept the words 'Chinese Communist Party' out of the disclosure papers."

And of course Goldman never told investors that the there was no independent corporate governance of the SOEs. "In our system, the board's primary loyalty is to the company, which includes shareholder interests," says tech investor Brian Costello. "But with these Chinese companies, loyalty is to the CCP. And why would they care if American investors are hurt if it's good for the CCP?"

What the China Mobile deal showcased was Paulson's ability to make big deals with the CCP, which clinched Goldman's reputation as the top China shop just as it was about to go public itself in the late 1990s. "All these IPOs with China's state-owned enterprise showed that Goldman had the inside track on China, the new growth market," says Costello. "That boosted the value of Goldman's IPO."

When Paulson found out that China National Petroleum Company (CNPC), the regime's biggest and most important energy concern, was contemplating going public in 1999, he courted its head by introducing the communist oilman to America's most prominent oilman, George H. W. Bush. Getting him a meeting was easy—Bush's cousin George Herbert Walker IV worked for Goldman Sachs. They took the CCP official to the ex-president's office, where Bush's son Neil was waiting, too. All of them old friends of China.[12]

The CNPC IPO met opposition from labor unions and human rights activists on account of its oil exploration in Sudan, where the company was alleged to be using prison labor.[13] "Our workers are used to eating bitterness," said a CNPC executive. "They can work 13 or 14 hours a day for very little. The quality isn't as high, but we charge less."[14]

Further, Beijing was selling arms to the Muslim-controlled government in Khartoum to prosecute its war against Christians and animists in the south. Sudan had been sanctioned by the Clinton administration as a state sponsor of terror.[15] Sudanese leadership had given sanctuary to Osama bin Laden from 1991 to 1996 and was implicated in the 1998 bombings of the US embassies in Kenya and Tanzania.[16]

Goldman spun a separate enterprise out of CNPC, named Petro-China. This had the additional benefit of deterring activists and avoiding possible Clinton administration actions, including blocking the IPO of a company dealing with a sanctioned regime. The day after PetroChina registered for the IPO, Goldman Sachs emailed select investors promoting the company with projections of earnings growth and net income. They weren't supposed to do that. There's a waiting period after registration and before the IPO when the investment bank underwriting the deal is supposed to stay quiet.

The bank claimed the emails had been sent by mistake, and got a slap on the wrist, forced to pay a $2 million fine after taking Petro-China public for more than $2 billion. Goldman had done the same before with several other Chinese IPOs.

"Registration provisions are designed to level the playing field and make it fair for everyone," said an official from the Securities and Exchange Commission."[17] And the early alerts would benefit Goldman's prestigious clients. "The banks get their clients in at the IPO price," says Costello. "Let's say that's $10 a share and then when trading starts it goes up $2 in a day. If you bought fifty thousand shares at the IPO price, you've made $100,000 overnight. It's like giving free money to your favorite clients." It was also a way for Goldman to get more rich people with clout invested in the firm's success and China's.

With other major IPOs—like Sinopec, China's second oil major, raising $3.5 billion just six months after the PetroChina deal—Goldman Sachs established itself as "the lead underwriter for major Chinese state-owned companies."[18] These IPOs won Goldman billions, and Paulson long-term relationships with top Chinese officials.

He used those ties to build one of the world's most prominent influence networks, which projected Beijing's power inside Washington. In 1999, he became chairman of the advisory board of Tsinghua University's School of Economics and Management, which offered senior CCP officials a chance to rub elbows with major American businessmen who had access to the White House.[19]

Paulson's successors as board chair include Walmart CEO H. Lee Scott Jr.; John Thornton, the former president of Goldman Sachs who left the Wall Street firm in 2003 to take a professorship at Tsinghua;[20] Biden friend and donor David Rubenstein, cochair of the Carlyle Group; Jim Breyer, CEO of Breyer Capital and Senator Mitch McConnell's brother-in-law; and Apple CEO Tim Cook.[21] Board members include big names from finance and tech, like

Raymond Dalio, founder of Bridgewater Associates, the world's largest hedge fund; BlackRock CEO Laurence Fink; and Blackstone CEO Steven Schwarzman.[22]

Schwarzman was so taken with Tsinghua that in 2015 he opened his own program there, Schwarzman Scholars, which funds students from the United States, China, and elsewhere for a one-year master's in global affairs at Tsinghua.[23] Chinese intelligence services presumably see Schwarzman's program as an opportunity to cultivate and recruit the rising generation of American professionals.

Similarly, Paulson's Tsinghua initiative is essentially a propaganda operation that gives party leadership, like Tsinghua alumnus Xi Jinping, an opportunity to showcase the number of high-profile Americans feeding from Beijing's hand. For instance, the 2017 board meeting was held in the Great Hall of the People in Beijing, where Paulson and the other Americans, including Schwarzman, Breyer, Cook, and Facebook founder Mark Zuckerberg, congratulated Xi for a recent speech he'd given to the Party. According to Chinese-state media, the US delegation praised China "for its achievement in poverty relief and efforts to promote innovation and development, as well as its robust development in economic and social areas."[24]

"All of the people on that Tsinghua board can get any White House, Democrat or Republican, on the phone," says Costello. "Xi or some senior official tells them what they want and that goes to the US president."

When President Bush first offered Paulson the Treasury job, the Goldman CEO declined. He explained to the head of China's central bank that he did not see how he could be effective in the last two years of an unpopular administration. That was too bad, said the CCP banker. He was speaking to Paulson as a friend. "It is a great honor to serve your country. More important, you never know what opportunity you may have to make a difference." He told Paulson: "I think you should become Treasury secretary."[25]

And just like that, the Party had an old friend on the inside.

THE OTHER SIDE'S GENERAL

Paulson's first move in his new post was to establish a conference series modeled after the advisory board he'd set up at Tsinghua. The strategic and economic dialogue (SED) made it look like the United States was getting somewhere with China when the purpose was to do nothing.

"The way the U.S. managed relations when I started at Treasury was simply too diffuse to be effective," Paulson wrote in his 2015 memoir, *Dealing with China*. "We maintained well-intentioned dialogues across many departments and agencies; partnerships on subjects ranging from commerce and trade to economic development and science and technology. But discussions got mired in detail, and people lost sight of the big-picture issues."[26]

China's top US benefactor took over the China file. Under his direction the United States would avoid compelling China to respond to specific American demands and instead focus on issues outside the scope of normal diplomatic talks, like "big-picture issues." Accordingly, as Paulson wrote: "We focused less on particular policies than on the process itself." That is, we talked for the sake of talking. Like the Tsinghua board, the SED was a staged production.

The Trump administration would later call the SED, which continued through two years of Bush and all eight years of the Barack Obama administration, "negotiation traps." These are snares, said Trump's deputy national security advisor Matt Pottinger, "that Beijing sets time and again." The point, Pottinger told the press, is "to lure the United States into a long, formal, midlevel bottoms-up negotiation."[27]

Lighthizer said this was one of his first instructions when he took over as Trump's US trade representative. "No more dialogues," he told me. "Under Bush and Obama, the Chinese just dragged us along, and we let it happen because the Chinese got to pick the other side's generals, like Paulson." Indeed, Paulson relieved pressure on Beijing when Congress wanted to punish the PRC for manipulating its currency.

The growing trade imbalance—China was up $202 billion in 2005—was fueled in part by the fact that China kept its currency at artificially low levels. According to Congress, this "gave China a significant trade advantage by making exports less expensive for foreign consumers and by making foreign products more expensive for Chinese consumers. The effective result is a significant subsidization of China's exports and a virtual tariff on foreign imports."[28]

And it was costing American jobs. After lawmakers threatened legislation in 2005 imposing a 27.5 percent tariff on all Chinese exports, the bill was shelved and then picked up again the following year, when Paulson started at Treasury. He'd said that "accelerating [China's] move to a market-based currency" was a goal of the SED but, he told lawmakers, threatening tariffs is "not the right way to negotiate with China."[29]

And for Paulson, China's artificially low currency wasn't the real problem. "China's currency," according to Paulson, "had become an oversimplified and misunderstood issue. It wasn't the main cause of our trade balance woes. After all, we ran negative balances with just about every major economy. Rather, the deficit with China stemmed from a range of structural issues that caused the U.S. to save too little and borrow too much."[30] Indeed SED's mandate wasn't just to address China's exchange rate but also increasing the United States' low savings rate.[31]

The US runs deficits around the world partly because our

leadership has fixated on the doctrine of free trade since the end of World War II. As for China in particular, the major factor is that US multinationals offshored manufacturing there—in order to supply the US market from Chinese export platforms that are very low cost, highly subsidized, and largely free of environmental and worker safety regulations. America spends more than it produces relative to China because China makes so many of the goods America once did. And a big reason China saves more relative to America is because its 1.3 billion people generally remain too poor to buy what China needs in order to keep growing, and because Beijing's policies have long suppressed consumption in favor of production. Implying that America's core problem is in fact middle-class Americans with reckless spending habits—who might learn a lesson from the thrifty Chinese—exculpates the political and corporate elites who betrayed the country to a communist regime.

"It's a self-serving argument from the establishment," says economist Alan Tonelson. "In the first place, the relationship between savings rates and trade balances is simply an identity arithmetically speaking. It says nothing about causation whatever, and certainly nothing about low savings rates deserving the blame for big trade deficits. Saying that the relationship is an identity means nothing more than that the level of savings and the level of the trade imbalance must be the same. In fact, rather than arguing that Americans' relatively spendthrift ways are responsible for the trade deficit, it's more accurate to say that the trade deficit is responsible for the low savings rate—because it's denied too many Americans jobs and therefore income-earning opportunities that make healthy savings possible in the first place."

Paulson went to Beijing in September to prepare for the first SED meeting in December, to be held in the Great Hall of the People. He met privately with Chinese president Hu Jintao and raised the currency issue. He "noted that outside of China—and to the U.S. Congress—currency flexibility was seen as an indicator of his country's reform efforts."[32]

He later wrote that he emphasized to Hu he "was not asking him to do something that wasn't good for China." In fact, the US official believed that moving the currency was very much in China's best interest. He came up with a number that he said would forestall US legislation. "Mr. President," said Paulson, "if your currency appreciated 3 percent against the dollar before the end of our first SED session this December, the result would be good for China and it would help me convince Congress that the SED is working."[33]

Hu allowed China's currency to appreciate by 1.3 percent in the last quarter of 2006, and 2.2 percent by the spring of 2007. By the time Paulson left Treasury, the currency was up 13.8 percent from his September 2006 meeting with Hu. "But the critics of China's foreign exchange policy were not satisfied," wrote Paulson. "Nor, frankly, should they be—until the value of China's currency is completely determined by the marketplace."[34] All he'd done in the meantime was buy the Chinese time by arranging for them to cheat a little less, and to inflict a little less pain on American workers.

By 2007, Paulson had turned the SED into a forum to discuss climate change, a pet interest of his but obviously of little importance to the Chinese—or else US companies wouldn't have offshored their operations to China partly to avoid costly environmental regulations.

THE CRISIS

In the aftermath of the 2007-8 financial crisis that he'd presided over, Paulson said that to avoid a similar near-extinction level event in the future, "we must create a systemic risk regulator to monitor the stability of the markets and with the power to step in and restrain or end activity at any financial firm that threatens the broader market."

That is, if only there'd been some way to know what was likely to destabilize the global financial system, US officials might have been able to defuse the situation before it became a crisis costing Americans their homes, jobs, and life savings.

But Paulson knew where the powder keg was long before he took the Treasury job. After all, he was CEO of a company that was pushing the very financial instruments that would unravel the market—mortgage-backed securities, or MBS. Among the several layers of mortgages the banks bundled together and sold as financial instruments, some included subprime mortgages, which are loans involving greater, or much greater, risk of default and foreclosures. That was a big problem. Common wisdom at the time was that people wouldn't walk away from their mortgages, but what if they did? What if people who shouldn't have been given big loans in the first place decided that when crunch time came buying food was more important than making their monthly mortgage payments? And that's what happened.

Years before the housing crash, there were plenty of public warnings about subprime mortgages. In September 2004, for instance, Chris Swecker, the head of the FBI's Criminal Division, gave a press conference in which he warned that rampant fraud in the mortgage industry had increased so sharply that the epidemic of financial crimes could cause multibillion-dollar losses to financial institutions.[35]

Many in the mortgage industry were also concerned. A San Jose real estate and mortgage broker named Michael Blomquist was so worried that mortgage fraud would lead to disastrous consequences that he wrote members of Congress warning of the problems in the housing industry. In 2005, Senator Dianne Feinstein wrote back to say she was "monitoring the situation closely." Eventually, Blomquist would sue Goldman Sachs and Paulson, among others who'd packaged risky mortgages as securities, alleging that they'd helped sustain the housing bubble.[36] The case was dismissed, but he was right to want to hold Paulson and his firm responsible.

More than half a year before Paulson started at Treasury, Goldman Sachs started to get antsy about the housing market. Until then, the bank had made a killing trading MBS, but then it began receiving reports of unprecedented defaults and fraud.[37] So, in December 2006, Goldman shifted strategy and started betting that the housing market would collapse.[38] Even as Goldman quietly built a large short position, the trading desk continued to facilitate MBS trades. It seems the firm had to cover its tracks, or else it would've tipped its hand to show it was shorting the housing market.

Is it possible Paulson didn't know what the bank that had employed him for more than thirty years and that he had led since 1999 was up to? Doubtful. But had he as Treasury secretary raised alarms about the housing market and taken steps to curb risky mortgage lending, he might have have left Goldman holding billions' worth of the bad financial instruments the bank was trying to unload. Instead, when the effects of the crisis hit fully in late 2007, Goldman's secret play netted the firm almost $4 billion—even as Americans who didn't have the inside dope suffered catastrophic losses in the worst economic disaster since the Great Depression.[39]

With Goldman safe, it was time for Paulson to take care of China.

By 2007 the US trade deficit with China had reached $295 billion.[40] Traditionally, the People's Bank of China (PBOC) invested the dollars it earned from the trade imbalance in US Treasuries, debt securities issued by the Treasury Department that are backed by the full faith and credit of the U.S. government and therefore among the safest investments in the world. But around the mid-2000s, the PBOC sought a better yield from its US investments and started to diversify.[41]

So Beijing started buying debt issued by the Federal National Mortgage Association, commonly referred to as Fannie Mae, and the Federal Home Loan Mortgage Corporation, or Freddie Mac, government-sponsored enterprises (GSE) established by Congress to facilitate financing for American home buyers. One assessment shows that by 2008, the Chinese held $700 billion in mortgage-backed securities issued by Fannie and Freddie.[42] According to Federal Reserve Chairman Ben Bernanke, foreign central banks like the PBOC "loaded up on Fannie and Freddie MBS because they were considered close substitutes for U.S. government debt."[43]

But they weren't the same. Treasuries were explicitly backed by the US government and the GSEs were not. Sure, "government-sponsored" is a tricky term, but that didn't make it a guarantee, not even an "implicit" one as Paulson and Bernanke claimed in their written accounts of the crisis. Nonetheless, according to Bernanke he and Paulson fielded calls during the crisis from central bank governors, sovereign wealth fund managers, and government officials in East Asia and the Middle East who "had not realized that the government did not already guarantee the GSEs." That's odd because according to a Federal Reserve Bank of New York staff report, there was "explicit language on these securities stating that they are not U.S. government obligations."[44]

Even without the warning label, it's obvious GSEs could not have been guaranteed like Treasuries because they represent a different level of risk, expressed in the fact that they yield more than Treasuries. Say that at the time China started gorging on GSEs the yield spread between them and comparable Treasuries was between 0.20 to 0.30 percent (since the crisis, the average of the spread has been 0.25 percent[45]), a relatively small difference thanks to high confidence in the US housing market. That spread might not mean much to a young father starting an account with a few thousand dollars for his newborn's college fund, but at $700 billion even a modest yield spread of 0.20 to 0.30 percent is worth between $1.4 to $2.1 billion. Look at it this way: If Treasuries and GSEs were both guaranteed by the government and involved the same amount of risk—virtually zero—and the latter paid better, no one would buy the former.

China and other foreign nations thought they'd gamed the American system. But the collapse of the housing market signaled a big problem. Fannie and Freddie are supposed to have very strict underwriting standards but they, too, had bought MBS bundled with subprime loans.[46] Once the housing market hit the skids and the crisis toppled banks and brand-name Wall Street firms, the fear was that Fannie and Freddie might be next to fall.

Paulson was worried about what foreign debt holders would conclude if the GSEs collapsed. "To them," he wrote, "if we let Fannie or Freddie fail and [foreign] investments got wiped out, that would be no different from expropriation. They had bought these securities in the belief that the GSEs were backed by the U.S. government. They wanted to know if the U.S. would stand behind this implicit guarantee—and what this would imply for other U.S. obligations, such as Treasury bonds."[47]

That's strange thinking. First, if US enterprises were failing and Americans were getting the worst of it, why would foreigners think that the housing crisis and the impending failure of the US economy was a plot to steal their wealth? Moreover, how did the reserve managers at the People's Bank of China, responsible for their country's economic well-being, and the success of the Party, buy $700 billion in Freddie and Fannie MBS without knowing that those securities, unlike Treasuries, were not explicitly backed by the US government? But they did know. Of course they knew. The Chinese bought them because they wanted a better yield on their investment. And when their bet went bad, they expected the pit boss to get them their money back.

Paulson wrote in his 2015 book *Dealing with China* that the PRC's vice premier Wang Qishan wanted him "to know that the financial crisis in the U.S. had affected the way he and others in the senior ranks of the Party saw us. 'You were my teacher,'" Wang told him, "'but now here I am in my teacher's domain, and look at your system, Hank. We aren't sure we should be learning from you anymore.'"[48]

It's not surprising that a Chinese official used the financial meltdown as an occasion to insult an old friend of the CCP who'd made the Party rich. And that Paulson seems to have defended neither his own honor nor the reputation of the country he was appointed to represent is evidence of the character of the men and women drawn from the China Class to safeguard American interests.

The Chinese assumed the Americans would ensure success for their friends, just as Beijing had done for its friends, like Richard Blum and Paulson. Sure, the United States had all sorts of laws and regulations, but if the capitalists really believed all their fine talk about democracy and rule of law, they wouldn't have showed the CCP how to cheat its way into US capital markets and raise billions for companies designed to defeat American firms and fund weapons systems pointed at US armed forces. If Paulson didn't help, Beijing had many ways to make the Americans feel pain—maybe they'd dump Treasuries as well as GSEs and plunge the Americans into an even worse crisis. Maybe they'd throw Goldman Sachs and all of Paulson's friends out of China and *expropriate* their money.

Paulson wrote that he "stressed" to the Chinese "that we understood our responsibilities."[49] In other words, he acknowledged that the PRC had to come out of America's crisis whole. The Chinese demonstrated their abilities to make sure Paulson prioritized their needs.

In both of Paulson's books dealing with the financial crisis he includes an important detail the public wasn't aware of at this time. In his 2010 book *On the Brink*, he relates how during an August 2008 trip to Beijing to attend the Olympics, he learned that

> *Russian officials had made a top-level approach to the Chinese suggesting that together they might sell big chunks of their GSE holdings to force the U.S. to use its emergency authorities to prop up these companies. The Chinese had declined to go along with the disruptive scheme, but the report was deeply troubling— heavy selling could create a sudden loss of confidence in the GSEs and shake the capital markets. I waited till I was back home and in a secure environment to inform the president.*[50]

In his 2015 book *Dealing with China*, Paulson retells the story but omits the nugget that he'd informed Bush of the intelligence he received—and that's probably because he never said anything to the president or anyone else about any sensitive information he'd gotten in Beijing.[51] Rather, the Treasury secretary would've just seen the numbers: China was already selling its GSEs. The Chinese had started selling them off in June, two months before Paulson says the Chinese alerted him to Russia's *secret* plan.[52] By the end of the year the PRC would dump $50 billion of its GSE debt, and Russia wound up selling $170 billion during the same period.

In public, Paulson said there was no plan for the government to take over Freddie and Fannie, but in private he said something else. In a secret mid-July meeting with financial executives, including several Goldman Sachs alumni who'd moved to others firms, Paulson said that he was thinking about putting the two GSEs under "conservatorship" in order to "allow the firms to continue operations."[53] That is, Paulson was planning to nationalize the two companies, which would wipe out their shareholders but give him the power to make sure China and the other foreign investors weren't hurt.

It's not clear if any of those who attended the secret meeting traded on the insider information Paulson had provided. But one hedge fund manager was told by his attorney that "Paulson's talk was material nonpublic information," and that he should immediately stop trading Fannie and Freddie shares. Perhaps one effect of the meeting was to contribute to the panic over the fate of the GSEs, because Paulson gave this as a key reason for his concern: The market was losing confidence in Fannie and Freddie, and Wall Street was nothing but a confidence game.

"By the end of August," he wrote, "neither could raise equity capital from private investors or in the public markets."[54] And Fannie and Freddie's collapse, he wrote, "would be catastrophic. Seemingly everyone in the world—little banks, big banks, foreign central banks, money market funds—owned their paper or was a counterparty. Investors would lose tens of billions; foreigners would lose confidence in the U.S. It might cause a run on the dollar."[55] And so in the first week of September, he put the two companies under conservatorship.

"There were options," says financial journalist Ira Stoll. "If only the government had just stopped talking about how troubled those entities were and stopped threatening to take them over."

Paulson critics say that the decision to invoke conservatorship was based not on a clear-cut capital failure but rather the expectation of further declines due to panic. Fannie and Freddie had met their regulatory capital requirements through mid-2008, which disproves the notion that the companies were insolvent prior to Paulson's intervention.[56]

"The free market could have found a market clearing price," says Stoll. "Freddie and Fannie were publicly traded stocks that people were buying early in the financial crisis because they thought it was a bargain and they were backed by home prices and the real estate prices, and eventually they came back."

Within a short time, both firms returned to profitability, calling into question just how broken their finances truly were when Paulson absorbed them in 2008. Fannie Mae earned more than $17 billion in 2012 and Freddie Mac made nearly $11 billion.[57]

"If you bought a house in 2008, it's now worth two or three times what it was then," says Stoll. "After Fannie and Freddie were taken over, they generated huge profits that went into the federal budget." By 2019, Fannie and Freddie paid the Treasury Department more than $300 billion.[58] To ensure the Chinese were made whole, Paulson ended up stripping shareholders of hundreds of billions of dollars.

"I've seen presentations showing that you could take them public and what they'd be worth if the government spun it out," says Stoll. "So not only would it have been possible, a lot of Fannie and Freddie shareholders were really hoping for that at the time. Paulson and George W. Bush screwed shareholders over by seizing control of something that was very valuable."

Maybe Paulson was right and taking over Fannie and Freddie prevented a run on the dollar and saved the international financial system. And in that light, it was a lucky stroke that China made their man Paulson make them whole. But, as Stoll says, "Paulson wasn't supposed to be there to represent the Chinese, he was supposed to be there to represent Americans."

But Paulson believed that his job was to defend the US-China relationship. He was, after all, the "custodian for this profoundly important relationship." In both the private and the public sector, he'd convinced himself he was doing the right thing. But like the rest of the China Class, he was operating under a false first principle:

The fact is that a prosperous Chinese Communist Party is not good for the world.

THE WAR AT HOME

In the fall of 2008, Paulson told Congress that the US banking system—and the world as we know it—would end if he didn't get $700 billion to bail out banks within seventy-two hours.[59] He got what he asked for, but succumbing to Paulson's emotional blackmail ended the worlds of millions of Americans and disrupted even more.

With the financial crisis and home foreclosures, it seemed America couldn't get a break in the new millennium. It was like a perfect storm of mostly self-inflicted catastrophes: Along with the financial crisis, there were the failed wars that followed 9/11, then the effects of the WTO, known as China Shock, as the Chinese picked off American industries.

For instance, North Carolina's furniture and textile industries were hit hard. From 1999 to 2009, furniture manufacturing employment fell by over 50 percent in the state as Chinese-made furniture flooded the market.[60] As the apparel and textile industries collapsed under import competition, North Carolina lost around 100,000 textile jobs and 70,000 apparel jobs between 1997 and 2002.[61]

In the Rust Belt and Great Lakes regions, Ohio, Michigan, Pennsylvania, Indiana, and Wisconsin saw steep job losses in steel, machinery, automotive parts, and appliances. Between 2001 and 2018, China Shock cost Pennsylvania about 137,300 jobs, Ohio around 136,700, and Michigan roughly 112,400.[62]

Americans had never seen anything like the path of devastation cut across the heartland, leaving towns and entire regions in ruins—except in war.

To help draw the Civil War to a close, Union General William Tecumseh Sherman marched his troops three hundred miles from

Atlanta to Savannah to target the Confederacy's center of gravity. Union forces consumed its resources, crippled its transportation and communications infrastructure, and destroyed its manufacturing, leaving the South incapable of defending itself. Some of the communities hardest hit in the CCP's scorched-earth policy that cost America 3.7 million jobs lost between 2001 and 2018 were those that are most relied on to send their sons and daughters to fight America's wars, including the global war on terror.[63]

"The financial crisis changed a lot of things," says a GWOT veteran who asked to be identified by the name he writes under, Lafayette Lee. "I had a college degree and I wanted to stay in the town near my grandparents where I spent some of my formative years, but when the financial crisis hit, I couldn't find a job. I worked odd jobs here and there, but things were tighter and tighter and finally I joined the military. I enlisted in 2011. I joined for patriotic reasons, too. I'd always wanted to do it, but I'd just got married and by then we were trying to hold on. I was trying to start my life, and it was a little hard. So I joined the military, but going back to where it all started has been really sobering."

Lee explains that the financial crisis was one in a series of crises that affected his small Western farming community where he lived with his grandparents—"there was NAFTA, the WTO, and by the time that the financial crisis hit, it was just a breakneck speed of change."

For young Americans in their twenties and thirties coming back from Iraq or Afghanistan to a community hit by China Shock was like watching a time-lapse account of your history from childhood to the new now unfold in real time. Small towns proud of what distinguished them from the neighboring communities—their histories, churches, leading families, sports rivalries—disappeared, absorbed into sprawling new tech communities. "All the family farms just got wrecked and were sold off very quickly and big corporations came in and transformed the entire landscape," says Lee. "And with these tech companies moving into these places, comes different people—these jobs are not for the local kids. They're H-1B foreigners or they're from California. And it completely changes the character of the place."

Issues that were irrelevant to the locals were urgent for the newcomers and the politics started to change, collapsing the local culture. "Our people had been farmers probably for—who knows?—thousands of years," says Lee. "Either farming or ranching, and the things that they knew, that my grandfather knew, just came naturally. There was this accumulation of wisdom and knowledge that had been handed down for a very long time, since even before the founding of the country. And it can disappear in one generation. You could have one person completely divorced from that and losing all that knowledge and understanding. We learned how to ride horses. And we knew things about cattle and pigs and crops, things that were just common knowledge in those communities. With the end of that agrarian backbone, the form of the community, the culture, changes."

And families are severed from their roots. "Every time I go back with my children so they can see family, it just it takes my breath away how unrecognizable it is," he says. "It keeps me up at night. It feels like a dream that's gone now. It's hard to go back to a place that you loved and felt in your soul and now you can't even recognize it. I met and courted my wife there. Some of the places that we used to go to be alone and enjoy nature together, it's all gone. I wanted to be able to take my kids one day and go up there and say, this is a place where your mom and I had long talks about the future, and tell them this was where everything started. When people can't be part of those stages of life that everyone for generations before went through in the same community with family and with neighbors and with people that they know and have long histories with, it deracinates people and cuts them off from these life-giving rituals and experiences and accelerates the decadence, the degradation that have already hit other parts of the country."

In communities hardest hit, other local enterprises, stores, restaurants, bars, etc., shut down for want of business and there were no new industries to absorb the displaced workers. Nor did many move away to find jobs elsewhere. And yet China Shock did not reduce the total number of US jobs: The loss of manufacturing jobs in low-skill regions was counterbalanced by gains in service sector jobs in high-skill regions.[64] Companies that offshored production to China became more profitable and were able to afford expanding their domestic operations in design, R&D, marketing, and retail. As the H-1B issue had made clear, all the talk of retraining workers was empty. The math was plain: with the advent of globalism, Red States lost jobs and Blue regions gained them.

The winners were glad the losers lost. What seemed surprising at first was that the winners were angry at the losers nonetheless. But the winners' anger was just their rationalization of the losers' suffering. It injected globalism with a sort of secular theodicy: The Red Staters deserved to suffer for all they'd ostensibly done and stood for—racism, war, patriotism. In this account, they'd earned hell.

GWOT veteran Samuel Finlay was recovering at Walter Reed Medical Center in Washington, DC, from combat injuries suffered in Afghanistan when he first heard how the tone of the country he'd returned to had changed. "First it was criticism of the Iraq War and Bush and then it went to Red Staters in general," says Finlay. "I remember reading this article in one of these small independent periodicals and the author really aired it out—he said the problem with the policies that led to Iraq are the result of Red Staters, people who live in rural areas and we need to pivot away from them toward multicultural urban cosmopolitanism. I remember reading that and getting really hot. I'm thinking, haji just tried to kill me and I can respect that—we were in his neighborhood. But this kind of vitriol, that Americans could openly talk about politically marginalizing people like me and my family. And if we say or do anything about it, then we're bigots lamenting our loss of privilege. But are we not supposed to take our own side in a fight? Being a wounded soldier from a Red State, that left a mark."

Those who lost in the globalism sweepstakes were left permanently poorer. The initial wave of China Shock starting with Beijing's 2001 accession to the WTO and the import surge leveled off around 2010, but its negative effects on manufacturing regions continued.[65] One study shows that the depressed conditions persisted at least through 2018—the end of the study's sample period.[66] It's still ongoing. The Joe Biden administration's open borders policy buried hope of recovery.

Long-term consequences from China Shock, the financial crisis, and other elements of the perfect storm include: declines in overall employment, lower earnings, rising poverty, increased use of disability and welfare benefits, tax base erosion, collapsed housing markets, and social distress, including an increase in single-parent households and a rise in so-called "deaths of despair," from drug and alcohol use, as well as opioid addiction.[67]

"From about 2006 to 2012 felt like the worst of the opioid crisis," says Army National Guard veteran Braxton McCoy. He was wounded in a suicide bombing attack in Iraq and spent a year recovering at Walter Reed. He took opioids to manage the pain and was hooked for a while. In 2017, he published a critically acclaimed memoir of his recovery and return home, *The Glass Factory*. McCoy says you can track the opioid crisis through popular culture. "There's

Greg Giraldo, the comedian, he died of an opioid overdose, and then Heath Ledger, and that's not to say anything of what was actually happening in the Rust Belt. I had two friends die of opioid overdoses at that time. One enlisted after I got wounded and the other was a civilian. I've never sat down and looked at the data, but anecdotally those years felt the worst."

He says that opening trade with China upended the local cattle industry in his Western town as ranchers stopped raising livestock and grew alfalfa to export. The full weight of the financial crisis hit him in 2009. "I ended up underwater on a house, which choked out every bit of wealth I had gathered by then. I basically ended up broke—not destitute but lost all our savings for sure."

The most noticeable effect of the dislocation that had uprooted his community was the darkness enveloping it. "There was this dark cloud feeling, depressiveness that I had not recognized before. When I was a young kid, we would go to downtown Salt Lake City to Temple Square at Christmas and look at the Christmas lights, and everything's bright and happy. It felt very safe, in retrospect almost like jumping out of a movie. But by the end of the 2000s, the main park was looking like a crap hole, filled with drug addicts and refugees."

He was raised in a religious home but the despair swallowing his community left him an atheist, briefly. "I came home from the war and feeling like perhaps the rest of your life is gone in your early twenties. Depression leads to nihilism, in my view. Getting off opioids was huge and then getting out of atheism was just recognizing finally how much evil there is in our culture and some of what I'd done and realizing just how evil and dark they were. And the moment you recognize that evil is real then obviously it means there is a counterforce."

The material as well as the spiritual world had been transformed. In 2012, Finlay wrote *Breakfast with the Dirt Cult*, a novel about the global war on terror and coming home through the eyes of a wounded US infantryman. What struck him was how the Chinese products ushered in by the WTO cheapened America and made it tinnier, uglier.

"I noticed it with lawn mowers," he says. "My dad is a city worker for thirty years, so he would have to deal with a lot of tools and equipment. They were craftsmen-made, die-hard. But he complains they're making them in China now, and they fall apart. American goods used to last all this time. If you can find tools that were made like thirty, forty years ago, they go at a premium. But now, there's this sort of like planned obsolescence kind of baked into the cake where you'll get maybe five years out of it and you'll have to replace it."

He says that in addition to being able to make things like ships, ammunition, and medicines there's another aspect to reshoring industry that doesn't get talked about much—American pride in making things. "I don't know how we rebuild that," he says. "In my grandfather's day, and even into my dad's, there was pride in American craftsmanship. And that doesn't really matter anymore. And if craftsmen were to try to turn things around, where would they begin? How do you even inculcate people with that pride again, like—I work in a factory, and I'm going to make the best lawn mower I can."

Finlay says his Oklahoma town wasn't much affected by China Shock. "We have an air force base, and the Oklahoma City area's big industry is oil." Oil was a central part of Trump's criticism of the GWOT. He thought America should've seized Iraq's energy resources. "You're not stealing anything," he said during the 2016 campaign. "We're reimbursing ourselves." Trump had a point: "We spend $3 trillion, we lose thousands and thousands of lives," and in return, "we get nothing."[68]

Trump came under fire for saying it, but the fact is that almost everyone else got paid, including China and Wall Street. Beijing secured a number profitable energy contracts in Iraq, including several deals for China National Petroleum Corporation, parent company of PetroChina, as well as Sinopec, both state-owned enterprises that Goldman Sachs made rich on US exchanges.[69] With less of an appetite for risk than China's SOEs, US firms tended to shy away from Iraq and the less promising energy deposits in Afghanistan because energy facilities were popular targets during the war and the only people defending them were US-led coalition forces. That is, Americans lost their lives in the GWOT defending, among other things, Chinese assets and Wall Street investments.

Is patriotism instrumental? "Well, we're not fighting for a people because that's racist," Finlay says acerbically. "We're not fighting for a place because that's xenophobic. And we're not fighting for our way of life because that's chauvinistic."

He reads out a passage from writer Robert Kaplan to make his point: "American patriotism—honoring the flag, July Fourth celebrations, and so on—must survive long enough to provide the military armature for an emerging global civilization that may eventually make such patriotism obsolete." In other words, says Finlay, "short-term disingenuous patriotism in the service of long-term global governance."

But that's not what Finlay believes. He says his novel partly grew out of his recognition that large parts of the country were angry at him and his kind, the men and women who believe in America and will keep fighting for it because you have to take your own side in a fight.

"My squad leader was a really salty, cynical kind of guy," Finlay remembers. "And one day we're reading the paper, and we came across this article on somebody burning a flag and he got really mad and I didn't really understand. This was a guy who'd seen a lot. When he was eighteen, he went off into the first Gulf War as a

Marine. But having that flag, and our country, there's something to that, and it's not something anybody would really talk about much, but it would sometimes come up because what you're feeling has to anchor itself in something tangible. So, I said, what's the big deal about someone burning the flag and he said, 'Because that's my goddamn flag.'"

CHAPTER NINE

Realigning America

That's not who we are as Americans.[1]
—Barack Obama

THE ESTABLISHMENT CONSENSUS WAS THAT CHINA HAD COME out of the financial crisis as the winner. "Today China has not only a more vigorous economy, but actually a better functioning government than the United States,"[2] George Soros said in a talk after the worst of the crisis had passed. "There is a really remarkable, rapid shift of power and influence from the United States to China."[3] He likened what he saw as the United States' foreseeable decline to Great Britain's after World War II.

Soros said that when the crisis finally hit in full force, China "benefited from being isolated from the rest of the world."[4] In other words, it is because Beijing ignored the chorus of US elites like Robert Zoellick, Henry Paulson, and Henry Kissinger that it came out of the crisis better than the United States did.

Soros threw in his lot with China and in 2009 poured hundreds of millions of dollars into Chinese investments. He'd been blamed for the Asian financial crisis a decade earlier when he shorted Thai and Malaysian currencies, so the Chinese distrusted him.[5] Now he praised them for their diligence and skill. He said Hong Kong did well fighting him a decade earlier when he tried to short its currency. "They actually did a very good job defending the Hong Kong dollar, so they deserve credit," he told an audience in Shanghai. "And my attack, if you call it that, was without success."[6]

He, too, had seen the bubble and warned beforehand of the worst financial market crisis in sixty years.[7] Estimates show that by betting against the housing market he made between $7 to $12 billion between 2007 and 2009.[8] The real issue underlying the crisis, he explained, was based on market fundamentalism, a theory "used to justify the belief that the pursuit of self-interest should be given free rein and markets should be deregulated."[9] To his mind, the doctrinaire belief in the financial system's inherent ability to repair itself exculpated greed. It's a pretty thesis, but one he could not fully embrace in practice, for by investing in China, all he'd done was move his chips to another place on the board to stake a different source of corruption.

American corporate and political elites purposefully mistook the lesson of the financial crisis to avoid being held accountable for it. They weren't the problem, they were just playing their part in the system, so the problem was the system. Some came to admire a system where the ruling party is blameless and beyond criticism and took China as a model.

"There is only one thing worse than one-party autocracy," wrote *New York Times* foreign affairs columnist Thomas Friedman, "and that is one-party democracy, which is what we have in America today."[10]

Friedman's 2009 article marks the moment when early in Obama's first term the country's establishment unified under a single political banner. According to one of Friedman's sources: "Globalization has neutered the Republican Party, leaving it to represent not the have-nots of the recession but the have-nots of globalized America, the people who have been left behind either in reality or in their fears. The need to compete in a globalized world has forced the meritocracy, the multinational corporate manager, the Eastern financier and the technology entrepreneur to reconsider what the Republican Party has to offer. In principle, they have left the party."

But the real divide wasn't between Republicans and Democrats. Rather, it separated America's self-anointed oligarchs, visionary tech entrepreneurs, and global trade consultants from the proles who didn't know or care about what was best for the country or even themselves. Maybe there was something to the China model.

"One-party autocracy certainly has its drawbacks," wrote Friedman. "But when it is led by a reasonably enlightened group of people, as China is today, it can also have great advantages." According to Friedman, "one party can just impose the politically difficult but critically important policies needed to move a society forward in the 21st century."

Friedman had long been supportive of US-China ties and was dismissive of US concerns over granting China permanent normal trade relations status and forfeiting leverage on China by delinking trade and human rights. "The AFL-CIO is free to argue that this bill will hurt U.S. workers," Friedman wrote in a May 2000 column.[11] "Republican hard-liners are free to argue that China's entry into the WTO will make it a more formidable geopolitical rival to the United States. But for either of them to say that this bill will hurt the cause of democratization in China, or that it won't help create more islands from which Chinese democrats can operate and more tools by which they can communicate, is to speak utter nonsense, and, one hopes, a majority of Congress will see it as such."

He'd acquired a reputation as a China cheerleader, even when it meant denigrating Americans. "Strategic focus," he wrote in a 2005 column, the ability "to meld strength and strategy—to thoughtfully plan ahead and to sacrifice today for a big gain tomorrow—seem to be such fading virtues in American life. Sadly, those are the virtues we now associate with China, Chinese athletes and Chinese leaders. Talk to U.S. business executives and they'll often comment on how many of China's leaders are engineers, people who can talk to you about numbers, long-term problem-solving and the national interest."[12]

But when I spoke with Friedman on the phone, he made it clear that the furthest thing from his mind was running interference for totalitarian regimes. "I am worried that America is not realizing its full potential to lead and innovate," he told me. "I am not above—shamelessly—using China to scare people into action. To that end, I often use China as today's 'Sputnik,'" he said, referring to the Soviet space program that inspired, and frightened, a generation of Americans to reach for the stars. "I will do whatever it takes to get Americans to understand that we can't just be dumb as we want to be forever and remain the world's biggest economy and strongest superpower."

He said he was disappointed in the failure of our system to deliver common sense reform.

"If you look at my books and writings since I left the Middle East, a lot of my focus has been on how America realizes its full potential in the twenty-first century," Friedman said. "I am not interested in China. I am interested in America. I think China has the worst political system in the world. I think America has the best political system in the world. But I think that China today is getting 80 percent out of its bad system and America is getting 20 percent out of its good system. And that worries me a lot."

But it's not clear to most Americans why it matters that, as Friedman wrote in the 2009 article, "China is committed to overtaking us in electric cars, solar power, energy efficiency, batteries, nuclear power, and wind power."[13] Americans tend to distrust the wisdom of government bureaucrats who believe they can decide which technologies are likely to succeed better than markets can.

For instance, the abject failure of Obama's environmental initiatives made obvious the considerable drawbacks of the common-sense statist model. Most famously, Obama's Department of Energy awarded Solyndra, a California solar panel manufacturer—one of whose investors was an Obama fundraiser—loan guarantees worth more than half a billion dollars only to see its investment go up in smoke when the price of a key ingredient used by its competitors dropped dramatically.[14]

Fracking, on the other hand, would usher in an age of cheap natural gas, turning the United States into a net energy exporter and creating jobs for millions of Americans. It wasn't bitter Red Staters who thwarted Obama's green initiatives; it was reality.

Few who thought America could stand to learn from China as a model wanted to check under the hood to see what made China work. It was enough that a CCP that could keep production lines running efficiently and cheaply was an irreplaceable part in the new economic order—globalism, the flat, borderless world that the *New York Times* columnist and others had written about with great optimism. What they imagined was a China that wanted to be more like America.

But most Americans had yet to realize that the Chinese-made goods they consumed—sneakers, clothing, electronic goods, and so on—were often manufactured in slave labor camps. Those who knew were making money from it, so they didn't discuss it. And almost no one outside of China had heard that the CCP chairman that had made so many Americans rich was harvesting organs from political prisoners.

THE ARCHITECTURE OF UTOPIA

Jiang Zemin was obsessed with crushing Falun Gong. At a joint press conference with Clinton in 2000, he was confronted by Falun Gong protestors and called them a "cult." Any government, he said, would crack down on "those who have done severe harm to the people."[15]

Falun Gong combines a traditional form of Chinese calisthenics known as Qigong with a spiritual practice developed by a Chinese national named Li Honghzi. Master Li, as the sect's members call him, moved to the US in 1996 and helped start a media and entertainment company that includes *The Epoch Times*, a daily newspaper modeled after American broadsheets like *The New York Times*.[16]

Beijing punished Western media that reported on the group. For instance, despite Time-Warner's friendly relations with Jiang, the party removed *Time* magazine from Chinese newsstands in 2001—while the media conglomerate was hosting a conference in Shanghai to celebrate China's WTO entry—because of a story reporting that Beijing was pressuring Hong Kong to ban the organization.[17]

After the PRC blocked the *New York Times* website in China the same year, publisher Arthur Sulzberger traveled to China in August 2001 to meet with Jiang for an interview.[18] Sulzberger brought with him a delegation of *Times* reporters, including Thomas Friedman. The foreign affairs columnist asked Jiang why China had blocked the *Times* website. Jiang, according to a *Times* report, "didn't appear to know, and agreed to look into it."[19]

It seems to have been related to the paper's coverage of Falun Gong. Just weeks before, on July 5, the paper had published a story on the front page of the print edition about Falun Gong, "A

Movement in Hiding: A Special Report. Sect Clings to the Web in the Face of Beijing's Ban."[20] Written by the paper's Shanghai bureau chief, Craig S. Smith, the article was about a thirtysomething tech worker who was a Falun Gong member, and an elderly professor, presumably a CCP official, who relayed the party's line that Falun Gong was a dangerous cult.

"On one side is a group that believes that it is engaged in a battle with evil beings for control of the universe," wrote Smith. "On the other is a government that promotes atheism and feels so threatened by a relative handful of people that it has marshaled the full force of its police power to bend them to its will." Falun Gong, he wrote, "represents the most sustained challenge to Communist Party authority in more than a decade."

The comparison to the Tiananmen Square uprising would have struck the Party, a paranoid cadre to start with, as exceedingly dangerous, perhaps even a threat, that originated not as a report from a foreign correspondent, but a warning from the US capital. Jiang himself, say Falun Gong members, saw the sect as a threat to his own authority.

"Falun Gong was very popular and spread all across China," says William Huang, an engineer who moved to the United States in 2008. He got his degree from Tsinghua University—"the MIT of China," he says—where students, professors, and administrators regularly practiced Falun Gong at various sites on campus. "There were even a lot of party members and CCP officials," says Huang. "Maybe in all of China there were more Falun Gong practitioners than party members at that time."

To Jiang, support for the movement showed that the people were losing faith in party ideology, or at least his ability to develop his own school of communist thought, as Mao and Deng had and Xi would.

"Falun Gong believes in higher beings. But the CCP believes only in communism, so they don't allow anyone to truly believe in any religion. And Falun Gong believes in traditional values based on five thousand years of Chinese civilization. But after the CCP took over, they systematically destroyed traditional Chinese culture through political movements like the Cultural Revolution."

Jiang believed he could wipe out Falun Gong, too. "He said he could destroy it in a short time," says Huang, "only three months." The crackdown started in July 1999, with PRC authorities rounding up Falun Gong members. Huang remembers he was corralled at the Shijingshan stadium with thousands of other Falun Gong practitioners on July 21, 1999, many of whom were beaten by police. They were warned to stop practicing the exercise and abandon the group but most, including Huang, kept at it. He was arrested in December 2000 and sentenced to a five-year term.

"Twenty inmates were squeezed in a small cell about 250 square feet," he remembers. "You did everything inside the cell—sleeping, eating, drinking, using the toilet. And every day was work, slave labor, at least eighteen hours a day. No holiday, no weekends. We were forced to make all kinds of products, like decorative plastic flowers. Also, Spider-Man toys and Christmas tree lights. The guards told us all the products would be exported to Western countries, including the USA. No one believed him. But after I came to the USA, I saw the exact same products we made here in the stores with a 'Made in China' label. Christmas tree lights. I was really shocked."

There were self-criticism sessions—"like the Cultural Revolution," says Huang. And torture. "I was forced to kneel down before hundreds of other prisoners with my hands cuffed behind my back and then I was shocked with high-voltage electric batons. I could feel the hot currents going everywhere through my body. I kept convulsing.

I almost died. They forced me to admit that I was a criminal, just because I practiced Falun Gong."

Huang says his blood was tested during his imprisonment. Obviously, it wasn't for his health, or the guards wouldn't have treated him badly. After he got out of prison and heard about forced organ harvesting from Falun Gong practitioners, he realized that the blood test was likely administered to see if he was a suitable candidate for organ harvesting.

Jiang defended his crackdown on the Falun Gong to Sulzberger, Friedman, and the others. According to Jiang, the group had "done great harm to people's physical and mental health" and no government could sit idly in the face of such an "out-and-out cult."[21]

Soon, the *Times* characterizations of Falun Gong would come to resemble the CCP's. According to a 2024 report from a media organization affiliated with Falun Gong, "the *New York Times* has been exceptionally silent on atrocities against Falun Gong practitioners, including the forced organ harvesting of prisoners of conscience." The paper, says the report, "ignored major reports by human rights groups and the 2019 London China Tribunal on forced organ harvesting, as well as ongoing high-profile individual cases of prison sentences and deaths in custody."[22]

The coarsening of American elites, increasingly acclimated to cruelty, and growing ever more comfortable expressing contempt for the have-nots it had impoverished, was an effect of how they idealized China's political system. Their class consciousness was further elevated by the fact that the president they'd newly elected was, according to their estimation of China, essentially a CCP elite—future looking, detail oriented, and strategically focused.

Obama's vision of America truly was transformative because it was not attached to anything recognizably American. When George W. Bush antagonized much of the world proclaiming in his speech immediately after the September 11 attacks that "either you are with us, or you are with the terrorists," his clumsy patriotism nonetheless struck a deeply American chord at a particular moment.[23] By contrast, Obama's version of a rallying cry, "That's not who we are as Americans," could be applied to anything—and he repeated it frequently—because it was anchored to nothing but the exigency of the moment in which he uttered it. It was grounded only in Obama, a schoolmaster shaming the underclassmen into his idiosyncratic idea of patriotism.

The divide he struck wasn't between Americans, never mind the two political parties. As Friedman's interlocutor had it, the split was between "the have-nots of globalized America" and those who would be part of the future.

And the future was what? One hundred percent clean and renewable energy—with half the country living below the poverty line? World peace—with US intelligence services exercising broad surveillance powers and the prerogative to censor speech when it challenged ruling class preferences? Environmental justice, as the Obama team called it, meant laying waste to vital economic sectors in order to remake America as a place where people who profess the "Green New Deal" climb the ladder to success, and others lose their jobs for being on the wrong side of history.

The architecture of their utopias was irrelevant, so long as those drawing the plans had the power to reward their friends and to punish those they identify as an enemy.

What has protected our fragile experiment in living together all these years is not the two-party system nor even the series of checks and balances written into the Constitution. Rather, it's the unspoken agreements that manifest themselves in national symbols, heroic tales, and sentimental myths. But Obama recast the American story as an epic tale of sectarian identity and grievance.

"We do not need to recite here the history of racial injustice in this country," he said in a 2008 speech during his first presidential campaign. "It's a racial stalemate we've been stuck in for years," but "working together we can move beyond some of our old racial wounds."[24]

And when Obama was done being president, it wasn't his fault that the country failed the task he'd given it. "Here's one thing I never believed," Obama told an interviewer in 2020, "was the fever of racism being broken by my election. That I was pretty clear about." He said he never subscribed to the idea "we live in a post-racial era. But I think that what did happen during my presidency was, yes, a backlash among some people who felt that somehow, I symbolized the possibility that they or their group were losing status not because of anything I did but just by virtue of the fact that I didn't look like all the other presidents previously."[25]

Obama's assessment of his presidential career was an audacious set piece, scripted to evoke the self-pity of the class whose ambitions and resentments he embodied: The progressive president who owned the mandate of a unified globalized elite was the victim of the victims of globalization.

PIVOT TO ASIA

Like George Soros in the wake of the financial crisis, the US president said he too was redirecting his attention to Asia.

"As the world's fastest-growing region—and home to more than half the global economy—the Asia Pacific is critical to achieving my highest priority, and that's creating jobs and opportunity for the American people," Barack Obama said in a November 2011 speech in the Australian capital, Canberra. "As President, I have, therefore, made a deliberate and strategic decision—as a Pacific nation, the United States will play a larger and long-term role in shaping this

region and its future, by upholding core principles and in close partnership with our allies and friends."[26]

The concept "Pivot to Asia," describing the administration's new
strategic focus, appears to have debuted in an October 2011 article
by Obama's secretary of state, Hillary Clinton. Since she was already
preparing to leave the administration to campaign for the presidency
in 2016, it seems less likely she was previewing Obama's policy than
laying out her own vision in anticipation that she'd be the next
inhabitant of the White House.

"As the war in Iraq winds down and America begins to withdraw its forces from Afghanistan, the United States stands at a pivot
point," she wrote. "Over the last 10 years, we have allocated immense
resources to those two theaters. In the next 10 years, we need to be
smart and systematic about where we invest time and energy, so that
we put ourselves in the best position to sustain our leadership, secure
our interests, and advance our values. One of the most important
tasks of American statecraft over the next decade will therefore be to
lock in a substantially increased investment—diplomatic, economic,
strategic, and otherwise—in the Asia-Pacific region."[27]

Compared to Obama's vague promises, Clinton's assessment was
far more clear-eyed and concrete. What she meant was that the Middle East is a sinkhole into which first Republicans and then Obama
had thrown American lives and money for no strategic purpose, and
now it's time to turn our attention to the looming threat. Candidate Nixon had made essentially the same case in his 1967 *Foreign
Affairs* article when the morass was Vietnam, but the pivot point was
the same: China. It didn't help Clinton or America that during the
intervening four decades her husband had supercharged Beijing by
ushering it into the WTO.

The underlying problem was that the WTO, like the George W.
Bush administration's freedom agenda for the Middle East,

demonstrated how the inability of US leaders to understand the national interest invariably leads to further disarray and corruption. Obama's White House would have needed more than a catchy brand name like Asia Pivot to recalibrate America's China policy. Instead, the initiative that was supposed to enhance diplomatic, economic, and military investment in the Indo-Pacific theater was little more than a communications campaign to make Obama look serious on China and deflect from the fact that what he really cared about was the Middle East.

Obama's Pentagon set a goal to deploy 60 percent of US naval and air assets to the Pacific by 2020 to ensure freedom of navigation through the South China Sea, a major trade route through which roughly one-third of global shipping passes yearly; reassure regional allies Japan, South Korea, Australia, the Philippines, and Thailand that treaty commitments were "sacrosanct"; and dissuade China's aggression.[28]

In fact, the White House failed on nearly every count as the PRC engaged in a campaign of aggressive actions challenging regional stability and US interests and allies.

In 2012 China seized Scarborough Shoal from the Philippines. A small group of rocks and reefs located about 120 miles west of the Philippine Island of Luzon, Scarborough Shoal is a strategically crucial military and maritime post in the South China Sea.

The Philippines also lays claim, along with China and others, to several disputed reefs and shoals in the Spratly Islands. The Chinese seized these in 2013 and dredged sand and rock to turn them into artificial islands, where they built airstrips, deep-water harbors, and military installations, with anti-ship cruise missiles, surface-to-air missile batteries, advanced radars, hardened hangars for combat aircraft, and runways long enough for bombers.[29]

"There were a few problems with the pivot to the Pacific, but foremost among them is that it never actually happened," says former Republican congressman Mike Gallagher, who chaired the House Committee on Strategic Competition between the United States and the Chinese Communist Party from 2023 until he left Congress in 2024. "There was no honest assessment of our military force structure and presence around the world that would suggest we did anything to increase our deterrent posture in the Indo-Pacific theater."

Rather, the PRC harassed US military assets at sea and in the air. In March 2009, five Chinese vessels surrounded the USNS *Impeccable*, an unarmed US Navy surveillance ship operating seventy-five miles south of Hainan Island. The Chinese warned the ship to leave or "suffer the consequences," forcing the US vessel to withdraw.[30]

Obama at last pushed back in 2013, when Beijing declared an Air Defense Identification Zone (ADIZ) covering much of the East China Sea, including airspace over the Japan-administered Senkaku Islands and overlapping with South Korea's long-standing ADIZs. China demanded that any aircraft, civil or military, flying through this zone submit flight plans to PRC authorities. The move was seen as a provocation, attempting to impose Chinese administrative control over international airspace and a disputed area. The United States responded by flying two B-52 bombers through China's new ADIZ, without informing Beijing, to demonstrate it would not recognize Chinese-imposed restrictions inconsistent with international norms.[31]

And yet in August 2014, a PLA air force fighter flew a barrel roll within yards of a US Navy plane over the South China Sea. In May 2016, two Chinese fighters intercepted a US spy plane, an EP-3 like the one the Chinese brought down in April 2001.[32] During the eight years of his presidency, the show of force that won the Obama administration most news was an agreement with Australia to rotate 2,500 US Marines through an Australian military base.[33]

"I just don't think that Team Obama believed in hard power," says Gallagher, a former Marine officer. "They weren't thinking in terms of actually building a bigger navy that could field a bunch of missile systems that could sink the PLA Navy if they try to take over Taiwan. There's just this persistent tendency in Democratic circles to relegate hard power to a secondary, if not tertiary position. They're saying we're going to divest of conventional hard power and make up for the gap by investing in technology, allies, and nonmilitary instruments of power. It's as if some magical AI software is going to allow us to win wars in the future—combined with nonmilitary instruments of power, as if sternly worded statements are going to affect the thinking of PRC leadership."

And China's new leader was also a big factor. "When Xi Jinping came to power," says Gallagher, "we thought he'd continue the whole strategy of hide your power and bide your time that started with Deng."

But a document distributed in spring 2013 by CCP leadership alarmed US policymakers. "The Communiqué on the Current State of the Ideological Sphere," known as Document 9, didn't sound like old friend Jiang Zemin who liked to recite the Gettysburg Address to gullible American audiences to prompt their admiration for his reformist credentials. The new man in charge was a committed communist.

Xi's father was Xi Zhongxun, a veteran of the Red Army and one-time vice premier who was jailed during the Cultural Revolution. His family was exiled to the countryside, where the fifteen-year-old Xi Jinping worked hard labor alongside the peasantry. Perhaps it's to redeem his family after their travails—his mother was forced to denounce her husband, and one of Xi's sisters seems to have taken her own life—or show that his loyalty, unlike his father's, is unimpeachable, that the premier is alight with the ideological zeal of the generation of 1949.

Document 9 enumerates the dangers facing the CCP—namely everything the United States says it stands for: constitutional democracy, universal values, civil society, independent journalism, and anything else designed to undermine the history of the CCP or compromise its ideological integrity.[34]

The Party was worried about internal and foreign foes. "Western anti-China forces and internal 'dissidents' are still actively trying to infiltrate China's ideological sphere and challenge our mainstream ideology," according to the memo. "Some people have disseminated open letters and declarations and have organized petition-signings to vocalize requests for political reforms, improvement of human rights, release of political prisoners,' 'reversing the verdict on [the Tiananmen Massacre]."

Document 9 was both a call to purify the party and a warning to its adversaries. "The position of Western anti-China forces to pressure for urgent reform won't change, and they'll continue to point the spearhead of Westernizing, splitting, and 'Color Revolutions' at China. In the face of these threats, we must not let down our guard or decrease our vigilance."

The use of "color revolutions"—policy slang for the various US-supported efforts through the 1990s up to Obama's presidency to topple foreign regimes—shows that the document was directed specifically at the United States. The message was: Confront us and you will have war—even at a moment when the Obama administration went out of its way to show it meant Beijing no harm. In other words, it was an instrument of political warfare, propaganda designed to keep the Americans on the defensive. Though Document 9 was widely distributed to party cadres, its real audience was Washington.

"When our adversaries say things, we should believe them and take them at their word," says Craig Singleton, a former US diplomat and now China program senior director at the Foundation for Defense of Democracies. "With Xi Jinping, what you see is what you get. He says what he means, and he means what he says. It's not like it was in the Soviet era, when US policymakers were hoping for snippets of secret Soviet speeches to understand Moscow's plans and intentions. Xi's ideological preferences are transmitted widely and publicly, he wants everyone, friend and foe alike, to internalize them. And, there should be no confusion at all about what Xi thinks and believes because he literally can't stop talking about his Marxist-Leninist views. What was so glaringly powerful about Document 9 was that it was just a clear articulation of his worldview."

It wasn't just talk, says Singleton. "Observers heard the first few speeches, what he was articulating, and then saw the actions he was taking to support what he had said." Xi waged a multipronged campaign against the United States, using nonmilitary assets.

"Xi turbocharged his espionage and United Front work efforts during the Obama years with little to no pushback," says Gallagher.

For instance, between 2011 and 2015, a Chinese intelligence operative named Christine Fang, or Fang Fang, enrolled in a California college and zeroed in on up-and-coming local politicians using campaign fundraising, extensive networking, and sexual relationships to capture their attention.[35] Among others she ensnared was Bay Area congressman Eric Swalwell, a member of the House Intelligence Committee until he was removed in 2023, seemingly because of his relationship with her.[36]

"The Swalwell case was another instance of how the Chinese subnational program looks for people they think are going to be potentially big or have potential access to people that are potentially big," says a former US intelligence official. "Swalwell says he didn't talk

but he's not the smartest guy in the world. He may not have understood what he was giving away."

The Chinese were playing a much bigger game as well, casting a
wide net across US communications systems to see what turned up.

In April 2015, US authorities discovered that in late 2013 Chinese operatives had hacked the Office of Personnel Management,
obtaining access to the records of 21.5 million current, former, and
prospective federal employees. The data stolen included information
required from government workers applying for security clearances,
like details about family members, foreign contacts, health history,
financial records, and even fingerprints. With a huge database of US
government employees involved in sensitive or classified work, Beijing was armed to use the information for blackmail, recruitment, or
espionage.[37] It was the largest and most serious hack of US government records in history.

In September, three months after the hack was made public, Xi
met with Obama in Washington where, side by side, they announced
a mutual understanding that "neither the U.S. or the Chinese government will conduct or knowingly support cyber-enabled theft of
intellectual property, including trade secrets or other confidential
business information for commercial advantage."[38] Xi was laughing
in America's face.

BIDEN'S PLUNDER

When Hunter Biden went into business with agents and institutions
of the Chinese state, he was capitalizing on his father's relationship with PRC officials. Sometimes Beijing pays in expectation of
future favors and at others it pays for services already rendered. In
this instance, it seems it was the latter, for the Chinese were grateful
to the vice president for having exposed Americans to the financial
fraud that fueled the growth of China's tech sector as well as PLA

weapons systems and other projects meant to ensure Chinese dominance of the United States.

Mitchell Silk is a corporate lawyer specializing in Chinese law and finance and author of the 2025 book *A Seat at the Table: The Unlikely Story of a Hassidic Jew in Trump's Treasury*. He learned Cantonese as a child when working at a Chinese restaurant in Florida and picked up Mandarin later. He served in the first Trump's administration's Treasury Department as assistant secretary for international markets, where he helped formulate the White House's economic and trade policy toward China.

"Foreign companies come to issue in the United States to tap into our capital markets to raise money because we have the largest and deepest capital markets in the world," he says. "People like our capital markets because, number one, of the liquidity and tenors available, and also because we're a self-reporting jurisdiction. The regulators will not generally bother you as long as you follow the rules. That translates to continued access to capital on the basis of ongoing conformance with all the disclosure, reporting, and compliance requirements."

For China, having its companies listed on prestigious exchanges like NASDAQ or the NYSE was a critical step in legitimizing the capitalist elements of its communist system. These listings weren't merely financial maneuvers; they symbolized global recognition and validated China's hybrid economic model on the international stage.

The first wave of Chinese companies tapped into the US capital markets in the mid- to late 1990s, thanks to the efforts of Henry Paulson and other Wall Street giants. "These were really big Chinese national conglomerates, like airlines, energy companies, and financial institutions," says Silk. "These were the blue chips, or rather red chips, doing global offerings where they were offering tranches in different financial markets. And the offerings tended to be in the billions. There was another group of corporates, mainly medium-size companies, that tapped into the US market, most of them on NASDAQ through a structure called a reverse merger."

In this process, a company buys a shell company, one still listed on US exchanges but dormant. Then the buyer would merge its existing China business into the shell.

As Silk explains, "When these Chinese companies started a reverse merger, the target corporate entity was already listed on the market, which obviated the need to go through the Securities and Exchange Commission's initial screening requiring disclosure of financial and audit reports and other information relating to the underlying China business to be merged into the shell." The Chinese companies grafted themselves onto existing but dormant companies to conceal material information, says Silk, "that would have altered investment decisions."

In 2011 the bottom fell out and Chinese companies were found to have perpetrated massive fraud. "All of these reverse merger issuers, lost very, very significant value," says Silk. "From 2011 to 2012, 28 of the 103 reverse merger issuers lost 90 percent of their value. Fifty-six of the 103 lost at least 80 percent of their value, 63 of the 103 lost at least 70 percent of their value, 76 of the 103 lost at least 60 percent, 83 lost at least 50 percent, and 89 lost at least 40 percent. So that is a very considerable amount of value that dropped out of the market, therefore very significantly impacting US investors."

One analysis estimated total investor losses around $100 billion; individual investors lost around $80 billion, institutional investors—including state and local pension funds—lost another $14 billion, and hedge fund losses made up the rest.

The SEC brought action against China's four major accounting firms for refusing to provide auditing documents that would've likely given evidence of fraud, but the Chinese accountants claimed they couldn't provide the information without violating Chinese privacy laws and exposing state secrets that could lead to their imprisonment or even execution.[39]

Despite the ridiculous hyperbole, the rationalization for hiding evidence of fraud highlights an important truth—the finances of Chinese companies are state secrets because the companies are state enterprises. The party has the decisive say in all corporate decisions. The party listed fraudulent companies on US exchanges to extract money from Americans and their institutions in order to fund PRC institutions, like the PLA.

It was clear that Chinese companies listed on US exchanges were not going to play by the rules, and there was no legal reciprocity in China to hold them accountable.

The capital markets were an invaluable source of income for the PRC, so Beijing wanted to keep its companies on the board. And they're also vital sources of income to Wall Street and elite investors. "When foreigners invest in China, there's only one real way for them to get their money out of China, by going public," says tech entrepreneur Brian Costello. "You can't just pull your money out as long as it's in China. That goes all the way to the top of the communist party for approval, and even then, good luck. But if the Chinese company lists on a US exchange, you can sell your shares freely. That's why Wall Street fights to keep that door open. Yes, the fees the banks get for initial public offerings are great, but more importantly, they need a way to get their very lucrative China investments out of the country."

The Obama administration wanted to work out a solution, one that would keep Wall Street and China happy. Vice President Joe Biden was at the center of what former US officials and finance experts say is the biggest financial scandal in US history. "The scandal," says Costello, "is that we again let Chinese companies that previously committed fraud with no repercussions list again on US capital markets without even having to follow our rules. It's absolute insanity."

Biden was fond of saying that he'd spent more time with Xi Jinping than any other world leader has.[40] And that may be accurate. The two became close during Biden's vice presidency when Xi, then the PRC's president-in-waiting, was also serving as vice president. Biden first met with him in Beijing in 2011 where his host pressed him on trade and investment issues.

Xi said that he wanted a "fair environment" for Chinese businesses and urged Biden to "eliminate the interferences of trade and investment protectionism." The accusation was dripping with historical irony. Since the start of the US-China relationship, Beijing had always protected its own companies while exploiting American vanity and greed. And in keeping with that American tradition, Biden promised "greater access and also continued development and investment both ways."[41]

Biden told the Beijing audience: "You have legitimate concerns about access to America. And I would argue we have legitimate concerns in reverse. But the trajectory of the relationship is nothing but positive, and it's overwhelmingly in the mutual interest of both our countries. And it's presumptuous to say this, but I think it's in the interest of the world. It's in the interest of the world that we increase the interaction between not only our business community, but our economies writ large."[42]

At the same time, US and Chinese regulators were trying to work out an agreement that would allow Chinese companies to list on American exchanges without violating US law while trying to account for China's demands to skirt US laws on account of the ostensible national security laws of a communist regime that had just stolen hundreds of billions of dollars from US investors. That is, the US government was negotiating over American law with a foreign government that had broken it.

Silk says that during the Trump administration he and other officials were unfazed by China's demands to treat their corporate enterprises unlike US companies or any other companies in the world. Silk says that the administration told the Chinese, "You can do whatever you want in China, but this is America, and if you want capital market access, you'll play by our rules, or you won't play at all." And, he adds, "if they refused to comply—if the rules in their country forbid that—then they could pick up their marbles and go home." But the Obama administration rolled over.

Negotiating for the US side there was the Public Company Accounting Oversight Board (PCAOB), which operates under the oversight of the SEC and is responsible for overseeing the audits of public companies to protect investors.

"As early as 2011, the US regulators wanted to have a go at the Chinese," says Silk. "Our SEC and others were debating with the Chinese securities regulators whether the Chinese auditors of the companies that listed in the United States had to disclose and produce their audit papers and audit notes." China pushed back—citing their national security laws but, says Silk, "knowing that their corporates and their regulators were going to get tagged for bad behavior."

The Americans had all the leverage. As former Ronald Reagan aide Roger Robinson told the press, "For those worried that forcing such compliance would cause China to simply move its companies' listings and equity and debt offerings elsewhere, U.S. global financial dominance is such that, to a large extent, there is no 'elsewhere' given China's huge annual fundraising requirements."[43]

"Wall Street didn't dare risk its cozy relationship with the CCP by exposing the fraud, let alone pushing to delist the companies," says Costello. "For the big banks and institutional investors, keeping those

Chinese firms listed on US exchanges is not only about short-term profit, it's their only real way they can get their money out of China. If the fraud comes to light, the door slams shut."

So, the White House caved to China and Wall Street.

In May 2013, the PCAOB signed a memorandum of understanding (MOU) with Chinese regulators that allowed Chinese companies to continue raising capital on US exchanges even though US regulators still couldn't inspect their auditors' work—an exception afforded no other companies in the world.

"The Chinese got away with not disclosing their auditors' papers, and that exposed US investors to more risk of the type that we saw in 2012 when so many US investors lost all or significant value in their investment," says Silk. "It was an untenable situation."

"The SEC's job is to enforce US laws and regulations to protect investors. It's not to selectively exempt anyone from them," says Costello. "They certainly shouldn't be creating loopholes for foreign adversaries to help them capitalize their companies."

That arrangement could only be greenlighted by top-level US officials, which points to the White House. "At the time, experienced leaders on the Senate Banking Committee who were responsible for overseeing the SEC, included Mark Warner, Elizabeth Warren, and Chuck Schumer," says Costello. "They never challenged the SEC's decision to grant China a pass on our regulations or what could otherwise be seen as a license to commit fraud. Their silence suggests cover from higher up."

Assorted former US officials from the last several administrations say it was likely Biden, prompted by the Chinese as well as Wall Street, who ensured the Chinese stayed on US capital markets. Costello agrees. "Biden was the primary interlocutor with Xi Jinping during this period," he says, "while simultaneously, his son was actively gearing up his investment fund, to invest in Chinese companies."

After Beijing's demands for access to US markets were satisfied, it put Hunter Biden in position to get rich in a closed system whose outcomes are determined by the CCP.

A month after the MOU between the US and PRC regulators, Hunter Biden signed his own memorandum of understanding with a Chinese counterpart, Jonathan Li, who ran a Chinese private-equity fund called Bohai Harvest. Hunter and his associates from Rosemont Seneca joined Li in a new company called BHR Partners that would invest Chinese capital companies outside China.[44] From the outset, BHR enjoyed significant CCP support, with the Bank of China owning 53 percent of Bohai's parent fund.[45] Soon after the vice president of the United States helped ensure Beijing continued access to US capital markets, the PRC staked his son to Chinese capital.

Hunter joined the vice president on a trip to Beijing where he introduced his father to his new partner, Jonathan Li.[46] The fund's initial capital was relatively modest, about $4.8 million, but by mid-2014 BHR was aiming to raise $1.5 billion.[47] Li said that the firm would focus on "ultra-large-scale and internationally influential projects," thanks to the "strong background of [BHR's] state-owned shareholders," like the Bank of China.[48] By the end of 2015, the fund was managing around $1.7 billion in assets.[49]

In December 2014, BHR invested in China General Nuclear Power Corporation, a state-owned nuclear energy company. The investment later drew scrutiny in 2016 when the Justice Department charged it with conspiracy to illicitly obtain US nuclear technology.[50] The deal underscored BHR's access to sensitive PRC industries.

In September 2015, BHR Partners teamed up with Aviation Industry Corporation of China (AVIC), a large Chinese state-owned aerospace and defense conglomerate, to acquire Henniges Automotive, a US-based auto parts manufacturer, for about $600 million.

BHR took a 49 percent stake while AVIC took 51 percent, giving the Chinese entities full ownership of Henniges, making it the biggest Chinese investment into US automotive manufacturing assets to date.[51] Because Henniges produced anti-vibration technologies with potential dual-use applications, the deal was reviewed by the Committee on Foreign Investment in the United States. Obama approved it while Republican lawmakers expressed unease that it tied the son of a politically prominent American to a PLA-linked company.[52]

Parallel to Hunter Biden's China successes, Chinese companies enjoyed a golden age on Wall Street after they were cleared to list on US capital markets.

In October, China's largest online classifieds platform went public and raised $215 million, and the following month a Chinese travel-booking site listed at $125 million.[53] An online car-sales marketplace and an online sports lottery provider were among the eight Chinese firms that listed in the United States in 2013, up from just three the year before.

The next year saw dozens of Chinese companies going public, including Alibaba's record-setting IPO in September 2014. The Chinese e-commerce giant raised $25 billion, making it the largest IPO in world history at that time.[54] The deal netted more than $300 million in fees for its underwriters, including Goldman Sachs and others. By year's end, Chinese firms had collectively raised tens of billions of dollars from US investors.[55]

And still American investors were flying blind because it was impossible to discern if the Chinese entities were legitimate. In 2016, the PCAOB began a pilot inspection program and, to no one's surprise, assessed that China was not allowing US regulators sufficient access.[56]

According to Silk, the Trump administration was working on

fixing the problem. "The brawl between the PCAOB and the Chinese regulator on access to audit papers had been going on for a decade," says Silk. "And right before we finished in Trump 45, there was nearly a deal that both sides found to be satisfactory on the access to auditor papers." But the Biden administration walked it all back. Biden's SEC head Gary Gensler, says Silk, "gave the Chinese their way in terms of disclosure."

And that's the other piece of circumstantial evidence pointing to Biden. As president, he did nothing to stop the CCP from defrauding US investors. In the early days of the second Trump administration, senior officials were determined to finally hold Beijing accountable. US Senator Rick Scott sent a letter to Trump's nominee for SEC chair Paul Atkins about the previous SEC chair Gary Gensler regarding the ongoing issues with Chinese companies listed on US exchanges. Scott wrote: "These companies consistently fail to meet the requirements of our markets—misleading American investors and putting their investments and U.S. national security and economic security at risk—and the Biden administration and SEC Chair Gensler consistently failed to enforce the Security and Exchange Commission's (SEC) accounting standards and disclosure requirements that are required by law."[57]

According to Scott, "there are currently 286 Chinese companies listed on U.S. Exchanges with a total market cap exceeding $1 trillion." The Biden administration's failure to enforce accounting and disclosure standards "allowed Chinese companies to continue trading on U.S. Exchanges without making the necessary financial disclosures, potentially putting American investors at risk."[58]

The more than a trillion dollars of American wealth extracted through US exchanges has been used to furnish the CCP with the latest AI technologies and advanced weapons systems pointed at US armed forces and American neighborhoods. Making China rich has made it an existential threat to America. And exposing the US public to a foreign Ponzi scheme for the purpose of enriching an American adversary is one of the biggest financial crimes in history. It's the backstory that gives the essential context to the Biden family's business dealings with the Chinese—making the CCP rich off the backs of Americans.

IRAN PIVOT

Obama let Biden handle China because it was never the president's priority. The pivot to Asia was a feint. Obama's real interest was in the Middle East—he wanted to strike a deal with Iran. As Obama deputy Ben Rhodes said in 2013 about the prospects of an agreement with the anti-US terror state, "It's a big deal. This is probably the biggest thing President Obama will do in his second term on foreign policy. This is healthcare for us, just to put it in context."[59]

The Asia pivot couldn't mean much if the Iran deal was as important for Obama's legacy as the Affordable Care Act. However, the geopolitical gambit that started the US relationship with China was of supreme importance to Obama, for the historic agreement he sought with Iran was modeled after the opening to China.

Ostensibly, the agreement Obama wanted with Iran was over its nuclear weapons program, but the purpose of the nuclear deal was to resolve a long-standing issue between the US and Iran in order to clear the way for a historic realignment. He wanted to bring Iran in from the cold, as Nixon and Kissinger had done with communist China. Obama would make history by opening to the country Washington cut off after Iran's revolutionary cadres stormed the US embassy November 4, 1979, and held fifty-two Americans hostage for 444 days. And as Kissinger had imposed a balance of power, so, too, would Obama, to establish what he called "geopolitical equilibrium" in the Middle East.[60]

For Kissinger the opening to China was the first move in a match where Russia, China, and the United States would keep each other in check. It was his modern-day version of the Concert System that put post-Napoleonic Europe on ice. From his perspective, stability and peace, especially in the nuclear age, required hobbling the major powers, including the country Nixon and Kissinger represented, America.

Obama wanted the same for the Middle East: to create a concert system balancing the region's strongest actors, Iran, Israel, and Saudi Arabia. Since the last two were the pillars of US power in the Middle East, geopolitical equilibrium meant collapsing America's regional position.

Obama aides and the broad network of publicists, journalists, and think experts tasked to sell the Iran nuclear deal—officially known as the Joint Comprehensive Plan of Action (JCPOA)—claimed that its purpose was to stop Iran from ever getting the bomb. It wasn't a perfect deal, they admitted, but it was better than nothing, and if something wasn't done, Iran would surely get the bomb.

But even a cursory glance at the JCPOA's clauses restricting Iranian nuclear and other activities reveals the truth—they are called "sunset clauses" because they were designed to expire. And once they expired, Iran's industrial-size nuclear weapons program would be entirely legal under the continuing protection of the United States. The JCPOA's true purpose, and the reason for the hundreds of billions of dollars Obama made available to the clerical regime in Tehran, was to facilitate the advancement of their nuclear program under the protective umbrella of an international agreement backed by the United States.

Obama wanted Iran to have the bomb. Without it there was little chance of balancing what he perceived to be the region's most disruptive force, neither the Iranian terror state nor Muslim extremists, but Israel, America's chief regional partner.

At the time that Obama proposed his plan, it seemed a far-fetched conspiracy theory that the president would mislead Americans about something as serious as legalizing the nuclear weapons program of a terror state to hobble a US ally that had proven its worth throughout the Cold War when it fought Soviet proxies like Egypt, Syria, and the various Palestinian factions that Moscow funded. It was bad enough that Iran had made clear its intent to destroy Israel, but it has been killing Americans since the 1979 Islamic revolution. Surely, Obama had some more conventional strategy in mind. And he did—Kissinger's celebrated opening to China.

As the Soviet Union seemed to Kissinger, in Obama's eyes Israel was the most dangerous actor. Iran was weak and needed to be bolstered to check Israel, as Nixon and Kissinger had elevated China. And by hobbling America's most important ally in the Middle East to realign with Iran, Obama weakened America, just as his predecessors had by balancing Moscow and Beijing against Washington. American money and patronage empowered China's revolutionary regime; so did the billions of dollars that Obama poured into Iran's war chest to fuel the revolutionary regime's ambitions, enflaming conflict from the Persian Gulf to the eastern Mediterranean. Like Kissinger, Obama weakened America to unleash a monster.

CHAPTER TEN

The Thirty Tyrants

China doesn't aspire to a strategic
partnership. It sees us as a rival.[1]

—Donald Trump

JUST MONTHS AFTER DONALD TRUMP'S 2016 VICTORY, FORMER
Defense Department official and founding dean of the Harvard
Kennedy School Graham Allison published *Destined for War: Can
America and China Escape Thucydides's Trap?* His thesis was derived
from a line in Thucydides's *History of the Peloponnesian War*: "What
made war inevitable was the growth of Athenian power and the fear
which this caused in Sparta." Allison applied it to the current state
of affairs, casting America as status quo Sparta and China as rising
Athens. His argument was that unless cooler heads on both sides
prevail, the two great powers of the moment are headed for conflict.

The book was endorsed by leading members of the China Class,
including its aging éminence grise, Henry Kissinger, who had been
Allison's thesis advisor at Harvard. Others who advertised their support on and inside the covers of Allison's book included: J. Stapleton

Roy, former US ambassador to China, former vice chair of Kissinger Associates, and later director of the Kissinger Institute on China and the United States at the Woodrow Wilson Center; William Cohen, secretary of defense under Bill Clinton, a board member of the US-China Business Council, and founder of the Cohen Group, with two offices in China; and Kurt Campbell, a top Asia hand in the Obama State Department, where he was Xi Jinping's main point of contact, a founder of the Asia group who would rotate back into government as the Biden administration's Asia czar.

Wall Street celebrities also vouched for Allison's insight and understanding, like Blackstone CEO Steven Schwarzman and Lloyd Blankenfein, Henry Paulson's successor at Goldman Sachs. So did David Rubenstein, cochair of the Carlyle Group, which has large investments in Chinese firms, including ByteDance, the parent company of TikTok, the social media app that shares US user data with CCP authorities.[2] Rubenstein's friend and frequent Thanksgiving dinner guest Joe Biden also recommended *Destined for War* and its author, whose "counsel" he often sought "both as a senator and vice president."

Despite the political and financial firepower backing *Destined for War*, Allison's thesis isn't true. The bulk of historical evidence shows that status quo powers have rarely warred against perceived threats, and for good reason—it is foolhardy to risk wealth, power, and prestige based on a hunch regarding what might constitute a future threat.

"Japan was the rising power in 1904 while Russia was long established," wrote China scholar Arthur Waldron in his review of Allison's book. "Did Russia therefore seek to preempt Japan? No: the Japanese attacked Russia in 1904. In 1941, the Japanese were again the rising power. Did ever-vigilant America strike out to eliminate the Japanese threat, even though Tokyo was already at war? No... In the 1930s Germany was also obviously the rising menacing power. Did France, Russia, England, and the other threatened powers move immediately? They could not even form alliances, so the USSR eventually joined Hitler rather than fight him."[3]

Indeed, Allison's theory doesn't even hold for the Peloponnesian War. Athens started a war that Sparta did not want. Thucydides, an Athenian general banished after a consequential defeat, wrote his now-classic chronicle in part to elicit sympathy for his people. His peerless narrative represents one of the few instances in which the vanquished rather than the victor got to write the history that informs the generations to come. And yet the losers' assessment of the causes of war are no more entitled to our confidence than those of the winners.

Most significant, Allison's analysis was dead wrong about the two powers his book was about. With WWII victories in the Atlantic and Pacific, the United States was indisputably the Cold War's leading power. As Henry Luce had predicted, it had truly become the American century. But Washington did not make war against the revolutionary regime that helped kill its young men in Korea and Vietnam and plotted to sow racial conflict at home. Nor did America even countenance nuclear threats made against Beijing by its communist rivals in Moscow. The US not only shielded China but raised it out of poverty and turned it nearly into a peer. The idea that Washington, never mind Wall Street or Silicon Valley, would in any way seek conflict with Beijing or happen into war was on its face ludicrous. Indeed, the various names endorsing Allison's book represented nearly five decades and trillions of dollars invested in the US-China pact.

And that was the point of Allison's book. With publication coinciding with the election of the first president in fifty years who recognized the threat China posed to America, the Harvard man's message was that disrupting the relationship was likely to usher in the end times. Accordingly, Trump must appease Beijing by continuing to transfer middle-class wealth to the CCP and its US allies or else. It was the China Class's ransom note. Trump's 2016 win was evidence they'd lost control. He was the candidate who spoke out against China and earned the right to represent the American people in the conflict that the CCP started.

Before Trump, Wall Street and Washington believed that the rise of China was inevitable. And US policy was to help it rise, encourage it to be a responsible stakeholder, and integrate the communist regime into the liberal international order that had guaranteed peace and security in the postwar period.

Because the political establishment assumed that American decline was as inevitable as China's rise, it wanted an accommodation with Beijing. Its leaders wanted to manage decline and make sure America declined slowly, at least while they were still around. Kissinger, the Bushes, Clinton, Paulson, Zoellick, and the rest of the China Class seem to have thought that the relationship with China would be like Great Britain's postwar mentorship of the US, with the sunset power explaining to the rising giant how the world works. Enlightened cooperation and comity and the mutual agreement that all states will pursue their interests, and satisfy their appetites, in moderation will ensure that the world will be a safe place. Globalism is peace.

But when their program was put to a vote in 2016, the China Class could not convince Americans to go along with it.

Jeb Bush was the Republican Party's early front-runner for the 2016 nomination. Like his father and brother before him, he believed in constructive engagement with China. He boasted how he'd been traveling to China since 2007 and was uniquely capable of explaining America to the Chinese and China to America.

And he believed that America should deal with China from a position of strength not weakness, echoing US presidents dating back to Nixon who despite their campaign promises turned a blind eye to the CCP's depredations.[4]

During a Republican primary debate in January 2016, he attacked Trump for wanting to tariff China. When Trump explained that the PRC won't buy from US companies unless they move their factories to China, Bush brushed it off to mislead the audience.[5] He was, after all, the China Class candidate. Thus, it hardly came as any surprise when a super PAC that backed his 2016 campaign was fined nearly a million dollars for accepting donations from a Chinese-owned company with the candidate's brother Neil on the board of directors.[6]

The China Class lost the presidency in 2016 because it failed to understand that Americans did not want to decline or elect a president who would manage decline to make room for a rising China. Given a choice, they voted against all that, because for Americans globalism is surrender.

The China Class had misread the Chinese, too. China doesn't believe in the liberal international order. The CCP is not interested in sitting in conference rooms with men like Paulson and Zoellick and other custodians of the US-China relationship. The Chinese reward their US interlocutors for the political capital spent to make China look good—while China enslaves and murders Tibetans, Uyghurs, and Falun Gong, jails and kills prodemocracy activists in Hong Kong, steals US nuclear secrets, compromises American officials, hacks our data, builds islands in the South Pacific, threatens US allies Taiwan and the Philippines, defrauds US investors, and points its weapons at American cities. The China Class vouches for Beijing, but the 2016 election was evidence that US voters see through the lies. The CCP isn't part of any order, they're communists.

FIFTH COLUMN

"Before Trump, we never had an America First president, a president who said that he was going to make sure that preventing the looting of America by China was a top priority," says Ezra Cohen. "So when I was appointed to the first Trump administration and asked to come up with the top five intelligence policy initiatives that I wanted to advance, I thought to myself, what is the number one America First thing in the intelligence world? And the answer was counterintelligence. That's all about protecting America, protecting our businesses from foreign espionage, protecting the government, protecting against intellectual property theft. This is how a large portion of the counter China initiative started."

Cohen was the national security council's senior director of intelligence in the first Trump administration. Along with other Trump aides, he discovered that the outgoing Obama administration was spying on the Trump transition team. To protect the privacy rights of US persons, American citizens, and green-card holders, intelligence officials redact their names in transcripts of foreign intelligence intercepts. It's not unusual for a US official to ask for a name to be redacted, but the Obama administration did it on an industrial scale.

For instance, during the period between Trump's election day victory and inauguration day, at least 40 Obama officials asked to have the name of Cohen's former boss Michael Flynn unmasked. It was evidence the Obama team was using intelligence resources to spy on the incoming administration. Cohen and others contacted House Intelligence Committee chair Devin Nunes, who built on the information and eventually uncovered the FBI's illegal spying campaign on the Trump team, including it seems the president himself.

Cohen was committed to stopping Chinese subterfuge. Previously, American officials had typically opposed counterintelligence targeting China since revealing what the Chinese were doing to undermine America would embarrass the Chinese and endanger trade relations. "The downside of not doing something about China was less than letting China continue doing what it was doing," says Cohen. "And that was true for some in the Trump administration, too. There was an enormous pressure from these Wall Street groups to try to make sure that my counterintelligence policy did not succeed."

Cohen explains that he discovered one of the biggest threats from China almost by accident. "When we were mapping out all the Chinese threats, we identified with the student visa issue. And the way it first came out was that we were talking about securing our national nuclear labs, the Department of Energy labs like Los Alamos, Lawrence Livermore, Argonne National Lab. They have partnerships with academic institutions. So scientists who have a DOE position also have appointments at a university. We started looking into this because those people were being targeted by the thousand talents program."

The Thousand Talents Plan program is part of the United Front Work Department. Its role is to recruit both Chinese nationals educated abroad and foreign experts to build China's technological and innovative capabilities. Targets are lured with offers of prestigious positions at Chinese universities and substantial amounts of money.

"These researchers had actually gone to China and helped set up a lot of the Chinese research institutes," says Cohen. "The professors were brought to China to help reproduce the environment and structure of American research institutes. So it wasn't just specific technology that the Chinese wanted. They wanted help reproducing the environment."

Cohen and his team put prohibitions in place for scientists receiving government funding, government grants, or anyone working in a US government-funded research program. "For instance," says Cohen, "they couldn't go to China without reporting it."

Cohen says this helped focus the attention of federal investigators who started looking more closely at Thousand Talents researchers, like the chair of Harvard's Department of Chemistry and Chemical Biology Charles Lieber.

A specialist in nanoscience, Lieber had received more than $15 million in grants from the National Institutes of Health and Department of Defense, which required him to disclose significant foreign financial conflicts of interest, including financial support from foreign governments. Starting in 2011, Lieber became a "Strategic Scientist" at Wuhan University of Technology (WUT) and a participant in China's Thousand Talents Plan from 2012 to 2017 that earned him $50,000 USD a month, living expenses, and more than $1.5 million to establish a research lab at WUT.

He never disclosed his participation in the Thousand Talents program to Harvard or the US government agencies that had funded his work. When federal agents started questioning him in 2018, Lieber lied about his involvement in the Thousand Talents Plan and affiliation with WUT. In 2023, he was convicted by a federal jury on two counts of making false statements to federal authorities, two counts of making a false income tax return, and two counts of failing to file reports of foreign bank and financial accounts with the IRS.[7]

Lieber was paid by Chinese intelligence operatives but the government couldn't prove he was a spy. "That's because of how the Espionage Act is written," says Cohen. "It requires you to prove the espionage, so you have to catch the agent in the act, or the handler giving the agent instructions. But with modern day encryption, they just can't get that. That's why nobody gets charged with actual espionage anymore. They get charged with procedural things like lying to federal agents, or illegal retention of classified information."

Cohen explains that after he and his team had made that channel a problem for the Chinese, they wanted to anticipate Beijing's next move. "If they can't get people to come to China, they'll get people who are already in the US," says Cohen. "So we knew the next move would be to harness the huge numbers of Chinese graduate students in the US. And when we started looking at foreign students in the national nuclear labs, what we got back was shocking. There were over twenty thousand Chinese foreign students affiliated to some degree with our national nuclear labs."

In the 2019-20 academic there were more than 370,000 Chinese nationals studying in the US on F-1 student visas, a historic high.[8]

"They were students, but many were also PLA officers," Cohen says, on the students affiliated with the national labs. "They weren't working on classified research, but what they were doing was adjacent to the classified research. There's supposed to be a very firm firewall, but it's not in practice. For instance, you could have classified research going on and then right outside that door you have Chinese graduate students working there."

Cohen's next move was to find a way to ban foreign students from a list of countries with China at the top. When Cohen and others took Trump the news about the number of Chinese students in America's nuclear labs, the president could scarcely believe it. Cohen says the president said to work together and get it done.

But there were traps set everywhere, inside and outside the administration. Russiagate was the outward-facing manifestation of the anti-Trump operation, joining the press and Washington, DC, institutions skilled in using the media to suit their ends, like the FBI, Justice Department, and CIA. But what was happening out of view was much larger, using powers and processes that few Trump supporters knew existed.

For instance, it was university researchers who threatened the

Trump administration over its plans to ban foreign students from China, Russia, and Iran. "They said they would terminate the relationships between the Department of Energy and the academic institutions," says Cohen. "That would destroy our national nuclear labs."

There were fights over Chinese students all through the administration, according to Theo Wold, who was deputy assistant to the president for domestic policy in the first Trump administration. "There was a faction inside the White House and throughout parts of the administration that were committed to shutting down China's access points to the visa system," says Wold, "which precipitated one of the more obvious ideological fault lines in the first term."

Wold says "there should be whole degree fields that Chinese nationals are not eligible to enter—computer science, advanced aeronautics, engineering, nuclear engineering, metallurgy. All the STEM subjects. The Chinese can build lots of things. They can copy lots of things. They're not capable of creating jet engines. When I went to places like Case Western and Michigan, I asked the chancellors for the matriculation rate from these programs and they would come back and it would be 88 percent Chinese national, 92 percent Chinese national. So, number one, restrict Chinese access to certain degree types."

But one faction fighting Trump initiatives believed that a purge of Chinese students from STEM would sacrifice the ability to recruit top-level Chinese nationals who excel in these fields.

"They believed that this might also be debilitating for U.S. corporate interests, like the tech industry. Another cadre believed that any curtailment of Chinese nationals coming through the F-1 student visa pipeline would mean the end of the American educational bubble. There were discussions about how the Chinese are building out their own post-university institutional capacity and pretty soon they won't need to come to the U.S. anymore and the attractiveness of a U.S. degree will start to subside and we will lose out to Australia and Canada as well as Oxbridge for these top-flight students. So, don't investigate and don't curtail, because the end of this will be a diminishment of a leading American industry."

Sometimes the universities stepped in directly. "The chancellor of the University of Texas system at the time was Admiral William McRaven," says Wold. "And he had already signaled that he was a Trump opponent. But this decorated Navy Seal, four-star admiral, war hero, he picked up the phone and said, 'I'm going to list for you all the programs that this is going to be detrimental to.' And McRaven didn't stop where most university presidents say it's sad, and this is going to hurt our bottom line here. He took an additional step and said, 'we have alumni who are invested in these programs, and I'm going to call each and every one of them, and we're going to mobilize them against this White House and this president to think twice about picking a fight with us over these visas.'"

There was one more group that fought Trump staffers on visas. "These were just panda huggers," says Wold. "The most charitable rendition of their argument was that the more cultural exchange, the more Chinese nationals allowed to come to the US will help propagate American values, both economic and cultural, in China. Of course they had to admit it hadn't been working, but you can't shut it off because who knows when the tide will turn and we'll start to see this this return on investment."

But for the America First side, says Wold, "whether it was the birth tourism question, the theft of intellectual property, the obvious gaming of our visa and immigration system to bring nefarious elements into the country, we felt we should at least take stock of how screwed we really are. And even that was almost a bridge too far."

China had become a leader for birth tourism. "The Russians have been using birth tourism since the fall of the Soviet Union," says Wold. "What is new is the number of high-level Chinese nationals or up-and-coming Chinese researchers, scholars, computer scientists who were arriving in the U.S. for graduate school programs and giving birth and then going back. These terminal master's degrees were less about stealing state secrets and more about securing U.S. passports."

The Mecca for Chinese birth tourism is California, where private home owners set up makeshift maternity wards and are paid lavishly for their assistance.[9] In 2019, Federal prosecutors in Santa Ana, California, charged nineteen people linked to schemes that helped thousands of Chinese give birth in US to secure birthright citizenship for their children.[10] Trump's DOJ was the first to bring federal criminal charges against operators and customers of birth tourism businesses.

According to the indictments, Chinese nationals were coached on how to pass the U.S. Consulate interview in China by falsely stating that they were going to stay in the US for only two weeks. They learned to trick U.S. Customs and Border Protection at ports of entry by wearing loose clothing that would conceal their pregnancies. The indictments also allege that the customers were directed to fly to Hawaii from China—instead of directly to Los Angeles—because it was easier to get by CBP in Hawaii.

The Chinese also use less high-profile US jurisdictions for birth tourism. In the Northern Mariana Islands, for instance, Chinese births have jumped in the last several decades. In 2009, there were only eight recorded child births from Chinese parents and in 2012 that number jumped 3,000 percent to 282. In 2014 the number rose to 314, rising to 383 in 2016.[11]

Wold explains that he first started to grasp the seriousness of the problem when he spoke with the governor of the Northern Marianas.

"They'd been hit by two devastating typhoons in a very short period," he says. "And they were looking for an expansion of a certain visa class so that they could bring in more Filipino construction workers for rebuilding and humanitarian interests. And as a point of curiosity, we asked to know more about the birth tourism industry. The numbers were shocking. They had built a new hospital facility with an obstetrics ward, and nearly 92 percent of total births in the hospital, the lone hospital in the city, were to Chinese nationals."

Even the newborns of US-based Chinese governmental officials are getting US citizenship. "It's pro forma behavior in some hospitals," says Wold. "They just hand the new parents applications for Social Security numbers and a passport and I think the Constitution's boundaries are pretty clear. The children of consular officials or representatives of foreign nations are not entitled to US citizenship."

It's nefarious, says Wold. "Some of these Chinese nationals ultimately will come to claim in-state tuition benefits or preferred homesteading residency tax benefits for their second homes or those things. But I don't think we've even arrived yet at the kind of scope of the fifth column activity that will occur when you have Chinese nationals who hold US passports and ostensibly US citizenship doing work here in our country on behalf of China."

He points to the August 2023 arrest of an American sailor charged with providing sensitive military information to China. Jinchao Wei was stationed at Naval Base San Diego where he was a machinist's mate on an amphibious assault ship. He held a US security clearance and had access to sensitive national defense information about the ship's weapons, propulsion, and desalination systems.[12] His mother had encouraged him to betray America to a Chinese intelligence officer, saying it might help him get a job with the Chinese government.[13] "She was proud of him for doing it," says Wold. "I think that's just the beginning of what we'll see as it comes home to roost, how manifest the Chinese exploitation of our immigration system is."

But the problem is so large that federal law enforcement authorities can't manage the sheer mass of Chinese nationals who are up to no good in the United States. "At one time there were eighty-seven active investigations at Ohio State alone," says Wold. "Think about that across every single campus that has a joint Department of Energy or Department of Health and Human Services lab or research facility."

Or they wander off campus for surveillance of sensitive sites. In October 2024, for instance, the FBI charged five Chinese students at the University of Michigan with espionage-related charges. They were caught taking photos of military equipment at Camp Grayling while the Michigan Army National Guard was hosting training for the Taiwanese military.[14]

FBI leadership spent the entirety of the first Trump administration trying to topple the commander in chief. But even if they'd been loyal to their mission, "the Bureau would not have anywhere near the amount of manpower to be able to look at all the Chinese nationals in the United States who are potentially spying on America," says Wold. "The size and scale of the fifth column would boggle the mind of most Americans."

And that massive CCP espionage operation was augmented by US leadership. "To get China into the Paris climate accord, one of the concessions the Obama team agreed to was to make it easier for Chinese nationals to get a visa," says Ezra Cohen. "Originally it was a single-entry visa for tourists or businessmen, it lets you in for one time and it lasts for six months. But one of the Chinese government's conditions for entering the agreement was that the US grant a ten-year entry visa for businesspeople and five-year visas for tourists. The Obama administration sacrificed national security and opened the door to the Chinese Communist Party in exchange for some crazy environmental thing that the Chinese never even followed. Just think about how sick and backwards these people's priorities are. It's catastrophic because all of these Chinese nationals can come in, ditch their identity, assume some new identity, and it's impossible to find them. The FBI doesn't have the bandwidth to track these people in the US."

Since China's massive espionage campaign is supported by a consortium of powerful and politically influential industries, like tech and academia, the fifth column is effectively a China Class auxiliary force.

THE THIRTY TYRANTS

It was coarse, un-American, of Harvard professor Graham Allison to liken America to slave-state Sparta, when the engine of China's rise was unregulated labor coerced from peasants, political dissidents, and minority populations. And by comparing the CCP to Athens, *Destined for War* further obscured the fact that there was a very clear lesson for the freeborn citizens of our constitutional republic to draw from the epic war between classical Greece's two most powerful city-states.

In chapter 5 of Niccolo Machiavelli's *The Prince*, the Italian Renaissance political philosopher who would define political modernity describes three options for how a conquering power might best treat those it has defeated in war. The first is to ruin them; the second is to rule directly; the third, he wrote, is to create "therein a state of the few which might keep it friendly to you."

The example Machiavelli gives of the last is the friendly government Sparta established in Athens upon defeating it after twenty-seven years of war in 404 BCE. For the upper caste of an Athenian elite already contemptuous of democracy, the city's loss confirmed that Sparta's system was preferable. It was a high-spirited military aristocracy ruling over a permanent servant class, the helots, who were periodically slaughtered to condition them to accept their subhuman status. From the perspective of Athenian elites, democracy gave too much power to the lowborn. And this oligarchic faction used Sparta's victory to undo the rights of Athenian citizens, and settle scores with their domestic rivals, exiling and executing them and confiscating their wealth.

The Athenian government disloyal to Athens's laws and contemptuous of its traditions was known as the Thirty Tyrants. The faction's leader was Critias, a poet and dramatist who was said to be one of the best students of Socrates, Athens's most esteemed philosopher. Critias may have helped save Socrates from the regime's wrath, and yet the philosopher appears to have regretted that his method, to question everything, fed Critias's sweeping disdain for tradition. Once in power, Critias turned his nihilism on Athens and destroyed the city. As with Athens's antidemocratic faction, America's best and brightest had long ago lost their way, and they, too, found occasion to unleash their wrath on their fellow citizens and destroy the candidate the citizens had chosen to free them from the deadly pact.

By the end of 2019, it looked like Trump was headed for a second term. The economy was soaring and unemployment was at record lows. He was rallying on the very field on which he'd chosen to confront his opponents—commerce.

"The objective was simple," says first term Trump Treasury official Mitchell Silk, "make China buy more of what we make."

In August, 2017 Trump had directed US trade representative Robert Lighthizer to determine "whether to investigate any of China's laws, policies, practices, or actions that may be unreasonable or discriminatory and that may be harming American intellectual property rights, innovation, or technology development."[15]

In March, Lighthizer released the results of his investigation, finding that China is conducting unfair trade practices related to technology transfer, intellectual property, and innovation. And in April, Trump announced $50 billion in tariffs on Chinese imports. Then Beijing retaliated, announcing its own list of $50 billion in US exports to be tariffed.

To appreciate Trump's commitment to protecting America from China's predatory trade practices, it's important to keep in mind that while he was contesting with Xi, the two of them raising the stakes in each round with more tariffs or the threat of more, Trump was defending himself from a domestic coup intended to push him out of office. As rogue US intelligence officials were illegally leaking classified information to advance the Russiagate narrative, as Robert Mueller's special counsel investigation disrupted the normal functioning of the US government, and as the media drove the American public into a manic frenzy alleging that the president was a Russian spy, Trump fought a trade war against America's chief adversary.

US companies knew Trump was serious about winning, for even as Democrats, the media, and intelligence officials plotted to impeach him, top tech firms like Dell and HP announced they were starting to shift some of their production outside of China.[16] Amazon, Microsoft, and Google said they were also planning to move some of their manufacturing elsewhere.[17]

In spring 2019, Lighthizer and other US negotiators had worked out a draft agreement with Beijing addressing the White House's key concerns, especially trade-deficit reduction, intellectual property protections, forced technology transfers, and industrial subsidies. Then in early May, China backed out of the deal. They'd removed key provisions from the draft, including commitments to change PRC laws around IP protection, tech transfer, and subsidies. Trump told his team to walk away.

At the end of June, Trump and Xi met at the G20 meeting in Japan and agreed to restart negotiations and pause further tariffs.[18]

In December Washington and Beijing announced an agreement and on January 15, 2020, China's Vice Premier Liu came to the White House to sign the Phase One trade deal, with China's pledges to boost U.S. imports by $200 billion over two years and commitments on IP and technology.[19]

"We secured commitments from the Chinese to buy more from us and sell less to us to reduce the trade deficit," says Silk. "We got them to make changes and reforms in their intellectual property laws and change numerous policies to allow in more of our agricultural products. And we got them to drop a bunch of non-tariff barriers, meaning laws and policies that kept US and other foreign service providers out of China, like financial services companies."

Trump had wanted more. He'd wanted to get everything back at once to even the playing field for Americans. Still, says Silk, "The Phase One trade agreement represents very considerable progress on the issues. It may not have delivered 100 percent of the way on all issues but it was demonstrable progress."

That's where things stood in the new year, an election year. But looming over Trump's successes was news of a respiratory disease sweeping out of Wuhan, China. Then Covid hit. And with that, the various institutions that had profited from and the ideas and concepts that were engendered by the last five decades of the US-China relationship seemed to cohere as one powerful force to oppose Trump. The coronavirus represented its dark culmination and made real the metaphor that opponents had long used to define it: It was true, after all—partnering with a totalitarian police state had made America sick.

In July 2019 the residents of Wuhan had begun to fill the streets, angry that officials responsible for the health and prosperity of the city's 11 million people had betrayed them. They were sick and feared getting sicker. The elderly gasped for breath. Marchers held up banners saying, WE DON'T WANT TO BE POISONED, WE JUST NEED A BREATH OF FRESH AIR. Parents worried for their children's lives. There was fear that the ill had suffered permanent damage to their immune and nervous systems.

Authorities censored social media accounts, as well as photos and videos of the protests. Undercover policemen watched for trouble-makers and detained the most vocal. With businesses forced shut, there was nowhere for protestors to hide. Some were carted off in vans. They'd been warned by the authorities: "Public security orga-nizations will resolutely crack down on illegal criminal acts such as malicious incitement and provocation."

But what had sent people to the streets of Wuhan wasn't Covid-19. In the early summer of 2019, what threatened public health in Wuhan was the plague of air pollution.[20]

To deal with the mounds of garbage poisoning the atmosphere, authorities planned to build a waste incineration plant—an initiative that rightly alarmed the people who lived there. In 2013, five incin-eration plants in Wuhan were found to emit dangerous pollutants.[21] Other cities had similarly taken to the streets to protest air pollution, including Shanghai in 2015. Each protest sent waves of panic through CCP leadership, who were fearful of the slightest echo of the 1989 prodemocracy protests in Tiananmen Square.[22] What if unrest spread from one city to the next, with the entire country, 1.4 billion people, eventually spinning out of control?

The way to keep unrest from going viral, the CCP had learned, was to quarantine it. The party has shown itself especially adept at neutralizing the country's minority populations, first the Tibetans, and then Uyghurs, through mass quarantines and incarcerations, managed through networks of electronic surveillance that paved the way to prisons and slave labor camps. By 2019, the grim fate of Chi-na's Uyghurs had become a matter of concern in the West—whether heartfelt or simply public relations oriented—even among many who profited hugely from their forced labor.

Prepare for a "smashing, obliterating offensive," Xi told the police and PLA troops.[23] His deputies issued sweeping orders: "Round up everyone who should be rounded up." Officials who showed mercy were themselves detained, humiliated, and held up as an example for disobeying "the party central leadership's strategy for Xinjiang."

According to a November 2019 *New York Times* report, Chinese authorities were most worried about Uyghur students returning home from school outside the province. The students had "widespread social ties across the entire country" and used social media whose "impact," officials feared, was "widespread and difficult to eradicate." The task was to quarantine news of what was really happening inside the detention camps. When the students asked where their loved ones were and what happened to them, officials were advised to tell "students that their relatives had been 'infected' by the 'virus' of Islamic radicalism and must be quarantined and cured."

But it wasn't just young men—those most likely to oppose the political measures—who were subject to China's lockdown policy. According to the documents, officials were told that "even grandparents and family members who seemed too old to carry out violence could not be spared."

When a real virus hit in the fall of 2019, Chinese authorities followed the same protocol, quarantining not just prospective troublemakers but everyone in Wuhan in the hope of avoiding an even larger public outcry than the one they'd quelled in the same city just months before.

There is a good reason why even during the Spanish flu pandemic from 1918 to 1920 Americans fought against lockdowns—mass quarantines of those who are not sick—as a public health measure. The leading members of a city, state, or nation do not imprison its own unless they mean to signal that they are imposing collective punishment on the population at large. US authorities had never used broad lockdown mandates previously because, as the Chinese demonstrated, it is widely recognized as an instrument of political repression.

At the end of December 2019, Chinese authorities began locking down social media accounts mentioning the new virus; doctors who warned of it or spoke about it with their colleagues were reprimanded; and another, allegedly infected by Covid-19, died.[24] All domestic travel in and out of Wuhan was stopped. If the purpose of the lockdowns was really to prevent spread of the contagion, the fact is that the PRC allowed international flights to continue. Rather, it appears that the domestic travel ban, like the social media censorship, was to keep news of the government's blunder from spreading throughout China and leading to massive, perhaps uncontrollable, unrest.

If Wuhan's streets had filled in June and July to protest the authorities' deadly incompetence when they concealed plans for an incinerator that would sicken the population of one city, how would the Chinese public respond upon discovering that the source for a respiratory illness destined to plague all of the country wasn't a freak accident of nature that occurred in a wet market, as officials claimed, but the CCP's own Wuhan Institute of Virology?

According to a State Department fact sheet, the United States "has reason to believe that several researchers inside the Wuhan lab became sick in autumn 2019, before the first identified case of the outbreak."[25] The fact sheet further explains that the Chinese government lab has conducted research on a bat coronavirus most similar to Covid-19 since 2016. Since at least 2017, the WIV has conducted classified research on behalf of the Chinese military. "For many years the United States has publicly raised concerns about

China's past biological weapons work, which Beijing has neither documented nor demonstrably eliminated, despite its clear obligations under the Biological Weapons Convention."[26]

Republican officials close to the Trump administration disputed Beijing's official account. "We don't know where it originated, and we have to get to the bottom of that," Senator Tom Cotton said in February. "We also know that just a few miles away from that food market is China's only biosafety level 4 super laboratory that researches human infectious diseases." Cotton said the Chinese had been duplicitous and dishonest. "We need to at least ask the question to see what the evidence says," Cotton said. "And China right now is not giving any evidence on that question at all."

The press disparaged Cotton's search for answers. *The Washington Post* claimed that Cotton was "fanning the embers of a conspiracy theory that has been repeatedly debunked by experts."[27] Trump was derided for contradicting American spy services when the president said he had a high degree of confidence that the coronavirus originated in a Wuhan lab. Senator Ted Cruz said that in dismissing obvious questions about the origins of the pandemic the press was "abandoning all pretenses of journalism to produce CCP propaganda."[28]

And so had the US establishment, even from inside the administration. Director of the National Institute of Allergies and Infectious Diseases Anthony Fauci had funded the Wuhan institute for apparently the same reason that US multinationals had been offshoring manufacturing to China since the 1980s—the work was cheaper with virtually no environmental and workplace regulations. "China was Fauci's candyland," one former Trump official told me. "They used it as playground because the Chinese let them do anything, as long as they offer knowledge and tech transfer."

Lockdowns aided Fauci's coverup, further disorienting and deracinating an already delirious population. In mid-March, with

Fauci's encouragement and Trump's initial acquiescence, US officials imposed the same repressive measures on Americans used by dictatorial powers throughout history to silence their own people.

US officials purposefully laid waste to our economy and society while arrogating more power to themselves. Destroying lives and ending thousands of them by sending the ill to infect the elderly in nursing homes was seemingly irrelevant to America's version of the Thirty Tyrants. It appears the point was to boost coronavirus casualties to defeat Trump.

In May, the drug-overdose death of a convicted African-American felon was blamed on a white Minneapolis police officer thereby fueling race riots spread across the country, with one of its most famous athletes volunteering for the Huey Newton role. The black revolutionary walked away from Beijing empty-handed but China had helped make LeBron James rich. The NBA legend and social justice activist draws millions of dollars a year from revenue streams originating in China, including a lifetime deal worth approximately $1 billion with Nike—"a brand of China and for China," according to its American CEO John Donahoe.[29] Other sponsorship deals and financial arrangements with corporations that have substantial interests in China include Walmart, PepsiCo, 2K Sports, AT&T, JP Morgan, Lyft, and Beats by Dr Dre, owned by Apple.

James had been criticized the year before when while in China he attacked Houston Rockets executive Daryl Morey after he tweeted in support of the Hong Kong protest movement. According to James, Morey was "either misinformed or not really educated on the situation." Given the NBA's financial ties to China, including a billion-dollar TV contract, James said that Morey hadn't understood the consequences of his support for prodemocracy protestors. "So many people could have been harmed, not only financially but physically, emotionally, spiritually," said James.

With George Floyd's death, James exercised none of that contemplative forbearance, even after protestors embarked on a nationwide campaign of looting, arson, assault, and murder. The basketball star posted an image on social media showing Floyd on his stomach with the Minnesota police officer later found guilty for murder kneeling on the back of his neck. James juxtaposed the picture with one of former NFL quarterback Colin Kaepernick, another Nike spokesman, kneeling during the national anthem. "This......Is Why," wrote James under the two images. "Do you understand NOW!!??!!?? Or is it still blurred to you?? #StayWoke."

Thus, Americans became prey to a society-wide elite—from the worlds of politics and business, sports and media—serving as Beijing's proxies who used the coronavirus to demoralize their fellow citizens; lay waste to small businesses; leave them vulnerable to rioters left free to steal, burn, and kill; keep their children from school and the dying from the last embrace of their loved ones; desecrate American history, culture, and society; and defame the country as systemically racist in order to furnish the predicate for why ordinary Americans in fact *deserved* the hell that the elite's private and public sector proxies had already prepared for them.

A month before the November vote, the Federal Bureau of Investigation hid the facts of Joe Biden's corruption to facilitate his election. America's premier law enforcement organization falsely briefed the press and social media platforms that the laptop belonging to the candidate's son Hunter, giving evidence of his financial arrangements with CCP agents and others, was "Russian disinformation."[30]

The Central Intelligence Agency hid China's efforts to interfere in the election. The Agency's top leadership—including, it seems, Director Gina Haspel—bullied intelligence analysts to alter their assessment of Chinese influence and interference in our political process so it wouldn't be used to support policies they disagreed with—Trump's policies.[31]

The China Class soon came to see the full range of benefits the lockdowns afforded. They made leading oligarchs richer while impoverishing Trump's small-business base. In imposing unconstitutional regulations by fiat, city and state authorities normalized autocracy. And not least, lockdowns gave the pro-China establishment a plausible reason to keep the cognitively impaired and often nearly comatose candidate stashed away in his basement for the duration of the presidential campaign. And yet it was true that Biden represented a return to normalcy—at least as it referred to the usual course of US-China relations dating back decades.

After Biden's election, China's foreign minister called for a reset of US-China relations, but Chinese activists said Biden policy toward China was already set.[32] "I'm very skeptical of a Biden administration because I am worried he will allow China to go back to normal, which is a 21st-century genocide of the Uyghurs," one human rights activist told *The New York Times* after the election. With Biden as president, said another, "it's like having Xi Jinping sitting in the White House."[33]

A video circulated on social media purporting to document a public speech given by the head of a Chinese think tank allegedly close to the Beijing government.[34] "Trump waged a trade war against us," he told a Chinese audience. "Why couldn't we handle him? Why is it that between 1992 and 2016, we always resolved issues with the US? Because we had people up there. In America's core circle of power, we have some old friends." The appreciative crowd laughed along with him. "During the last three to four decades," he continued, "we took advantage of America's core circle. As I said, Wall Street has a very profound influence...We used to rely heavily on them. Problem is they have been declining since 2008," he said, referring to the financial crisis. "Most importantly after 2016 Wall Street couldn't control Trump... In the US-China trade war they tried to help. My friends in the US told me that they tried to help, but they couldn't. Now with Biden winning the election, the traditional elites, political elites, the establishment, they have a very close relationship with Wall Street."

Thus Biden's inauguration marked the restoration of an American ruling party that saw its relationship with China as a shield and sword against their own countrymen. Like Athens's Thirty Tyrants, they are not simply contemptuous of a political system that recognizes the natural rights of all its citizens that are endowed by our creator; they despise in particular the notion that those they rule have the same rights they do.

Like Critias and the pro-Sparta faction, America's China Class believed that democracy's failures are proof of their own exclusive right to power—and they are happy to rule in partnership with a foreign regime that will help them destroy their own countrymen. The rule of the Thirty Tyrants lasted less than a year. Trump's exile ended after four.

EPILOGUE

Reversing Kissinger

China's current government has contempt for our way of life.[1]

—Donald Trump

NOT LONG AFTER DONALD TRUMP'S 2024 ELECTION VICTORY, THE Washington foreign policy establishment theorized that at the heart of the president's second-term China policy was a "Reverse Kissinger."

A late February meeting at the White House between Trump and Ukrainian President Volodymyr Zelensky devolved into what nearly became a shouting match, leaving many observers wondering if the newly reelected president had staged the flare-up for an audience of two: Xi Jinping and Vladmir Putin. Was the spectacle meant to illustrate that Trump would tilt against Ukraine to accommodate Putin and thereby drive a wedge between Russia and China?

Diplomats, think-tank experts, and journalists contended that Trump was using the same tactic employed by Richard Nixon's chief foreign policy aide when he encouraged his boss to open relations with Beijing and thereby play the China card against the more powerful Soviet Union. Trump, they argued, was doing the same, except in the other direction.

Kissinger himself had prophesied the coming of the Reverse Kissinger, for as he told Nixon only days before their fateful 1972 trip, a future American president "if he's as wise as you, will wind up leaning towards the Russians against the Chinese."[2]

Kissinger reportedly suggested the idea to Trump in 2017.[3] And Trump had told me that lots of people agreed it was a bad idea to let Russia and China get close. There were many in that first administration who wanted to see if there was a way to work with Moscow to hobble Beijing, but there was no way to get around Russiagate. The surveillance and propaganda operation managed by Barack Obama's spy chiefs who alleged that the Trump circle had illicit ties to Russia consumed most of Trump's first term and made it impossible for him to engage with Putin on most meaningful issues.

What about for his second term? Trump's critics said that there's nothing now analogous to the fault line underlying the 1972 opening, no obvious breathing space between Moscow and Beijing like the growing ideological divide between the increasingly radical Chinese Communist Party and the relatively staid Soviet politburo known as the Sino-Soviet split.

Others are less sure. "I'm not convinced that China and Russia have a shared worldview outside of a mutual loathing for the United States," says former US diplomat Craig Singleton. "The Xi and Putin dynamic has driven a partnership that they classify as being 'without limits,' but the partnership is not all it seems. There is little indication that China is willing to put Russia's interests above its own. And, it certainly hasn't thus far. China appears primarily opportunistic right now. Xi made a decision that he was willing to sacrifice relations with the Europeans, a prime market for Chinese goods and a geopolitical power in and of itself, in exchange for embracing Russia's desire to disrupt the current US-led global order. The Chinese are realizing that if they want to achieve their broader objectives and keep the US out of Asia, they have to create these little fires everywhere, to distract, divide, and drain U.S. resources in theaters outside of the Indo-Pacific."

Take the Red Sea, for instance, where the Houthis, an Iranian-backed terror group, closed shipping lanes by firing on the US Navy, while allowing Chinese ships safe passage. Also in the Middle East, there are Israel's conflicts with Hezbollah and Hamas, again supported by Iran, the third leg alongside China and Russia in the anti-US bloc. Without those small upheavals, spurred by China or its partners, says Singleton, "all of our attention would be rredirected to East Asia, and confronting Chinese revisionism and revanchism."

Until Trump, the PRC didn't need troubles elsewhere to keep American presidents from focusing on China. From Vietnam to Tiananmen and provocation in the South China Sea to Covid, Republicans and Democrats alike have incentivized, enabled, rationalized, and turned a blind eye to China's mischief in Asia and further abroad. The record shows there is virtually nothing Beijing could have done to make US presidents consider China a threat and act accordingly. Instead, starting with Nixon, US leaders have given China free rein throughout the world. Insofar as China poses a threat to the US, it's because the US has been helping China every step of the way.

Indeed, from the very start, the United States raised China while hobbling itself. Nixon and Kissinger sought to draw Beijing into an international order of cooperation and commerce, which in the ensuing years made China rich and powerful as its cheap labor pool became the basis for what we now call globalism. Kissinger is its intellectual father, the theorist and apologist for the very order that the America First president seeks to undo. Accordingly, it's more accurate to think of Trump's overall strategy not as Reverse Kissinger but rather as reversing Kissinger.

Since China grew rich and powerful, thanks at first to its enormous trade surpluses with the United States, reversing the deadly pact meant attacking its center of gravity—the doctrine of free trade. Making America great again, defending the middle class, and rebuilding our industrial base meant returning to the country's protectionist roots.

"What motivates Trump—the first thing to know about Trump," says Robert Lighthizer, Trump's first-term US trade representative, "is that he's very much bothered by situations where Americans are treated unfairly. So forget economics, he's a fairness guy. So, we're getting screwed. My team is getting screwed, right? That's what he said in the '70s, '80s, and '90s—it was all 'We're getting screwed,' largely by Japan at that point. And we were getting screwed and there aren't that many options for what you can do. But if you have to change the economics of the imports and exports, there's no question in my mind that the simplest, clearest way is tariffs, and that's what he picked."

Trump's promise to tariff China and others convinced some US and other companies to come to America only months after his inauguration. "Thanks to our America First policies we're putting into place, we have had $1.7 trillion of new investment in America in just the past few weeks," Trump said in his March 2025 joint address to congress. "SoftBank, one of the most brilliant anywhere in the world, announced a $200 billion investment. OpenAI and Oracle—Larry Ellison—announced [a] $500 billion investment. Apple announced [a] $500 billion investment. Tim Cook called me. He said, 'I cannot spend it fast enough.' It's going to be much higher than that, I believe. They'll be building their plants here, instead of in China. And just yesterday, Taiwan Semiconductor—the biggest in the world, most powerful in the world, has a tremendous amount—97 percent of the market, announced a $165 billion investment to build the most powerful chips on Earth right here in the USA."[4]

Trump's tariffs make the choice clear: Keep your factories in China and face devastating tariffs or come home, employ Americans, pay your taxes, and make America wealthy again. "'Produce here' is Trump's message to all companies that manufacture overseas," says policy analyst Alan Tonelson. "Whatever production you bring to the United States we will help you because there will be no tariffs. Plus, I'm only going to charge you a corporate income tax of 15 percent. Which is very competitive by global standards." Tonelson admits he's awed by the boldness of Trump's program: "It clashes with practically every major organized economic and financial interest in this whole country."

Some of the counterattacks are coming from the right. During the first Trump administration, David Koch, who died in 2019, and Charles Koch waged war on Trump's tariff regime; by spring 2025, two Koch-linked groups had already brought two lawsuits against Trump for his new tariff regime. Despite Trump's warnings to keep Koch affiliates out of his second administration, several Koch-sponsored foreign policy experts were pushed into the Pentagon, including one inserted into a position in the Office of the Director of National Intelligence, where he is in place to shape Trump's intelligence briefings.[5]

One big difference between the first and second terms is that there is no equivalent to Russiagate, the all-purpose instrument used to tie Trump down with an internal espionage and propaganda campaign, designed in part to keep him from focusing on China. As a result, the second-term attacks related to his China policy have been direct and raw, thus shriller, angrier, and more likely to amplify fear and panic as the dominant moods.

First-time Trump supporters from the finance and tech worlds were among those most publicly distressed after he imposed the broad tariff regime April 2—what the president called Liberation Day. To them there was no discernible program. Why, they wondered, bring the hammer down on friends, like Japan, as well as China? Surely there must be a bigger plan. The president is supposed to have a grand strategy, like Nixon when he played the China card against the Soviet Union. What was Trump's grand strategy? We win, as Reagan said, they lose.

Trump's immediate goal is to free America from a trade regime that has been preying on the American middle class for decades.

"Why did they let this happen?" says the president, referring to the commanders in chief who preceded him, from Nixon to Biden. The Chinese, Trump tells me at Mar-a-Lago, "were just taking total advantage of us. They charge tariffs on cars that we make, sending them to China. And we wouldn't charge them anything. They would say, 'Well, we'll buy your cars, but you have to make them in China.' We would say, 'We'll buy your cars even if you make them in China.' So it didn't help us. So they said, 'Well, if you want to avoid the tariff, build a plant in China.' And that's what happened. That's why all this stuff comes out of China. Why did they allow it to happen? It's so basic. It's common sense."

Trump's first-term plan was to go big. "We had something where we were going to have the right to go into China and compete and really do a job in China, without all of the tariffs and all of the many other breaks that they put on which made it impossible for our companies to do business," says the president, referring to the comprehensive agreement his administration started negotiating months after his January 2017 inauguration.

"The Chinese are phenomenal negotiators," the president says. "When I was negotiating with China, I said, no, we have to have a 50 percent tariff on this. And they said, 'No, no, no.' But they acted like it didn't matter. 'No, the tariffs don't have any impact.' And I said good, if they have no impact, I want them on. So one of my guys came back and says, 'Listen, here's the story: The only thing they care about are the tariffs. That was just a negotiation. That the only thing they care about are the tariffs. They got to have the tariffs taken off.' I said, I can't do it."

The tariffs were the deal's enforcement mechanism, ensuring that Beijing didn't break its word, as it's done repeatedly over the last half century. "And then," says the president, "they broke the deal."

In early May 2019, Chinese negotiators told Trump's team that the issues they wanted resolved once and for all—like the theft of US intellectual property, forced technology transfers, and currency manipulation—were off the table.

"We had a deal that was so great and we were ready to sign it," says Trump, "and President Xi could not get it approved, which was very strange because I thought he was really—and he is—a very powerful guy. But I was shocked, because we were negotiating with his people. At the last moment they said we won't be able to do much of the stuff that was agreed and President Xi was unable to get it approved, which was shocking to me. And I believe that's true. And I don't say that from any point of disparagement."

Trump wanted to get America off the China fix. "They were making $500 billion a year off the United States," he says. The Trump team believes that the trade deficit with China should account for its trade proxies, like Vietnam, making the number much higher than the roughly $300 billion figure usually cited.

"Not sustainable," says the president. "That $500 billion a year has built a very powerful military. And I said we're going to eventually end up going cold turkey with China. We're not going to do any business with China. We're not going to give you $500 billion a year."

Then the Chinese came back with another offer. "They wanted to make any kind of a deal because I was going to cut off all business with China." The smaller deal was the Phase One trade agreement signed January 2020. Trump didn't get exactly what he wanted, but he saw something important, something that would factor into his plans, assuming he'd get another shot at China.

"I think you have some very powerful forces in China. President Xi is a very smart and powerful man, but you have other forces that are strong," says the president. "I saw it firsthand. He viewed my relationship with him and my position as president as very important. They were very embarrassed when they said this to us, because this was like having a deal ready to be signed and the deal was virtually ready to be signed. And then they withdrew it. And I believe that they had some additional forces in China that did not want to. I have no doubt in my mind. But that deal didn't happen."

Whether it was Xi or other political forces in the shadows who collapsed the big deal, it's hard to see how the Chinese Communist Party could have accepted Trump's terms. No more subsidies for its industries? No more stealing IP or forced transfers of technology? No more currency manipulation? No more trade imbalance worth hundreds of billions at America's expense? These are all weapons the Chinese have employed for decades to make China richer and more powerful and America poorer and weaker. The Chinese can't afford to forfeit weapons of war. It's not a normal country but a parasite regime—cutting a deal with Beijing that would leave both parties satisfied would only greenlight a continuation of the decades-long destruction of America. Thus, protecting the peace and advancing the prosperity of the Americans who'd elected him could only mean rolling back the CCP.

After all, Xi's rejection of the deal is evidence the Party can't compete in a global system that won't let it cheat, lie, and steal; for like all communist powers, it sucks up wealth created by others. The CCP grew out of a peasant population, and Mao wasted its already limited capital and enormous human resources on totalitarian fantasies that led to famine and mass death. The regime was impoverished and tilting on the edge of the abyss, until the Americans stepped in to save it with money, technology, and arms. US elites repeated Nixon and Kissinger's crime repeatedly over the years, from George H. W. Bush to Bill Clinton and Henry Paulson to Joe Biden, rescuing the regime and then enriching it, gorging Beijing on the wealth of the American middle class.

The problem isn't just the trade regime—for Americans, it was even more fundamentally the political regime that grew from it and altered the character of US society, politics, and culture.

The US system "is an entrepreneurial system," says President Trump. "It's a good system. It's become very corrupt. It's become very corrosive. It's become much different than it should be. It's a great system, but it's become incredibly corrupted."

The corruption was built in at the start: Kissinger's secret trip and Nixon's summit with Mao gave the Chinese early evidence that the Americans would abase themselves for relations with a cruel and backward regime that prided itself on killing Americans in Vietnam. With Tiananmen, Washington showed there was nothing Beijing could do that would compel the Americans to change course, for there was too much money at stake. China's accession to the WTO brought the US elite into partnership with the CCP to dismantle the American middle class, the first in a series of scorched-earth campaigns, later the financial crisis, that destroyed communities across the country and reconfigured others, while the income gap widened, and America's China Class began to consolidate its power.

When the middle class elected a leader who promised to redeem them and restore America, elites from the political and corporate establishments and the worlds of media, academia, and entertainment joined as one to meet the common threat and unleashed their furies to drive him from the White House: Russiagate, impeachment, weaponized lockdowns, race riots, election interference to shield the candidate who would protect *their* interests, a second impeachment, and finally charges of fomenting an insurrection against the government he led forced Donald Trump into exile. The raid of his Mar-a-Lago home and a lawfare campaign that included two federal cases were meant to intimidate, impoverish, and imprison him. He returned, survived two assassination attempts, and won a mandate to complete the work that had first earned him the wrath of the China Class—to undo the economic and political arrangements with a communist regime that had furnished the US establishment with its wealth, power, and prestige, and shatter the deadly pact that had corrupted our constitutional republic and devastated its citizenry.

For twenty-five years, Trump has warned that the Chinese Communist Party is a destabilizing force in the world.[6] Because its partnership with the US establishment has drained the lifeblood of American ingenuity and invention, by making America great again the president is almost certain to drive China out of the international system and isolate it, as it was before Nixon and Kissinger brought it in from the cold more than half a century ago.

"We are so stupid to have allowed this to happen," says the president. "And nobody did anything about it until I came along."

Acknowledgments

Thanks to my editors at *Tablet* magazine, where some of this material was previously published in different form. Thanks to Price Sukhia and Penny Zhou, who helped sort through enormous amounts of research and shaped my thinking on important issues in the US-China relationship. Thanks to my agent and friend, Keith Urbahn, who fought for this book, along with lawyer Steven Biss. Thanks to my editor, Alex Pappas, who believed in it. Thanks to everyone who spoke with me for it, especially Tony Badran, Brian Costello, Jan Jekielek, Bradley Thayer, and Alan Tonelson—all of whom helped me see and understand. I am most thankful, as ever, for the love of my wife, Catherine, and the laughter of my son, Augie.

Notes

Chapter One: The Deadly Pact

1. Donald Trump with Dave Shiflett, *The America We Deserve* (St. Martin's Press, 2000), 106.

2. Barack Obama, "Remarks by the President at PBS NewsHour Town Hall Discussion with Gwen Ifill for Elkhart, IN Residents," Barack Obama *White House Archives*, June 2, 2016, https://obamawhitehouse.archives.gov/the-press-office/2016/06/02 /remarks-president-pbs-newshour-town-hall-discussion-gwen-ifill-elkhart.

3. Donald J. Trump, "Remarks by President Trump at APEC CEO Summit, Da Nang, Vietnam," Donald J. Trump *White House Archives*, November 10, 2017, https:// vn.usembassy.gov/20171110-
remarks-president-trump-apec-ceo-summit/.

4. Donald J. Trump, "Remarks by President Trump in Meeting with Dr. Henry Kissinger," Donald J. Trump *White House Archives*, October 10, 2017, https://trump whitehouse.archives.gov/briefings-statements/remarks-president-trump-meeting -dr-henry-kissinger/.

5. Sara Fritz, "New China Lobby Is Big Business: U.S. Firms Fight for Their Interests," *The Seattle Times*, May 12, 1997, https://archive.seattletimes.com/archive /?date=19970512&slug=2538720.

6. The White House, "Fact Sheet: President Donald J. Trump Imposes Tariffs on Imports from Canada, Mexico and China," February 1, 2025, https://www.whitehouse .gov/fact-sheets/2025/02/fact-sheet-president-donald-j-trump-imposes-tariffs-on -imports-from-canada-mexico-and-china/.

7. Lee Edwards, "The Legacy of Mao Zedong is Mass Murder," The Heritage Foundation, February 2, 2010, https://www.heritage.org/china/commentary/the-legacy -mao-zedong-mass-murder.

8. Edwin Chen, "Entry Likely to Be an Issue in U.S. Elections Next Year," *Los Angeles Times*, November 16, 1999, https://www.latimes.com/archives/la-xpm-1999-nov-16-mn -34079-story.html.

9. AFL-CIO Executive Council, "Taking Action to Challenge Communist China's Unfair Trade Practices," AFL-CIO, March 12, 2004, https://aflcio.org/about/leadership /statements/taking-action-challenge-communist-chinas-unfair-trade-practices.

10. Melissa Zhu, "Pelosi's Taiwan Visit: China Halts Cooperation with US on Key Issues," *BBC News*, August 5, 2022, https://www.bbc.com/news /world-asia-china-62343675.

11. Richard A. Gephardt, "Remarks on China's Trade Status and WTO Membership," speech delivered at Webster University, St. Louis, MO, April 19, 2000, U.S. Department of State Archive, https://usinfo.org/wf-archive/2000/000419/epf304.htm.

12. Meredith Lee Hill and Gavin Bade, "Who Reined in the China Committee's Trade-War Proposal?" *Politico*, December 13, 2023, https://www.politico.com/news/2023/12/13/agriculture-lawmakers-lobbyists-quietly-challenge-china-hawks-on-trade-00131451.

13. Trump with Shiflett, *The America We Deserve*, 107.

14. "President Biden Holds News Conference in Vietnam," C-SPAN, September 10, 2023, video, https://www.c-span.org/video/?530300-1/president-biden-holds-news-conference-vietnam.

15. Brian Mann, "In 2023 Fentanyl Overdoses Ravaged the U.S. and Fueled a New Culture War Fight," NPR, December 28, 2023, https://www.npr.org/2023/12/28/1220881380/overdose-fentanyl-drugs-addiction.

16. Sebastian Rotella, Clifton Adcock, Garrett Yalch, Kirsten Berg, "Gangsters, Money and Murder: How Chinese Organized Crime Is Dominating Oklahoma's Illegal Medical Marijuana Market," *Frontier*, March 14, 2024, https://www.readfrontier.org/stories/gangsters-money-and-murder-how-chinese-organized-crime-is-dominating-oklahomas-illegal-medical-marijuana-market/.

17. Trading Economics, "United States Imports from China of Pharmaceutical Products," https://tradingeconomics.com/united-states/imports/china/pharmaceutical-products.

18. Stephen Sorace, "Chinese Spy Balloon Was Equipped with Tech from at Least 5 US Firms: Report," *Fox News*, February 9, 2023, https://www.foxnews.com/us/chinese-spy-balloon-equipped-tech-from-least-5-us-firms-report.

19. "*The Buy American, Hire American President*," Donald J. Trump White House Archives, October 2020, https://trumpwhitehouse.archives.gov/wp-content/uploads/2020/10/Donald-J-Trump-Buy-American-Hire-American-President.pdf.

20. "CPA Applauds Rubio-Miller Bill to Prohibit Chinese Companies from Receiving Inflation Reduction Act 45X Tax Credits," Coalition for a Prosperous America, December 13, 2023, https://prosperousamerica.org/cpa-applauds-rubio-miller-bill-to-prohibit-chinese-companies-from-receiving-inflation-reduction-act-45x-tax-credits/.

21. "Russia, China and Iran Finish Drills in Gulf of Oman," USNI News, March 14, 2024, https://news.usni.org/2024/03/14/russia-china-and-iran-finish-drills-in-gulf-of-oman.

Chapter Two: Unbalancing America

1. Krystal Hu, "Henry Kissinger: A Permanent U.S.-China Conflict Will Be 'Catastrophic,'" *Yahoo! Finance*, November 15, 2019, https://finance.yahoo.com/news/henry-kissinger-a-permanent-us-china-conflict-will-be-catastrophic-155631408.html.

2. Nicholas Thompson, "How Google's China Strategy Went Astray," *Wired*, January 19, 2010, https://www.wired.com/2010/01/google-china-engagement/.

3. Gerald R. Ford, "Remarks on the Death of Mao Tse-tung," The American Presidency Project, September 9, 1976, https://www.presidency.ucsb.edu/documents/remarks-the-death-mao-tse-tung.

4. Jimmy Carter, "How to Repair the U.S.-China Relationship—and Prevent a

Modern Cold War," *Washington Post*, December 31, 2018, https://www.washingtonpost
.com/opinions/2018/12/31/jimmy-carter-us-china-relationship-modern-cold-war/.

5. Ronald Reagan, "Remarks to Chinese Community Leaders in Beijing, China,"
Ronald Reagan Presidential Library, April 29, 1984, https://www.reaganlibrary.gov
/archives/speech/remarks-chinese-community-leaders-beijing-china.

6. George H. W. Bush, *The China Diary of George H. W. Bush: The Making of a Global
President*, ed. Jeffrey A. Engel (Princeton University Press, 2008), xv.

7. William J. Clinton, "Remarks by the President in Address on China and the
National Interest," Bill Clinton White House Archives, October 24, 1997, https://
clintonwhitehouse4.archives.gov/WH/New/html/19971024-3863.html.

8. George W. Bush, "Remarks at Tsinghua University in Beijing, China," George
W. Bush White House Archives, February 22, 2002, https://georgewbush-whitehouse
.archives.gov/news/releases/2002/02/20020222.html.

9. Charlie Campbell, "Obama: The U.S. Welcomes China's Rise," *Time*, April 28,
2014, https://time.com/78779/obama-philippines-china/.

10. Barack Obama, "Remarks by President Obama and President Xi Jinping in
Joint Press Conference," Barack Obama White House Archives, November 12, 2014,
https://obamawhitehouse.archives.gov/the-press-office/2014/11/12/remarks-president
-obama-and-president-xi-jinping-joint-press-conference.

11. Felicia Sonmez, "Biden Says China Is 'Not Competition for Us,' Prompting
Pushback from Republicans," *Washington Post*, May 1, 2019, https://www.washington
post.com/politics/biden-says-china-is-not-competition-for-us-prompting-pushback
-from-republicans/2019/05/01/4ae4e738-6c68-11e9-a66d-a82d3f3d96d5_story.html.

12. Walter Isaacson, *Kissinger: A Biography* (Simon and Schuster, 1992), 344, Kindle.

13. "Memorandum of Conversation Between Henry A. Kissinger and Zhou Enlai,
July 9, 1971," in *Kissinger's Secret Trip to China*, National Security Archive Electronic
Briefing Book No. 66, ed. William Burr, February 27, 2002, https://nsarchive2.gwu.edu
/NSAEBB/NSAEBB66/ch-34.pdf, 1.

14. Ibid., 4.

15. Zhou Enlai, "Memorandum of Conversation with President Richard Nixon,"
May 29, 1971, in *Getting to Beijing: Henry Kissinger's Secret 1971 Trip*, USC U.S.-China
Institute, https://china.usc.edu/sites/default/files/article/attachments/19710529-zhou
-nixon.pdf.

16. Richard M. Nixon, "Asia After Viet Nam," *Foreign Affairs* 46, no. 1 (October
1967): 111–125, https://www.foreignaffairs.com/articles/united-states/1967-10-01/asia
-after-viet-nam.

17. Bernard Gwertzman, "U.S. Papers Tell of '53 Policy to Use A-Bomb in Korea,"
New York Times, June 8, 1984, https://www.nytimes.com/1984/06/08/world/us-papers
-tell-of-53-policy-to-use-a-bomb-in-korea.html.

18. John Pomfret, *The Beautiful Country and the Middle Kingdom: America and China,
1776 to the Present* (Henry Holt, 2016), 256.

19. Jay Taylor, *The Generalissimo: Chiang Kai-shek and the Struggle for Modern China*
(Belknap Press of Harvard University, 2009), 91.

20. U.S. Department of State, *United States Relations with China, with Special Reference*

to the Period 1944–1949 (Washington, DC: Government Printing Office, 1949), archived at https://archive.org/details/UnitedStatesRelationsWithChinaWhitePaper1949.

21. Alden Whitman, "The Life of Chiang Kai-shek: A Leader Who Was Thrust Aside by Revolution," *New York Times*, April 6, 1975, https://www.nytimes.com/1975/04/06/archives/the-life-of-chiang-kaishek-a-leader-who-was-thrust-aside-by.html.

22. Pomfret, *Beautiful Country and the Middle Kingdom*, 390.

23. Ibid., 391.

24. Ibid., 391–92.

25. Ibid., 392.

26. Clayton D. Brown, "China's Great Leap Forward," *Education About Asia* 17, no. 3 (Winter 2012): 29–34, https://www.asianstudies.org/publications/eaa/archives/chinas-great-leap-forward/.

27. Pomfret, *Beautiful Country and the Middle Kingdom*, 392.

28. Henry Kissinger, *Diplomacy* (Simon and Schuster, 1994), 24.

29. Henry Kissinger, *World Order* (Penguin Press, 2014), 60 Kindle.

30. Nikita Khrushchev, "On the Cult of Personality and Its Consequences," speech delivered to the 20th Congress of the Communist Party of the Soviet Union, February 25, 1956, archived at Marxists Internet Archive, https://www.marxists.org/archive/khrushchev/1956/02/24.htm.

31. Editorial Departments of *Renmin Ribao* (People's Daily) and *Hongqi* (Red Flag), "On the Question of Stalin," September 13, 1963, archived at Marxists Internet Archive, https://www.marxists.org/subject/china/documents/polemic/qstalin.htm.

32. "Editorial Note," in U.S. Department of State, *Foreign Relations of the United States, 1969–1976*, vol. 34, *National Security Policy, 1969–1972*, Document 59, https://history.state.gov/historicaldocuments/frus1969-76v34/d59.

33. Henry A. Kissinger, "Memorandum from the President's Assistant for National Security Affairs (Kissinger) to President Nixon," March 2, 1973, in U.S. Department of State, *Foreign Relations of the United States, 1969–1976*, vol. 18, *China, 1973–1976*, Document 18, https://history.state.gov/historicaldocuments/frus1969-76v18/d18.

34. Henry A. Kissinger, "Memorandum from the President's Assistant for National Security Affairs (Kissinger) to President Nixon," September 29, 1969, in U.S. Department of State, *Foreign Relations of the United States, 1969–1976*, vol. 12, *Soviet Union, January 1969–October 1970*, Document 88, https://history.state.gov/historicaldocuments/frus1969-76v12/d88.

35. U.S. Department of State, "State Department Cable 143440 to U.S. Consulate Hong Kong," August 25, 1969, in *The Sino-Soviet Border Conflict, 1969: U.S. Reactions and Diplomatic Maneuvers*, National Security Archive Electronic Briefing Book No. 49, ed. William Burr, https://nsarchive2.gwu.edu/NSAEBB/NSAEBB49/sino.sov.13.pdf; William Burr, ed., *The Sino-Soviet Border Conflict, 1969: U.S. Reactions and Diplomatic Maneuvers*, National Security Archive Electronic Briefing Book No. 49, June 12, 2001, https://nsarchive2.gwu.edu/NSAEBB/NSAEBB49/.

36. Henry Kissinger, *On China* (Penguin Books, 2012), 221.

37. Robert B. Semple Jr., "President Ends 21-Year Embargo on Peking Trade; Authorizes Export of $50-Million in Goods," *New York Times*, June 11, 1971, https://

www.nytimes.com/1971/06/11/archives/president-ends-21year-embargo-on-peking
-trade-authorizes-export-of.html.

38. My discussion of Kissinger and the balance of power that follows was influenced by the late Angelo Codevilla, especially his essay "The Courage of His Contradictions," *Claremont Review of Books*, Spring 2015, https://claremontreviewofbooks.com /the-courage-of-his-contradictions/.

39. Hedley Donovan, Henry Grunwald, Hugh Sidey, and Jerrold Schecter, "The Nation: An Interview with the President: The Jury Is Out," *Time*, January 3, 1972, https://content.time.com/time/subscriber/article/0,33009,879011-5,00.html.

40. "Conversation Between President Nixon and his Assistant for National Security Affairs," February 14, 1972, in U.S. Department of State, *Foreign Relations of the United States, 1969–1976*, vol. 17, *China, 1969–1972*, Document 192, https://history.state.gov /historicaldocuments/frus1969-76v17/d192.

41. Kissinger, *World Order*, 302.

42. Francis P. Sempa, "Nixon and China: 50 Years Later," *The Diplomat*, February 21, 2022, https://thediplomat.com/2022/02/nixon-and-china-50-years-later/.

43. Tom Phillips, "The Cultural Revolution: All You Need to Know About China's Political Convulsion," *The Guardian*, May 11, 2016, https://www.theguardian.com /world/2016/may/11/the-cultural-revolution-50-years-on-all-you-need-to-know-about -chinas-political-convulsion.

44. Isaacson, *Kissinger: A Biography*, 345.

45. Ibid., 766.

46. Bonnie Girard, "Nixon's China Sell-Out," *The Diplomat*, July 6, 2018, https:// thediplomat.com/2018/07/nixons-china-sell-out/.

47. Joseph Bosco, "The One China Policy: What Would Nixon Do?" *The Diplomat*, January 5, 2017, https://thediplomat.com/2017/01/the-one-china-policy -what-would-nixon-do/.

48. U.S. Department of State. *Memorandum of Conversation: Zhou Enlai, Henry Kissinger*, Beijing, July 9, 1971, declassified document, National Security Archive Electronic Briefing Book No. 66, https://nsarchive2.gwu.edu/NSAEBB/NSAEBB66 /ch-34.pdf, 17–34.

49. Ibid., 15.

50. "Memorandum from the President's Assistant for National Security Affairs (Kissinger) to President Nixon," July 14, 1971, in U.S. Department of State, *Foreign Relations of the United States, 1969–1976*, vol. E–13, *Documents on China, 1969–1972*, Document 9, https://history.state.gov/historicaldocuments/frus1969-76ve13/d9.

51. Ibid.

52. Michael E. Ruane, "Richard Nixon's Visit to China: His Mao Zedong Meeting in 1972 Stunned World," *Washington Post*, February 20, 2022, https://www.washington post.com/history/2022/02/20/nixon-china-mao-visit-1972/.

53. "Memorandum of Conversation Between Chairman Mao Zedong and President Richard Nixon," Beijing, February 21, 1972, in U.S. Department of State, *Foreign Relations of the United States, 1969–1976*, vol. 17, *China, 1969–1972*, Document 194, https:// history.state.gov/historicaldocuments/frus1969-76v17/d194.

54. WWD Staff, "Celebrating Henry Kissinger," *WWD*, October 29, 2013, https://wwd.com/fashion-news/fashion-features/celebrating-henry-kissinger-6967416/.

55. Bosco, "The One China Policy."

56. U.S. Department of State, "Memorandum of Conversation Between President Nixon and Premier Zhou Enlai," February 22, 1972, in *The Kissinger Transcripts: A Verbatim Record of U.S. Diplomacy, 1969–1977*, National Security Archive, https://nsarchive2.gwu.edu/nsa/publications/DOC_readers/kissinger/nixzhou/17-08.htm.

57. Bosco, "The One China Policy."

58. Clyde V. Prestowitz, *The World Turned Upside Down: America, China, and the Struggle for Global Leadership* (Yale University Press, 2021), 190.

Chapter Three: Maoist Chic

1. Robert Penn Warren, interview with Malcolm X, in *Who Speaks for the Negro?* (Vanderbilt University Library, 1964), https://whospeaks.library.vanderbilt.edu/interview/malcolm-x.

2. Michael L. Burgoyne, "Lessons from Peru: Counterinsurgency in the 21st Century," *Military Review* 90, no. 5 (September–October 2010): 68–77, https://www.armyupress.army.mil/Portals/7/military-review/Archives/English/MilitaryReview_20101031_art011.pdf.

3. Mbulelo Musi and Cedric Masters, "The Long-Standing Friendship Between the Chinese PLA and the South African Liberation Forces," *Friends of Socialist China*, February 14, 2023, https://socialistchina.org/2023/02/14/the-long-standing-friendship-between-the-chinese-pla-and-the-south-african-liberation-forces/.

4. Roger Kimball, "A Nostalgia for Molotovs: 'The New York Review,'" *New Criterion*, April 1998, https://newcriterion.com/issues/1998/4/a-nostalgia-for-molotovs-ldquothe-new-york-reviewrdquo.

5. "Revisit to Peking," *New York Times*, October 6, 1971, https://www.nytimes.com/1971/10/06/archives/revisit-to-peking.html.

6. Joshua Bloom and Waldo E. Martin Jr., "The Forbidden History of the Black Panther Party," *Utne Reader*, March 26, 2013, https://www.utne.com/politics/black-panther-party-ze0z1303zwar/.

7. Ruodi Duan, "Black Power in China: Mao's Support for African American Racial Struggle as Class Struggle," Harvard University, Fairbank Center for Chinese Studies, September 13, 2022, https://fairbank.fas.harvard.edu/research/blog/black-power-in-china-maos-support-for-african-american-racial-struggle-as-class-struggle/.

8. Ruodi Duan, "Black Nationalism and Maoism: Revisiting the Relationship," *Made in China Journal*, February 23, 2024, https://madeinchinajournal.com/2024/02/23/black-nationalism-and-maoism-revisiting-the-relationship/.

9. Hua Chunying (@SpokespersonCHN), "I can't breathe," X (formerly Twitter), May 30, 2020, https://x.com/spokespersonchn/status/1266741986096107520.

10. "Explainer: What Is the New Hong Kong National Security Law?" *BBC News*, July 1, 2020, https://www.bbc.com/news/world-asia-china-52765838.

11. Nicole Gaouette and Kylie Atwood, "Pompeo Condemns China's Proposed Hong Kong National Security Law," CNN, May 22, 2020, https://www.cnn.com/2020/05/22/politics/pompeo-hong-kong-national-security-legislation/index.html.

12. Hu Xijin, "US Should Stand with Minnesota Violent Protesters as It Did with HK Rioters," *Global Times*, May 29, 2020, https://www.globaltimes.cn/content/1189945.shtml.

13. Zhou Jin, "Black Lives Matter, and Their Human Rights Should Be Guaranteed," press briefing, June 1, 2020, quoted in *China Daily*, June 1, 2020, https://www.chinadaily.com.cn/a/202006/01/WS5ed4eb56a310a8b24115a010.html.

14. Jo Kim, "With Support for Black Lives Matter, China Crosses a Thin Line," *The Diplomat*, June 9, 2020, https://thediplomat.com/2020/06/with-support-for-black-lives-matter-china-crosses-a-thin-line .

15. Erin-Atlanta Argun, "10 Facts About Andy Warhol's Mao," *MyArtBroker*, February 19, 2025, https://www.myartbroker.com/artist-andy-warhol/10-facts/10-facts-about-andy-warhols-mao.

16. Ibid.

17. Charlie Finch, "A Nostalgia for Molotovs: 'The New York Review,'" *Artnet Magazine*, September 8, 2008, http://www.artnet.com/magazineus/features/finch/finch9-8-08.asp.

18. Chao Ren, "Concrete Analysis of Concrete Conditions: A Study of the Relationship Between the Black Panther Party and Maoism," *Constructing the Past* 10, no. 1 (2009): Article 7, archived at Marxists Internet Archive, https://www.marxists.org/history/erol/ncm-1/bpp-maoism.pdf.

19. Tom Wolfe, *Radical Chic and Mau-Mauing the Flak Catchers* (Farrar, Straus and Giroux, 1970), 46, Kindle.

20. Robin D. G. Kelley and Betsy Esch, "Black Like Mao: Red China and Black Revolution," *Souls* 1, no. 4 (1999): 6–41, https://politicaleducation.org/wp-content/uploads/2018/07/Black-like-Mao-Kelley-and-Esch.pdf, 105.

21. Ibid.

22. Huey P. Newton, "Huey Newton in Conversation with *Sechaba*," *SFAQ / NYAQ / AQ*, March 14, 2016, https://www.sfaq.us/2016/03/huey-newton-in-conversation-with-sechaba/.

23. Wolfe, *Radical Chic*, 19–20.

24. Kelley and Esch, "Black Like Mao."

25. Valeria Ricciulli, "How the Young Lords Brought the Revolution to Drug Treatment," *Curbed*, October 25, 2021, https://www.curbed.com/2021/10/young-lords-acupuncture-detox-bronx-lincoln-hospital.html.

26. Chao Ren, "Concrete Analysis of Concrete Conditions: A Study of the Relationship Between the Black Panther Party and Maoism," *Encyclopedia of the Revolutionary Left*, archived at Marxists Internet Archive, https://www.marxists.org/history/erol/ncm-1/bpp-maoism.pdf.

27. Bethany Allen-Ebrahimian, "When China Stood with African American Activists," *Axios*, June 16, 2020, https://www.axios.com/2020/06/16/china-racism-black-panthers.

28. Wolfe, *Radical Chic*, 27.

29. Ibid., 47–48.

30. Richard Nixon Presidential Library and Museum, "White House Special Files: Box 53, Folder 11," Nixon Presidential Returned Materials Collection, National Archives

and Records Administration, accessed April 16, 2025, https://www.nixonlibrary.gov
/sites/default/files/virtuallibrary/documents/jul10/53.pdf.

31. Duan, "Black Power in China."

32. Manning Johnson, *Color, Communism, and Common Sense*, 1958, https://www
.heritage-history.com/site/hclass/secret_societies/ebooks/pdf/johnson_color.pdf.

33. Hongshan Li, "Building a Black Bridge: China's Interaction with African-American
Activists During the Cold War," *Journal of Cold War Studies* 20, no. 3 (Summer 2018): 116.

34. "Mao Tse-tung Greets W. E. B. Du Bois and Shirley Graham Du Bois,"
Voices & Visions, http://vandvreader.org/mao-tse-tung-greeting-w-e-b-du-bois-and
-shirley-graham-du-bois-1959/; "W. E. B. Du Bois in China," *New York Times*, November 5, 2000, https://archive.nytimes.com/www.nytimes.com/books/00/11/05/specials
/dubois-china.html.

35. Li, "Building a Black Bridge," 123.

36. "W. E. B. Du Bois in China."

37. W. E. B. Du Bois, "China and Africa," speech delivered in Peking, China, May
1959, reprinted in *Black Agenda Report*, April 4, 2012, https://www.blackagendareport
.com/speech-china-and-africa-w-e-b-du-bois-1959.

38. Li, "Building a Black Bridge," 134.

39. Ibid., 124.

40. Ibid., 131–32.

41. Mao Tse-tung. "Statement Supporting the American Negroes in Their Just Struggle Against Racial Discrimination by U.S. Imperialism," *Peking Review*, no. 33 (August
12, 1966): 12–13, archived at Marxists Internet Archive, https://www.marxists.org
/subject/china/peking-review/1966/PR1966-33h.htm.

42. Zhenxing Zhu, "Pilgrimage for Revolutionary Spirit: African American Activists,
the People's Republic of China, and Chinese American Leftists in the Cold War-Civil
Rights Era," *Doshisha American Studies*, April 2018.

43. Li, "Building a Black Bridge," 132.

44. Zhu, "Pilgrimage for Revolutionary Spirit."

45. Duan, "Black Power in China."

46. Kelley and Esch, "Black Like Mao."

47. Thubten Samphel, "The Dalai Lama's China Experience and Its Impact," *Central Tibetan Administration*, April 16, 2015, https://tibet.net/the-dalai-lamas-china
-experience-and-its-impact/.

48. Bradley A. Thayer, *The Strategic Consequences of Chinese Racism: A Strategic Asym-
metry for the United States*, submitted to the Office of Net Assessment, U.S. Department
of Defense, January 7, 2013, https://www.esd.whs.mil/Portals/54/Documents/FOID
/Reading%20Room/Litigation_Release/Litigation%20Release%20-%20The%20
Strategic%20Consequences%20of%20Chinese%20Racism%20%20201301.pdf, 15.

49. Ibid.

50. Anwar Ouassini, Mostafa Amini, Nabil Ouassini, "#ChinaMustexplain: Global
Tweets, COVID-19, and Anti-Black Racism in China," *Review of Black Political Econ-
omy* 49, no. 1 (March 2002): 61–76, https://www.ncbi.nlm.nih.gov/pmc/articles
/PMC8914295/.

51. Ibid.; Human Rights Watch, "China: Covid-19 Discrimination Against Africans," May 5, 2020, https://www.hrw.org/news/2020/05/05/china-covid-19 -discrimination-against-africans#.

52. Mao Zedong, "A New Storm Against Imperialism," in *Selected Works of Mao Tse-tung*, April 16, 1968, archived at Marxists Internet Archive, https://www.marxists .org/reference/archive/mao/selected-works/volume-9/mswv9_80.htm.

53. Ibid.

54. "1968 Riots: Four Days That Reshaped Washington, D.C.," *Washington Post*, March 27, 2018, https://www.washingtonpost.com/graphics/2018/local/dc-riots-1968/.

55. Karen Grigsby Bates, "Bobby Hutton: The Killing That Catapulted the Black Panthers to Fame," NPR, April 6, 2018, https://www.npr.org/2018/04/06/600055767 /bobby-hutton-the-killing-that-catapulted-the-black-panthers-to-fame.

56. Mingwei Huang, "Between Men: Vying Masculinities in 1970s U.S.–China Rela-tions," *The Scholar and Feminist Online* 14, nos. 1–2 (2017), https://sfonline.barnard .edu/between-men-vying-masculinities-in-1970s-u-s-china-relations/2/#identifier_7 _3686.

57. Huey P. Newton, *Revolutionary Suicide* (Harcourt Brace Jovanovich, 1973), 351.

58. Ibid., 347.

59. Eveline Chao, "Let One Hundred Panthers Bloom," *ChinaFile*, July 1, 2013, https://www.chinafile.com/viewpoint/let-one-hundred-panthers-bloom.

Chapter Four: Trading in Blood

1. George H. W. Bush, "Address to the 44th Session of the United Nations General Assembly," U.S. Department of State Archive, September 25, 1989, https://2009-2017. state.gov/p/io/potusunga/207266.htm.

2. George H. W. Bush, *The China Diary of George H. W. Bush: The Making of a Global President*, ed. Jeffrey A. Engel (Princeton University Press, 2008).

3. Zhang Shasha and Wang Dong. "Mourning George H. W. Bush: His Deep Bond with China." *China.com.cn*, December 7, 2018. http://news.china.com.cn /live/2018-12/07/content_267371.htm. This passage is an original translation.

4. Richard Nixon and Henry Kissinger, "Telephone Conversation, April 27, 1971," National Security Archive, https://nsarchive2.gwu.edu/news/20020211/telcon.pdf.

5. "Ronald Reagan's View of China," *Taiwan Today*, March 1, 1981, https://taiwanto-day.tw/news.php?unit=4&post=4845.

6. "Statement by Secretary of State Kissinger," September 19, 1974, in U.S. Department of State, *Foreign Relations of the United States, 1969–1976*, vol. 38, part 1, *Foundations of Foreign Policy, 1973–1976*, Document 45, https://history.state.gov/historicaldocuments /frus1969-76v38p1/d45.

7. Hal Brands, "The Vision Thing," Miller Center, January 14, 2016, https://millercenter .org/issues-policy/foreign-policy/the-vision-thing.

8. U.S. Department of State, "*Reagan Doctrine 1985*," Office of the Historian, https://2001-2009.state.gov/r/pa/ho/time/rd/17741.htm.

9. Michael Pillsbury, *The Hundred-Year Marathon: China's Secret Strategy to Replace America as the Global Superpower* (St. Martin's Griffin, 2016), 101.

10. U.S. Department of State, "The U.S.-China Joint Communiqué (1982)," Office of the Historian, https://history.state.gov/milestones/1981-1988/china-communique.

11. Ted Chan, "Bush Ends China Visit," UPI Archives, May 9, 1982, https://www.upi.com/amp/Archives/1982/05/09/Bush-ends-China-visit/5840389764800/.

12. Clyde V. Prestowitz, *The World Turned Upside Down* (Yale University Press, 2021), 65.

13. John Pomfret, *The Beautiful Country and the Middle Kingdom: America and China, 1776 to the Present* (Henry Holt, 2016), 71.

14. Ibid., 68.

15. Ibid., 74.

16. U.S. Census Bureau, *Trade in Goods with China*, https://www.census.gov/foreign-trade/balance/c5700.html.

17. Michael Lind, "Why Tariffs Are Good," *Tablet*, March 7, 2025, https://www.tabletmag.com/sections/news/articles/tariffs-good-trump-china.

18. Robert E. Lighthizer, "Grand Old Protectionists," *New York Times*, March 6, 2008, https://www.nytimes.com/2008/03/06/opinion/06lighthizer.html.

19. Pomfret, *Beautiful Country and the Middle Kingdom*, 11.

20. For a history of American involvement in the opium trade, see Eric Jay Dolin, *When America First Met China: An Exotic History of Tea, Drugs, and Money in the Age of Sail* (Liveright Publishing, 2012).

21. Ibid., 123.

22. Walter Isaacson, *Kissinger: A Biography* (Simon and Schuster, 1992) 732, Kindle; Judith Miller, "Kissinger Means Business," *New York Times Magazine*, April 20, 1986, https://www.nytimes.com/1986/04/20/magazine/kissinger-means-business.html.

23. David L. Marcus, "The New China Lobby Goes to Bat for Beijing," *The Spokesman-Review*, March 25, 1997, https://www.spokesman.com/stories/1997/mar/25/the-new-china-lobby-goes-to-bat-for-beijing/.

24. Miller, "Kissinger Means Business."

25. Memorandum of Conversation: President Bush's meeting with Deng Xiaoping, Wilson Center Digital Archive, February 26, 1989, https://digitalarchive.wilsoncenter.org/document/116507.

26. Jeffrey T. Richelson and Michael L. Evans, eds., *Tiananmen Square, 1989: The Declassified History*, National Security Archive Electronic Briefing Book No. 16 (Washington, DC: The National Security Archive, June 1, 1999), https://nsarchive2.gwu.edu/NSAEBB/NSAEBB16/index.html.

27. U.S. Embassy Beijing, "Situation Report No. 24," cable, June 5, 1989, in Richelson and Evans, eds., *Tiananmen Square, 1989: The Declassified History*, https://nsarchive2.gwu.edu/NSAEBB/NSAEBB16/docs/doc10.pdf.

28. U.S. Embassy Beijing, "Situation Report No. 32," cable, June 4, 1989, in Richelson and Evans, eds., *Tiananmen Square, 1989: The Declassified History*, https://nsarchive2.gwu.edu/NSAEBB/NSAEBB16/docs/doc14.pdf.

29. Ibid.

30. U.S. Embassy Beijing. "Situation Report No. 24," cable, June 5, 1989, in Richelson and Evans, eds., *Tiananmen Square, 1989: The Declassified History*, https://nsarchive2.gwu.edu/NSAEBB/NSAEBB16/index.html#d10; U.S. Embassy Beijing. "Situation Report

No. 34," cable, June 5, 1989, in Richelson and Evans, eds., *Tiananmen Square, 1989: The Declassified History*, https://nsarchive2.gwu.edu/NSAEBB/NSAEBB16/docs/doc16.pdf.

31. Pillsbury, *Hundred-Year Marathon*, 107.

32. Richard C. Bush, "30 Years After Tiananmen Square: A Look Back on Congress' Forceful Response," Brookings Institution, June 3, 2019, https://www.brookings.edu/blog/order-from-chaos/2019/05/29/30-years-after-tiananmen-square-a-look-back-on-congress-forceful-response/.

33. Pillsbury, *Hundred-Year Marathon*, 108.

34. George H. W. Bush, "Remarks at a White House Briefing on the Situation in China," George Bush Presidential Library and Museum, June 5, 1989, https://bush41library.tamu.edu/archives/public-papers/494.

35. "China, Tiananmen Square & the U.S. Response," George & Barbara Bush Foundation, June 2019, archived at https://web.archive.org/web/20230402052526/www.georgeandbarbarabush.org/2019/06/china-tiananmen-square-the-u-s-response/.

36. "George H.W. Bush, Press Conference, June 5, 1989," USC US-China Institute, June 5, 1989, archived at https://web.archive.org/web/20241119155439/china.usc.edu/george-hw-bush-press-conference-june-5-1989.

37. Sheila Rule, "Reagan Gets a Red Carpet from British," *New York Times*, June 14, 1989, https://www.nytimes.com/1989/06/14/world/reagan-gets-a-red-carpet-from-british.html.

38. "Document of 1989: President Bush's Secret Cable to Beijing," Standoff at Tiananmen, June 2012, http://www.standoffattiananmen.com/2012/06/document-of-1989-president-bushs-secret.html.

39. "Memorandum of Conversation: Deng Xiaoping and Brent Scowcroft, July 2, 1989," *The Wire China*, https://www.thewirechina.com/wp-content/uploads/2020/06/Deng_Scowcroft_July_2_1989_Meeting.pdf.

40. Ibid.

41. Martin Tolchin, "House, Breaking with Bush, Votes China Sanctions," *New York Times*, June 30, 1989, https://www.nytimes.com/1989/06/30/world/house-breaking-with-bush-votes-china-sanctions.html.

42. "Memorandum of Conversation: Deng Xiaoping and Brent Scowcroft."

43. Maureen Dowd, "2 U.S. Officials Went to Beijing Secretly in July," *New York Times*, December 19, 1989, https://www.nytimes.com/1989/12/19/world/2-us-officials-went-to-beijing-secretly-in-july.html.

44. Isaacson, *Kissinger*, 751.

45. Peter Schweizer, "How Henry Kissinger Became an 'Old Friend' of China Who Rendered Great Help to the CCP," *Breitbart*, November 30, 2023.

46. Henry A. Kissinger, "The Caricature of Deng as a Tyrant Is Unfair," *Washington Post*, August 1, 1989, https://www.washingtonpost.com/archive/opinions/1989/08/01/the-caricature-of-deng-as-a-tyrant-is-unfair/4da436a0-0c52-44cc-995a-4894691aa8ad.

47. David Skidmore and William Gates, "After Tiananmen: The Struggle over U.S. Policy Toward China in the Bush Administration," *Presidential Studies Quarterly* 27, no. 3 (Summer 1997): 529.

48. Richard Nixon, "Memorandum on U.S.-China Policy," May 12, 1989, U.S.

Institute of Peace, archived at https://web.archive.org/web/20240504173613/www.usip.org
/sites/default/files/china/1989_Nixon_China_Memo.pdf.

49. Ibid.

50. Kerry Dumbaugh, *China's Most-Favored-Nation (MFN) Status: Congressional Consideration, 1989–1998*, Congressional Research Service Report 98-603 F, August 1, 1998, https://www.everycrsreport.com/reports/98-603.html.

51. Skidmore and Gates, "After Tiananmen," 530.

52. Ibid., 532.

53. Isaacson, *Kissinger*, 220–21.

54. Richard Nixon Presidential Library and Museum, Alexander M. Haig Jr. White House Special Files: Staff Member and Office Files, National Archives and Records Administration, https://www.nixonlibrary.gov/finding-aids/alexander-m-haig-jr-white-house-special-files-staff-member-and-office-files.

55. Skidmore and Gates, "After Tiananmen," 529.

56. Ibid., 532.

57. Ibid., 532–3.

58. Dumbaugh, *China's Most-Favored-Nation (MFN) Status*; Bush, "30 Years After Tiananmen Square."

59. Skidmore and Gates, "After Tiananmen," 518.

60. Isaac Stone Fish, *America Second: How America's Elites Are Making China Stronger* (Knopf, 2022), 48.

61. Isaacson, *Kissinger*, 750.

62. Prestowitz, *World Turned Upside Down*, 202.

63. Ibid., 1–2.

64. Ibid., 2.

65. "China & the Bush Family: Middle Kingdom Rainmakers," *ExcellenTRap*, May 11, 2015, https://excellentrap.wordpress.com/2015/05/11/china-the-bush-family-middle-kingdom-rainmakers/.

66. Peter Schweizer, *Redhanded: How American Elites Get Rich Helping China Win* (Harper, 2022), 189.

67. "China & the Bush Family"; Schweizer, *Redhanded*, 189–190.

68. "Few Speakers Are in Bush's League," *Tampa Bay Times*, May 31, 1997, https://www.tampabay.com/archive/1997/05/31/few-speakers-are-in-bush-s-league/.

69. William Safire, "Essay; The Biggest Vote," *New York Times*, May 18, 2000, https://www.nytimes.com/2000/05/18/opinion/essay-the-biggest-vote.html.

Chapter Five: Business with Friends

1. "Feinstein Repeatedly Defended China Against Human Rights Accusations as Husband Got Rich off Chinese Companies," *Fox News*, September 10, 2021, https://www.foxnews.com/politics/feinstein-repeatedly-defended-china-against-human-rights-accusations-as-husband-got-rich-off-chinese-companies.

2. Richard C. Blum, Oral History Interview, conducted by Martin Meeker, Regional Oral History Office, Bancroft Library, University of California, Berkeley, 2015, https://digitalassets.lib.berkeley.edu/roho/ucb/text/blum_richard_2015.pdf, 218.

3. James Areddy, "A Conversation with Dianne Feinstein," *Wall Street Journal China Real Time Report*, June 6, 2010, https://blogs.wsj.com/chinarealtime /2010/06/06/a-conversation-with-dianne-feinstein/.

4. Glenn F. Bunting and Dwight Morris, "Husband's Business Ties Pose Dilemma for Feinstein," *Los Angeles Times*, October 28, 1994, https://www.latimes.com/archives /la-xpm-1994-10-28-mn-55837-story.html.

5. Connie Bruck, "The Inside War," *New Yorker*, June 22, 2015, https://www.newyorker.com/magazine/2015/06/22/the-inside-war.

6. Lee Smith, "China Queen Dianne Feinstein Used Her Senate Power to Push Most-Favored-Nation Status for the CCP's Corrupt Dictatorship. Why?," *Tablet*, April 20, 2020, https://www.tabletmag.com/sections/news/articles/lee-smith-china -coronavirus-1.

7. Lance Williams, "Husband Invested in China as Feinstein Pushed Trade," *SFGate*, August 27, 2000, https://www.sfgate.com/news/article/Husband-invested-in-China -as-Feinstein-pushed-3051244.php.

8. Blum, Oral History Interview, 282.

9. Anthony Spaeth, "China: Meet Jiang Zemin," *Time*, October 27, 1997, https://time .com/archive/6731679/china-meet-jiang-zemin/.

10. Areddy, "A Conversation with Dianne Feinstein."

11. Blum, Oral History Interview, 217.

12. Martine Panzica, "Richard Blum, Founder of the American Himalayan Foundation, Dies at 86," Lion's Roar, February 28, 2022, https://www.lionsroar.com /richard-blum-founder-of-the-american-himalayan-foundation-dies-at-86/.

13. Blum, Oral History Interview, 218.

14. Ibid., 218–19.

15. "Dianne Feinstein to Lead China Trip," UPI, June 1, 1979, https://www.news papers.com/clip/64935868/the-sacramento-bee/.

16. Senator Dianne Feinstein, Speech: "Managing the Triangular Relationship: The U.S., China & Taiwan," May 11, 2005, https://asiasociety.org/managing-triangular -relationship-us-china-taiwan.

17. Sam Tran, "San Francisco Welcomes 45th Anniversary of Relations with Shanghai," Asia Matters for America, June 22, 2024, https://asiamattersforamerica.org/articles /san-francisco-welcomes-45th-anniversary-of-relations-with-shanghai.

18. Thilo Hanemann, *Chinese Direct Investment in California: 2017 Update*, Rhodium Group, 2017, https://rhg.com/wp-content/uploads/2018/03/web_Chinese-Direct -Investment-in-California_2017-update.pdf.

19. Katherine Wimble, "San Francisco Chinatown," *SAH Archipedia*, Society of Architectural Historians, https://sah-archipedia.org/buildings/CA-01-075-9010.

20. Matt Stirn, "What Archaeologists Are Learning from the Lives of Chinese Immigrants Who Built the Transcontinental Railroad," *Smithsonian Magazine*, April 2022, https://www.smithsonianmag.com/history/archaeologists-learning-lives -chinese-immigrants-transcontinental-railroad-180979786.

21. Gerry Groot, "The Rise and Rise of the United Front Work Department under Xi," *China Brief* 18, no. 7 (April 24, 2018), https://jamestown.org/program/the-rise-and-rise

-of-the-united-front-work-department-under-xi/; Koh Ewe and Laura Bicker, "United Front: China's 'Magic Weapon' Caught in a Spy Controversy," *BBC News*, December 18, 2024, https://www.bbc.com/news/articles/c878evdp758o.

22. U.S. House of Representatives, Select Committee on the Chinese Communist Party, "Select Committee Unveils CCP Influence Memo on United Front," October 1, 2023, https://selectcommitteeontheccp.house.gov/media/press-releases/select-committee -unveils-ccp-influence-memo-united-front-101; Alexander Bowe, *China's Overseas United Front Work: Background and Implications for the United States*, U.S.-China Economic and Security Review Commission, August 24, 2018, https://www.uscc.gov/sites/default /files/Research/China%27s%20Overseas%20United%20Front%20Work%20-% 20Background%20and%20Implications%20for%20US_final_0.pdf.

23. Larry Diamond and Orville Schell, *Chinese Influence and American Interests: Promoting Constructive Vigilance* (Hoover Institution Press, 2018), sec. 3, https://www .hoover.org/sites/default/files/research/docs/06_diamond-schell_sec03_2ndprinting _web.pdf.

24. John S. Van Oudenaren, "Beijing's 'Peaceful Evolution' Paranoia," *The Diplomat*, September 1, 2015, https://thediplomat.com/2015/09/beijings-peaceful -evolution-paranoia/.

25. Office of the Director of National Intelligence, National Counterintelligence and Security Center, *People's Republic of China (PRC) Subnational Influence Efforts: Issues for Congress*, July 6, 2022, https://www.dni.gov/files/NCSC/documents/SafeguardingOur Future/PRC_Subnational_Influence-06-July-2022.pdf.

26. Craig S. Smith, "Blum Associate's Link to China Hinders Plans to Convert Base," *Wall Street Journal*, March 26, 1997, https://www.wsj.com/articles /SB859334036309889000.

27. Bunting and Morris, "Husband's Business Ties Pose Dilemma for Feinstein."

28. Ibid.

29. Ibid.

30. Andrew Murray and Timothy Nerozzi, "Feinstein Defended China Against Human Rights Violations as Husband Got Rich off Chinese Companies," *Fox News*, January 26, 2022, https://www.foxnews.com/politics/feinstein-repeatedly-defended-china -against-human-rights-accusations-as-husband-got-rich-off-chinese-companies.

31. Bunting and Morris, "Husband's Business Ties Pose Dilemma for Feinstein."

32. Clive Hamilton and Mareike Oldberg, *Hidden Hand: Exposing How the Chinese Communist Party Is Reshaping the World* (Oneworld Publications, 2020), 144.

33. Peter Hasson, "All Signs Point to One Man as Chinese Spy in Feinstein's Offfice," *The Daily Caller*, August 6, 2018, https://dailycaller.com/2018/08/06 /feinstein-chinese-spy/; Zach Dorfman, "How Silicon Valley Became a Den of Spies," *Politico Magazine*, July 27, 2018, https://www.politico.com/magazine/story/2018/07/27 /silicon-valley-spies-china-russia-219071/.

34. Murray and Nerozzi, "Feinstein Defended China Against Human Rights Violations."

35. "Senator Attacks 'Hypocrisy' as MFN Hearing Begins," *South China Morning Post*, June 27, 1997, https://www.scmp.com/article/162552/senator -attacks-hypocrisy-mfn-hearing-begins.

36. Bunting and Morris, "Husband's Business Ties Pose Dilemma for Feinstein."

37. Peter Schweizer, *Redhanded: How American Elites Get Rich Helping China Win* (Harper, 2022), 51.

38. Glenn F. Bunting, "Feinstein, Husband Hold Strong China Connections," *Los Angeles Times*, March 28, 1997, https://www.latimes.com/archives/la-xpm-1997-03-28-mn-43046-story.html.

39. Smith, "China Queen Dianne Feinstein."

40. Dianne Feinstein, "Most-Favored Status Is Not a Perk," *Los Angeles Times*, May 19, 1996, https://www.latimes.com/archives/la-xpm-1996-05-19-op-5907-story.html

41. Ibid.

42. Craig S. Smith, "Blum Associate's Link to China Hinders Plans to Convert Base," https://www.wsj.com/articles/SB859334036309889000.

43. Chriss Street, "Trump Administration Forces China to Sell the Port of Long Beach," *American Thinker*, May 7, 2019, https://www.americanthinker.com/blog/2019/05/trump_administration_forces_china_to_sell_the_port_of_long_beach.html.

44. Robert Pear, "FBI Warned of Donations from China, Senator Says," *New York Times*, March 10, 1997, https://archive.nytimes.com/www.nytimes.com/library/politics/0310campaign-finance.html.

45. Bunting, "Feinstein, Husband Hold Strong China Connections."

46. Ibid.

47. Pear, "FBI Warned of Donations from China, Senator Says."

48. Smith, "China Queen Dianne Feinstein."

49. David G. Savage and Richard A. Serrano, "Clinton Not Told of China Donation Plan, Aides Insist," *Los Angeles Times*, March 10, 1997, https://www.latimes.com/archives/la-xpm-1997-03-10-mn-36717-story.html.

50. Brad Meikle, "Newbridge Closes Second Asia Fund," Buyouts, August 9, 1999, https://www.buyoutsinsider.com/newbridge-closes-second-asian-fund/; Richard Simon and Greg Krikorian, "Husband's Business Ties to China Dog Feinstein," *Los Angeles Times*, October 20, 2000, https://www.latimes.com/archives/la-xpm-2000-oct-20-mn-39450-story.html.

51. John Howard, "Green Party Protestors Add Spice to Debate," *Berkeley Daily Planet*, October 28, 2000, https://berkeleydailyplanet.com/issue/2000-10-28/article/1874.

52. Ibid.

53. Ibid.

54. Smith, "China Queen Dianne Feinstein."

55. Peter S. Goodman, "U.S. Firm to Control Chinese Bank," *Washington Post*, June 1, 2004, https://www.washingtonpost.com/wp-dyn/articles/A5136-2004May31.html.

56. Simon Rabinovitch and Samuel Shen, "Ping An to Buy Newbridge Stake in Shenzhen Bank," Reuters, June 12, 2009, https://www.reuters.com/article/legal/government/ping-an-to-buy-newbridge-stake-in-shenzhen-bank-idUSSHA332330/.

57. "World Business Quick Take," *Taipei Times*, March 14, 2003, https://www.taipeitimes.com/News/worldbiz/archives/2003/03/14/0000197995.

58. Ibid.

59. Washington Mutual, Inc., *Exhibit 99.1: WaMu to Strengthen Capital Position, Raising $7 Billion Anchored by a TPG Capital Investment*, U.S. Securities and

Exchange Commission, April 8, 2008, https://www.sec.gov/Archives/edgar/data
/933136/000095013408006239/v39678aexv99w1.htm.

60. Cleary Gottlieb Steen & Hamilton LLP, "Newbridge Capital in First Foreign
Control Investment in Chinese Banking Sector," press release, April 4, 2005, https://
www.clearygottlieb.com/news-and-insights/news-listing/newbridge-capital-in-first
-foreign-control-investment-in-chinese-banking-sector115.

61. "Senators Plan Bill to Press China on Currency," *Los Angeles Times*, June 13, 2007,
https://www.latimes.com/archives/la-xpm-2007-jun-13-fi-china13-story.html.

62. William Lowther and Flora Wang, "Chinese Lobbying Outshines Taiwan,"
Taipei Times, January 11, 2010, https://www.taipeitimes.com/News/front/archives
/2010/01/11/2003463187.

63. Schweizer, *Redhanded*, 59.

64. Ibid., 57.

65. Michael Kaplan, "Dianne Feinstein's Stunning Properties—and Feud-
ing Family," *New York Post*, September 29, 2023, https://nypost.com/2023/09/29
/dianne-feinsteins-stunning-properties-and-feuding-family/.

66. Robin Hill-Gray, "Richard Blum, Billionaire Husband of Senator Dianne Feinstein, Dies at Age 86," *Market Realist*, February 28, 2022, https://marketrealist.com/p
/richard-blum-net-worth/.

Chapter Six: The Greatest Theft

1. Nick Gass, "Trump: 'We Can't Continue to Allow China to Rape Our Country,'"
Politico, May 2, 2016, https://www.politico.com/blogs/2016-gop-primary-live-updates
-and-results/2016/05/trump-china-rape-america-222689.

2. Jim Zarroli, "Looking Back: Trump Has Been a Hard-Liner on Trade for a
Long Time," KCUR, August 23, 2018, https://www.kcur.org/2018-08-23/looking
-back-trump-has-been-a-hard-liner-on-trade-for-a-long-time.

3. Donald Trump with Dave Shiflett, *The America We Deserve* (St. Martin's Press,
2000), 108, Kindle.

4. Ibid.

5. Stuart Auerbach, "Gephardt Hits Japan on Trade Practices," *Washington Post*,
September 11, 1991, https://www.washingtonpost.com/archive/business/1991/09/11
/gephardt-hits-japan-on-trade-practices/c3b46108-bf2c-4d70-85ad-bb9389bf4a65/.

6. Ibid.

7. Robin Toner, "Gephardt Presses Double Theme: Nationalism and Economic
Worry," *New York Times*, March 3, 1988, https://www.nytimes.com/1988/03/03
/business/gephardt-presses-double-theme-nationalism-and-economic-worry.html.

8. Ibid.

9. Kerry Dumbaugh, *China's Most-Favored-Nation (MFN) Status: Congressional Consideration, 1989–1998*, Congressional Research Service Report 98-603, August 1, 1998,
https://www.everycrsreport.com/reports/98-603.html.

10. William Saletan and Ben Jacobs, "A Troubling Story About Dick Gephardt,"
Slate, September 10, 2003, https://slate.com/news-and-politics/2003/09/a-troubling
-story-about-dick-gephardt.html.

11. Stephen Labaton, "Gephardt Raises Japan Challenge," *New York Times*, December 7, 1991, https://www.nytimes.com/1991/12/07/us/gephardt-raises-japan-challenge.html.

12. Adam Clymer, "Gephardt Will Denounce Trade Policy Toward China," *New York Times*, May 27, 1997, https://www.nytimes.com/1997/05/27/us/gephardt-will-denounce-trade-policy-toward-china.html.

13. John E. Yang, "Gephardt Bashes U.S. Policy on China," *Washington Post*, May 28, 1997, https://www.washingtonpost.com/archive/politics/1997/05/28/gephardt-bashes-us-policy-on-china/b52b87da-3e5d-4507-b4fa-f283c7fb50c4/.

14. "Memorandum of Conversation Between Chairman Mao and Dr. Kissinger," Beijing, February 17–18, 1973, in U.S. Department of State, *Foreign Relations of the United States, 1969–1976*, vol. 18, *China, 1973–1976*, Document 12, https://history.state.gov/historicaldocuments/frus1969-76v18/d12.

15. "Joint Statement Following Discussions With Leaders of the People's Republic of China (Shanghai Communiqué)," February 27, 1972, in U.S. Department of State, *Foreign Relations of the United States, 1969–1976*, vol. 17, *China, 1969–1972*, Document 203, https://history.state.gov/historicaldocuments/frus1969-76v17/d203.

16. Neil Thomas, "For Company and for Country: Boeing and US-China Relations," MacroPolo (Paulson Institute), February 26, 2019, https://archivemacropolo.org/analysis/boeing-us-china-relations-history/.

17. Commission on Presidential Debates, "October 11, 1992 First Half Debate Transcript," https://www.debates.org/voter-education/debate-transcripts/october-11-1992-first-half-debate-transcript/.

18. U.S. Census Bureau, "Trade in Goods with China," https://www.census.gov/foreign-trade/balance/c5700.html.

19. Elaine Sciolino, Thomas Friedman, and Patrick E. Tyler, "Clinton and China: How a Promise Self-Destructed," *New York Times*, May 29, 1994, https://www.nytimes.com/1994/05/29/world/clinton-and-china-how-promise-self-destructed.html.

20. John Kruger and Charles Lewis, "Bill's Long March," *Washington Post*, November 7, 1993, https://www.washingtonpost.com/archive/opinions/1993/11/07/bills-long-march/87bbbe72-db14-4dc7-9621-79a0d5dd7060/.

21. Bill Clinton, "Statement by the President on Most Favored Nation Status for China," USC U.S.-China Institute, May 28, 1993, archived at https://web.archive.org/web/20240908220813/china.usc.edu/statement-president-clinton-most-favored-nation-status-china-1993.

22. Bill Clinton, "President Clinton Press Conference on Human Rights in China," USC U.S.-China Institute, May 26, 1994, archived at https://web.archive.org/web/20240909042328/china.usc.edu/president-clinton-press-conference-human-rights-china-1994.

23. Henry A. Kissinger and Cyrus R. Vance, "The Right Decision on China," *Washington Post*, June 6, 1994, https://www.washingtonpost.com/archive/opinions/1994/06/06/the-right-decision-on-china/d05a4d41-fc0a-4065-8fdf-3e7ef859e986/.

24. Ibid.

25. Alan C. Miller, "Democrats Return Illegal Contribution," *Los Angeles Times*, September 21, 1996, https://www.latimes.com/archives/la-xpm-1996-09-21-mn-46051-story.html.

26. Brian Duffy and Bob Woodward, "FBI Probes China-Linked Contributions," *Washington Post*, February 28, 1997, https://www.washingtonpost.com/archive/politics/1997/02/28/fbi-probes-china-linked-contributions/67d857a8-247b-40e6-9ac8-f4ee39afbbf6/.

27. John F. Harris, "White House Unswayed by China Allegations," *Washington Post*, July 20, 1997, https://www.washingtonpost.com/archive/politics/1997/07/20/white-house-unswayed-by-china-allegations/0431e12c-3e8a-4c32-8ae6-cf2e32f625ab/.

28. "Campaign Finance Key Player: John Huang," Campaign Finance Special Report, *Washington Post*, July 24, 1997, https://www.washingtonpost.com/wp-srv/politics/special/campfin/players/huang.htm.

29. Bob Woodward, "Justice Dept. Was Warned on Fund-Raiser," *Washington Post*, February 10, 1998, https://www.washingtonpost.com/wp-srv/politics/special/campfin/stories/cf021098.htm.

30. William Safire, "Essay; China's Spy Ring," *New York Times*, February 16, 1998, https://www.nytimes.com/1998/02/16/opinion/essay-china-s-spy-ring.html.

31. Seth Mydans, "Family Tied to Democratic Party Funds Built an Indonesian Empire," *New York Times*, October 20, 1996, https://www.nytimes.com/1996/10/20/world/family-tied-to-democratic-party-funds-built-an-indonesian-empire.html.

32. Bob Woodward, "Findings Link Clinton Allies to Chinese Intelligence," *Washington Post*, February 10, 1998, https://www.washingtonpost.com/archive/politics/1998/02/10/findings-link-clinton-allies-to-chinese-intelligence/87265d5d-7452-41f2-ad2f-aa4abe7e579e/.

33. Wenzhou Grassroots Online, "This Man from Wenzhou Once Helped Clinton Become President of the United States!" *Sohu*, October 23, 2017, https://www.sohu.com/a/199613450_355996. *Sohu* is Chinese state media.

34. U.S. Senate Committee on Governmental Affairs, "Johnny Chung and the White House 'Subway,'" in *Investigation of Illegal or Improper Activities in Connection with 1996 Federal Election Campaigns: Final Report*, 105th Cong., 2nd sess., March 10, 1998, vol. 1, sec. 10, https://irp.fas.org/congress/1998_rpt/sgo-sir/1-10.htm.

35. David Jackson and Lena H. Sun, "Liu's Deals with Chung: An Intercontinental Puzzle," *Washington Post*, May 24, 1998, https://www.washingtonpost.com/wp-srv/politics/special/campfin/stories/liu052498.htm.

36. U.S. Department of Justice, "Ernest G. Green Pleads Guilty to Tax Violations," press release no. 01-662, December 21, 2001, https://www.justice.gov/archive/opa/pr/2001/December/01_crm_662.htm.

37. Terry Frieden, "Former Democratic Fund-Raiser John Huang Pleads Guilty," CNN/AllPolitics, August 12, 1999, archived at https://web.archive.org/web/20010502205200/http://www.cnn.com/ALLPOLITICS/stories/1999/08/12/huang.sentence/.

38. U.S. Department of Justice, "Ernest G. Green Pleads Guilty to Tax Violations."

39. Harris, "White House Unswayed."

40. James Risen and Jeff Gerth, "Breach at Los Alamos: A Special Report; China Stole Nuclear Secrets for Bombs, U.S. Aides Say," *New York Times*, March 6, 1999, https://www.nytimes.com/1999/03/06/world/breach-los-alamos-special-report-china-stole-nuclear-secrets-for-bombs-us-aides.html.

41. Harris, "White House Unswayed."

42. "Campaign Fund Probe to Widen: China Plot Theory Cited," *Roanoke Times*, February 17, 1997, https://scholar.lib.vt.edu/VA-news/ROA-Times/issues/1997/rt9702/970217/02170102.htm.

43. Anita Kumar, "Foreign Cash Pours into Clinton Family Foundation," *Miami Herald*, February 19, 2015, https://www.miamiherald.com/news/nation-world/article10677056.html.

44. Mark Tapscott, "Clinton Foundation Got $2 Million from Firm Linked to Chinese Intelligence," *Washington Examiner*, March 16, 2015, https://www.washingtonexaminer.com/news/1869775/clinton-foundation-got-2-million-from-firm-linked-to-chinese-intelligence/.

45. Harris, "White House Unswayed."

46. Robert E. Lighthizer, "What Did Asian Donors Want?" *New York Times*, February 25, 1997, https://www.nytimes.com/1997/02/25/opinion/what-did-asian-donors-want.html.

47. Robert E. Lighthizer, "A Deal We'd Be Likely to Regret," *New York Times*, April 18, 1999, https://www.nytimes.com/1999/04/18/opinion/a-deal-wed-be-likely-to-regret.html.

48. Robert E. Lighthizer, "Donald Trump Is No Liberal on Trade," *Washington Times*, May 9, 2011, https://www.washingtontimes.com/news/2011/may/9/donald-trump-is-no-liberal-on-trade/.

49. Roxanne Roberts and Tamara Jones, "Business Mixes with Pleasure," *Washington Post*, October 30, 1997, https://www.washingtonpost.com/archive/lifestyle/1997/10/30/business-mixes-with-pleasure/f3a268b3-7276-47be-af09-8f87d061e35d/.

50. Ibid.

51. White House Office of the First Lady, White House State Dinner for the President of China, October 29, 1997, https://clintonwhitehouse3.archives.gov/WH/EOP/First_Lady/html/102997.html.

52. Roberts and Jones, "Business Mixes with Pleasure."

53. Proposition One Committee, "White House Tibet Protest, October 30, 1997," http://prop1.org/protest/tibet/971030wt.htm.

54. Roberts and Jones, "Business Mixes with Pleasure."

55. Ibid.

56. Ibid.

57. John Chartier, "Unions Oppose Trade Pact," CNN Money, May 22, 2000, https://money.cnn.com/2000/05/22/news/china_trade/.

58. Ibid.

59. Robert E. Scott, "A Conservative Estimate of 'The Wal-Mart Effect': Wal-Mart's Growing Trade Deficit with China Has Displaced More Than 400,000 U.S.

Jobs," Economic Policy Institute, December 9, 2015, https://www.epi.org/publication/the-wal-mart-effect/.

60. Richa Naidu and Siddharth Cavale, "Walmart Shifts to India, Cuts China Imports," Reuters, November 29, 2023, https://www.reuters.com/business/retail-consumer/walmart-shifts-india-china-cheaper-imports-2023-11-29/.

61. OpenSecrets, "Walmart Inc. PAC Contributions to Federal Candidates: 2024 Cycle," https://www.opensecrets.org/political-action-committees-pacs/walmart-inc/C00093054/candidate-recipients/2024.

62. United for Respect, "Walmart's 2024 Political Spending," https://united4respect.org/reports/walmart-political-spending-2024/.

63. Robert E. Scott, "Growing U.S. Trade Deficit with China Cost 2.8 Million Jobs Between 2001 and 2010," Economic Policy Institute, September 20, 2011, https://www.epi.org/publication/growing-trade-deficit-china-cost-2-8-million/.

64. Hidenobu Tokuda, Takayuki Miyajima, and Miho Takase, "How Will U.S.-China Trade Friction Affect the Japanese Economy?," Mizuho Research Institute, April 6, 2017, https://www.mizuhogroup.com/binaries/content/assets/pdf/information-and-research/insights/mhri/mea170510.pdf.

65. Ibid.

66. Ibid.

67. Statista, "Share of Foreign-Invested Enterprises in China's Total Imports and Exports from 2000 to 2022," https://www.statista.com/statistics/1288326/china-foreign-invested-companies-share-in-total-import-and-export/.

68. Vote Smart, "HR 4444—U.S.-China Relations Act of 2000," https://justfacts.votesmart.org/bill/3035/7879/us-china-relations-act-of-2000.

69. "Secretary of State Madeleine K. Albright, President Clinton, President Jimmy Carter, President Gerald Ford, Vice President Al Gore, Dr. Henry Kissinger, and Mr. James Baker, Remarks in Support of China PNTR, East Room, The White House, Washington, DC, May 9, 2000," U.S. Department of State Archive, https://1997-2001.state.gov/statements/2000/000509.html.

70. Eric Schmitt and Joseph Kahn, "China Trade Vote: Clinton Triumph; House, 237–197, Vote Approves Normal Trade Rights," *New York Times*, May 25, 2000, https://www.nytimes.com/2000/05/25/world/china-trade-vote-clinton-triumph-house-237-197-vote-approves-normal-trade-rights.html.

71. U.S. Senate Committee on Foreign Relations, *Giving Permanent Normal Trade Relations Status to Communist China: National Security and Diplomatic, Human Rights, Labor, Trade, and Economic Implications*, 106th Cong., 2nd sess., July 18–19, 2000, S. Hrg. 106-744, https://www.govinfo.gov/content/pkg/CHRG-106shrg67840/html/CHRG-106shrg67840.htm.

72. Nick Gass, "Trump: 'We Can't Continue to Allow China to Rape Our Country.'"

Chapter Seven: Paper Tigers

1. Robert B. Zoellick, "Whither China: From Membership to Responsibility?" (remarks to the National Committee on U.S.-China Relations, New York City, September 21, 2005), U.S. Department of State Archive, https://2001-2009.state.gov/s/d/former/zoellick/rem/53682.htm.

2. Kim Zetter, "Burn After Reading: Snowden Documents Reveal Scope of Secrets Exposed to China in 2001 Spy Plane Incident," *The Intercept*, April 10, 2017, https:// theintercept.com/2017/04/10/snowden-documents-reveal-scope-of-secrets-exposed-to -china-in-2001-spy-plane-incident/.

3. Donald Rumsfeld, *Known and Unknown: A Memoir* (Sentinel, 2011), 314 Kindle.

4. Steven Mufson and Philip P. Pan, "Spy Plane Delays Irk President," *Washington Post*, April 3, 2001, https://www.washingtonpost.com/archive/politics/2001/04/03 /spy-plane-delays-irk-president/6625680b-5d4a-4444-80ad-94defb0f6fff/.

5. "Text of Letter from U.S. to China," CNN.com, April 11, 2001, https://www.cnn. com/2001/WORLD/asiapcf/east/04/11/prueher.letter.text/.

6. Charles Krauthammer, "Two Very Sorries . . . ," *Washington Post*, April 12, 2011, https://www.washingtonpost.com/archive/opinions/2001/04/12/two-very-sorries/0ee47 d4b-202c-4446-930f-498abc4827f1/.

7. Rumsfeld, *Known and Unknown*, 314.

8. Joseph Kahn, "World Trade Organization Admits China, Amid Doubts," *New York Times*, November 11, 2001, https://www.nytimes.com/2001/11/11/world/world-trade -organization-admits-china-amid-doubts.html.

9. John Pomfret, "Jiang Has Caution for U.S.," *Washington Post*, March 24, 2001, https://www.washingtonpost.com/archive/politics/2001/03/24/jiang-has-caution-for-us /4c7429b5-c02d-4d44-849f-ddc86fd438a6/.

10. "Bush's Brother Was Consultant to Firm That Won China Contract," CNN.com, November 25, 2003, https://www.cnn.com/2003/ALLPOLITICS/11/25/bush.brother. reut/.

11. Thomas W. Lippman, "The Tables Turn as a Bush Criticizes Clinton's Policy Toward China," *Washington Post*, August 20, 1999, https://www.washingtonpost.com /archive/politics/1999/08/20/the-tables-turn-as-a-bush-criticizes-clintons-policy-toward -china/4f9f7aad-ca6d-49ea-9838-9fc02d8541fe/; George W. Bush, "U.S. China Policy Must Have Clear Purpose, Strategic Vision," *Washington Post*, October 18, 2000, https://www.washingtonpost.com/wp-srv/onpolitics/elections/wwb2000/1018/bush /question/.

12. Alex Frew McMillan and Major Garrett, "U.S. Wins Support from China," CNN, October 19, 2001, https://www.cnn.com/2001/WORLD/asiapcf/east/10/19/bush.jiang .apec/index.html.

13. John J. Tkacik Jr. and Nile Gardiner, "China Will 'Stand Aside' on Iraq," The Heritage Foundation, February 12, 2003, https://www.heritage.org/middle-east /commentary/china-will-stand-aside-iraq.

14. James Griffiths, "They Were Sent to China's Worst Jails. Then China Turned Them Over to the U.S.," CNN, May 15, 2021, https://www.cnn.com/2021/05/15/china /china-xinjiang-guantanamo-uyghurs-intl-hnk/index.html.

15. "Eastern Turkistan Islamic Movement Revealed," China.org.cn, January 21, 2002, http://www.china.org.cn/english/2002/Jan/25582.htm.

16. U.S. Department of State, "Determination Pursuant to Section 1(b) of Executive Order 13224 Relating to the Eastern Turkistan Islamic Movement," *Federal Register* 67, no. 173 (September 6, 2002): 57076, https://www.federalregister.gov

/documents/2002/09/06/02-22737/determination-pursuant-to-section-1b-of
-executive-order-13224-relating-to-the-eastern-turkistan.

17. Human Rights Watch, "How Mass Surveillance Works in Xinjiang, China,"
May 2, 2019, https://www.hrw.org/video-photos/interactive/2019/05/02/china
-how-mass-surveillance-works-xinjiang.

18. Human Rights Watch, "'Break Their Lineage, Break Their Roots': China's
Crimes Against Humanity Targeting Uyghurs and Other Turkic Muslims," April 19,
2021, https://www.hrw.org/report/2021/04/19/break-their-lineage-break-their-roots
/chinas-crimes-against-humanity-targeting#_ftn8.

19. Lindsay Maizland, "China's Repression of Uyghurs in Xinjiang," Council on
Foreign Relations, updated September 22, 2022, https://www.cfr.org/backgrounder
/chinas-repression-uyghurs-xinjiang.

20. Ibid.

21. Dylan Carlson and Marin Weaver, *Disentangling the Knot: Identifying U.S. and
Global Exposure to Xinjiang Cotton*, Working Paper ID-094, Office of Industries, U.S.
International Trade Commission, October 2022, https://www.usitc.gov/publications
/332/working_papers/disentangling_the_knot_final_102522-compliant.pdf.

22. U.S. Department of Labor, Bureau of International Labor Affairs, *List
of Goods Produced by Child Labor or Forced Labor*, 3 https://www.dol.gov-/
agencies/ilab/reports/child-labor/list-of-goods-print?items_per_page=10&
combine=china&field_exp_exploitation_type_target_id_1=All&tid=All&field_exp
_good_target_id=All&order=name&sort=desc#:~:text=ILAB%20has%20reason%20
to%20believe,origin%20cotton%20to%20produce.

23. Finbarr Bermingham, "Xinjiang Exports to US Doubled in 2021 First Quarter Despite Cotton Ban and Sanctions," Business & Human Rights Resource Cen-
tre, April 22, 2021, https://www.business-humanrights.org/en/latest-news/xinjiang
-exports-to-us-doubled-in-2021-first-quarter-despite-cotton-ban-and-sanctions/.

24. U.S. House of Representatives, Select Committee on the Chinese Communist
Party, Letter to John Donahoe, President and CEO of Nike, Inc., Regarding Supply
Chain Practices in China, Washington, DC, May 2, 2023, https://selectcommitteeon
theccp.house.gov/sites/evo-subsites/selectcommitteeontheccp.house.gov/files/evo-media
-document/05.02.2023-letter-to-nike-china-select.pdf.

25. Patricia Wilson, "Bush Urges 'Yes' Vote on China Trade," Institute for Agriculture and Trade Policy, May 4, 2000, https://www.iatp.org/news/bush-urges-yes-vote
-on-china-trade.

26. "Kissinger Warning on U.S.-China Ties," CNN.com, April 15, 2002, https://
edition.cnn.com/2002/WORLD/asiapcf/east/04/15/kissinger.china/index.html.

27. Ibid.

28. Ibid.

29. Robert B. Zoellick, "The United States, China and the Era of Globalization,"
speech, U.S. Embassy in Beijing, Office of the United States Trade Representative,
May 24, 2002, https://ustr.gov/archive/Document_Library/USTR_Speeches/2002/The
_United_States_China_in_the_Eras_of_Globalization.html.

30. Stephen Foley, "How Goldman Sachs Took Over the World," *The Independent*, July 21, 2009, https://www.the-independent.com/news/business/analysis-and-features /how-goldman-sachs-took-over-the-world-873869.html; Henry M. Paulson, Jr., "Statement by Secretary Henry M. Paulson, Jr. on China's Strategic and Economic Dialogue," U.S. Department of the Treasury, press release, December 14, 2007, https://home .treasury.gov/news/press-releases/hp430.

31. Zoellick, "The United States, China and the Era of Globalization."

32. "Former U.S. Ambassador to China Winston Lord: Kissinger 'Made History'; Secret Talks with Zhou Enlai Before Nixon's Visit," *Sohu*, January 8, 2013, http://news .sohu.com/20130108/n362724321.shtml. (Original translation.)

33. Ibid.

34. Paul Blustein, "The Untold Story of How George W. Bush Lost China," *Foreign Policy*, October 4, 2019, https://foreignpolicy.com/2019/10/04/the-untold-story-of-how-george -w-bush-lost-china/.

35. George W. Bush, "President Discusses Free Trade with Central American Leaders," George W. Bush White House Archives, January 17, 2003, https:// georgewbush-whitehouse.archives.gov/news/releases/2003/01/text/20030117-4.html.

36. U.S. Census Bureau, "Trade in Goods with China," Foreign Trade: Data, https:// www.census.gov/foreign-trade/balance/c5700.html.

37. Mao Zedong, "Talk with the American Correspondent Anna Louise Strong," in *Selected Works of Mao Tse-tung*, vol. 5, archived at Marxists Internet Archive, https:// www.marxists.org/reference/archive/mao/selected-works/volume-5/mswv5_52.htm.

38. John Miller, "Interview: Osama Bin Laden," *Frontline*, PBS, originally aired May 2001, https://www.pbs.org/wgbh/pages/frontline/shows/binladen/who/interview.html.

39. Robert B. Zoellick, "Whither China: From Membership to Responsibility?," remarks to the National Committee on U.S.-China Relations, New York City, September 21, 2005, U.S. Department of State (archived), https://2001-2009.state.gov/s/d/former /zoellick/rem/53682.htm.

40. Ibid.

41. William J. Clinton, "Remarks by the President on China Trade Bill," The White House, April 4, 2000, Bill Clinton White House Archives, https://clintonwhitehouse4 .archives.gov/WH/Work/040400.html.

42. Eric Weinstein, "How and Why Government, Universities, and Industry Create Domestic Labor Shortages of Scientists and High-Tech Workers," working draft, National Bureau of Economic Research, 2002, https://users.nber.org/~sewp/references /archive/weinsteinhowandwhygovernment.pdf.

Chapter Eight: Masters of the Universe

1. Henry M. Paulson, *Dealing with China: An Insider Unmasks the New Economic Superpower* (Grand Central Publishing, 2015), 180 Kindle.

2. U.S. Senate Committee on Finance. *China's Accession to the WTO: Hearing Before the Committee on Finance, United States Senate, One Hundred Sixth Congress, Second Session, March 23, 2000*, S. Hrg. 106–545 (Washington, DC: U.S. Government

Printing Office, 2000), https://www.govinfo.gov/content/pkg/CHRG-106shrg66498/html /CHRG-106shrg66498.htm.

3. Paulson, *Dealing with China*, 195.

4. Ibid., 25.

5. Ibid., 178–180.

6. Knowledge at Wharton Staff, "Why the U.S. Should Engage More Deeply with China," *Knowledge at Wharton*, Wharton School of the University of Pennsylvania, April 12, 2016, https://knowledge.wharton.upenn.edu/article/henry -paulson-on-engaging-with-china/.

7. Henry M. Paulson Jr., *On the Brink: Inside the Race to Stop the Collapse of the Global Financial System* (Grand Central Publishing, 2010), 32, Kindle.

8. Fiona Lau and Elzio Barreto, "Goldman Exits China's ICBC Seven Years and Billions Later," Reuters, May 21, 2013, https://www.reuters.com/article/us-goldman -icbc/goldman-exits-chinas-icbc-seven-years-and-billions-later-idUSBRE94J0822 0130521/.

9. Goldman Sachs, "1997: China Telecom Privatization Shines Through the Shadow of the Asian Financial Crisis," https://www.goldmansachs.com/our-firm/history /moments/1997-china-telecom-privatization.html.

10. Paulson, *Dealing with China*, 6.

11. Ibid., 39.

12. Ibid., 66–67.

13. Michael M. Phillips, "PetroChina's IPO Roadshow Opens, While Opposition Forces Rally," *Wall Street Journal*, March 23, 2000, https://www.wsj.com/articles /SB95374979284750553.

14. Ian Johnson, "U.S. Groups Oppose China IPO," *Wall Street Journal*, December 17, 1999, https://www.wsj.com/articles/SB945285475375546693.

15. Human Rights Watch, *Sudan, Oil, and Human Rights* (New York: Human Rights Watch, 2003), chap. 26, https://www.hrw.org/reports/2003/sudan1103/26.htm.

16. Eyder Peralta, "Sudan, Who Once Sheltered Bin Laden, Removed from U.S. Terrorism List," NPR, December 14, 2020, https://www.npr.org/2020/12/14/946 207797/sudan-who-once-sheltered-bin-laden-removed-from-u-s-terrorism -list.

17. Lauren Bayne Anderson, "Goldman Settles Charges of Illegally Promoting Stock," *Washington Post*, July 2, 2004, https://www.washingtonpost.com/archive /business/2004/07/02/goldman-settles-charges-of-illegally-promoting-stock/1c8f8c50 -ddbd-44db-ba31-a6b5e7443daf/.

18. "Sinopec's IPO Is Projected to Raise Some $3.5 Billion," *Wall Street Journal*, October 10, 2000, https://www.wsj.com/articles/SB971028714539246295; Landon Thomas Jr. and Joseph Kahn, "Co-President at Goldman Announces His Retirement," *New York Times*, March 25, 2003, https://www.nytimes.com/2003/03/25/business/co -president-at-goldman-announces-his-retirement.html.

19. Knowledge at Wharton Staff, "Why the U.S. Should Engage More Deeply with China."

20. Thomas Jr. and Kahn, "Co-President at Goldman Announces His Retirement."

21. Tsinghua University School of Economics and Management, Advisory Board, "Introduction," https://www.sem.tsinghua.edu.cn/en/About_SEM/Advisory_Board/Introduction.htm.

22. Tsinghua University School of Economics and Management, "Advisory Board Members," https://www.sem.tsinghua.edu.cn/en/About_SEM/Advisory_Board/Advisory_Board_Members.htm.

23. Schwarzman Scholars, "About," https://www.schwarzmanscholars.org/about/.

24. "President Xi Jinping Meets with Members of Tsinghua SEM Advisory Board," *Tsinghua Global MBA*, July 13, 2020, http://gmba.sem.tsinghua.edu.cn/info/1080/1692.htm.

25. Paulson, *On the Brink*, 37.

26. Paulson, *Dealing with China*, 185–86.

27. Eva Fu, "Don't Fall for China's 'Negotiation Traps': Former Trump Advisor," *Epoch Times*, February 4, 2021, https://www.theepochtimes.com/china/dont-fall-for-chinas-negotiation-traps-former-trump-advisor-3685716.

28. U.S. Congress. Senate. *A Bill to Authorize Appropriate Action if the Negotiations with the People's Republic of China Regarding China's Undervalued Currency Are Not Successful*, S. 295, 109th Cong., 1st sess., introduced February 3, 2005, https://www.congress.gov/109/bills/s295/BILLS-109s295is.pdf.

29. Paulson, *Dealing with China*, 184–85; "Threats 'Not Way to Deal with China,'" *China Daily*, September 29, 2006, https://www.chinadaily.com.cn/china/2006-09/29/content_699223.htm.

30. Paulson, *Dealing with China*, 190–91.

31. U.S. Department of the Treasury, "The First U.S.-China Strategic Economic Dialogue December 14–15, Beijing Fact Sheet," Press Release HP-205, December 15, 2006, https://home.treasury.gov/news/press-releases/hp205.

32. Paulson, *Dealing with China*, 196.

33. Ibid., 196–97.

34. Ibid., 198.

35. Terry Frieden, "FBI Warns of Mortgage Fraud 'Epidemic,'" CNN, September 17, 2004, https://edition.cnn.com/2004/LAW/09/17/mortgage.fraud/.

36. Greg Gordon, "Real Estate Agent's Warnings of Housing Bubble Unheeded," McClatchy DC, September 25, 2008, https://www.mcclatchydc.com/news/nation-world/national/economy/article24596194.html.

37. Alison Frankel, "Is This the Inside Info That Triggered Goldman's MBS 'Big Short'?," Reuters, July 30, 2014, https://www.reuters.com/article/world/is-this-the-inside-info-that-triggered-goldmans-mbs-big-short-idUS4014561534/.

38. *Goldman Sachs Group, Inc., et al., Petitioners v. Arkansas Teacher Retirement System, et al.*, No. 20-222, Joint Appendix, vol. 1, filed January 25, 2021, Supreme Court of the United States, https://www.supremecourt.gov/DocketPDF/20/20-222/167109/20210125121017755_Goldman%20Joint%20Appendix%20Volume%201.pdf.

39. "How Hank Paulson's Inaction Helped Goldman Sachs," *The Real News Network*, October 10, 2010, https://therealnews.com/gordonblack.

40. U.S. Census Bureau, "Trade in Goods with China," 2007 year-end data, https://
www.census.gov/foreign-trade/balance/c5700.html.

41. Keith Bradsher, "China Defends Pace of Change in Yuan," *International Herald Tribune*, March 5, 2007, archived at https://web.archive.org/web/20070307100612
/http://www.iht.com/articles/2007/03/05/business/yuan.php.

42. Robert N. McCauley, "Safe Assets: Made, Not Just Born," BIS Working Papers
No. 769. Basel: Bank for International Settlements, February 2019, https://www.bis.org
/publwork769.pdf.

43. Ibid.

44. W. Scott Frame, Andreas Fuster, Joseph Tracy, and James Vickery, *The Rescue of Fannie Mae and Freddie Mac*, Staff Report no. 719, Federal Reserve Bank of New York, March
2015, https://www.newyorkfed.org/medialibrary/media/research/staff_reports/sr719.pdf.

45. Collin Martin, "U.S. Agency Bonds: What You Should Know," Charles
Schwab, October 11, 2024, https://www.schwab.com/learn/story/us-agency-bonds
-what-you-should-know.

46. Federal Housing Finance Agency Office of Inspector General, *A Brief History of the Housing Government-Sponsored Enterprises* (Washington, DC: FHFA OIG,
March 31, 2011), https://www.fhfaoig.gov/Content/Files/History%20of%20the%20
Government%20Sponsored%20Enterprises.pdf.

47. Paulson, *On the Brink*, 159.

48. Paulson, *Dealing with China*, 240.

49. Ibid., 128.

50. Ibid., 161.

51. Ibid., 249–50.

52. Benn Steil and Dinah Walker, "The Dangers of Debt: Russia and China's GSE
Dumping," Council on Foreign Relations, June 15, 2010, https://www.cfr.org/blog
/dangers-debt-russia-and-chinas-gse-dumping.

53. Richard Teitelbaum, "How Henry Paulson Gave Hedge Funds Advance
Word of 2008 Fannie Mae Rescue," Bloomberg, November 29, 2011, https://www
.bloomberg.com/news/articles/2011-11-29/how-henry-paulson-gave-hedge-funds
-advance-word-of-2008-fannie-mae-rescue.

54. Paulson, *On the Brink*, 3.

55. Ibid., 4.

56. Federal Housing Finance Agency. "FHFA Announces Suspension of Capital Classifications During Conservatorship," news release, October 9, 2008, https://
www.fhfa.gov/news/news-release/fhfa-announces-suspension-of-capital-classifications
-during-conservatorship.

57. Kevin M. Clermont and Theodore Eisenberg, "Foreigners' Fate in America's
Courts: Empirical Legal Research," Cornell Law Faculty Publications, no. 1322 (2006):
237–267, https://scholarship.law.cornell.edu/cgi/viewcontent.cgi?article=2864&context
=facpub.

58. Congressional Budget Office. "Effects of Recapitalizing Fannie Mae and Freddie Mac Through Administrative Actions," August 2020, https://www.cbo.gov
/publication/56511.

59. Luigi Zingales, "Capitalism After the Crisis," *National Affairs*, no. 1 (Fall

2009), https://www.nationalaffairs.com/publications/detail/capitalism-after-the-crisis; Charles Haywood, "Book Review: *Naked Money* (Charles Wheelan)," *The Worthy House*, July 21, 2017, https://theworthyhouse.com/2017/07/21/book-review-naked-moneycharles-wheelan/.

60. John Mullin, "The Rise and Sudden Decline of North Carolina Furniture Making," *Econ Focus*, Fourth Quarter, 2020, Federal Reserve Bank of Richmond, https://www.richmondfed.org/publications/research/econ_focus/2020/q4/economic_history.

61. Neil Caudle, "When the Needles Went to China," *Endeavors*, Fall 2004, https://endeavors.unc.edu/fall2004/textiles.html.

62. Robert E. Scott and Zane Mokhiber, *Growing China Trade Deficit Cost 3.7 Million American Jobs Between 2001 and 2018: Jobs Lost in Every U.S. State and Congressional District*, Economic Policy Institute, January 30, 2020, https://www.epi.org/publication/growing-china-trade-deficits-costs-us-jobs/.

63. Robert E. Scott and Zane Mokhiber, *Growing China Trade Deficits Cost U.S. Jobs: Jobs Lost by State and Congressional District*, Economic Policy Institute, January 30, 2020, https://www.epi.org/publication/growing-china-trade-deficits-costs-us-jobs/.

64. Scott Kennedy and Ilaria Mazzocco, "The China Shock: Reevaluating the Debate," Big Data China, October 14, 2022, https://bigdatachina.csis.org/the-china-shock-reevaluating-the-debate/.

65. David Autor, David Dorn, and Gordon Hanson, "On the Persistence of the China Shock," *Brookings Papers on Economic Activity*, Fall 2021, 381–447, https://www.brookings.edu/articles/on-the-persistence-of-the-china-shock/.

66. Ibid.

67. Ibid.

68. Julian Borger, "Donald Trump: 'You Heard Me, I Would Take the Oil,'" *The Guardian*, September 21, 2016, https://www.theguardian.com/us-news/2016/sep/21/donald-trump-iraq-war-oil-strategy-seizure-isis.

69. John Calabrese, "Beijing to Baghdad: China's Growing Role in Iraq's Energy Sector," Middle East Institute, June 7, 2023, https://www.mei.edu/publications/beijing-baghdad-chinas-growing-role-iraqs-energy-sector.

Chapter Nine: Realigning America

1. Barack Obama, "Remarks by the President on American-Made Energy," Barack Obama *White House Archives*, March 22, 2012, https://obamawhitehouse.archives.gov/the-press-office/2012/03/22/remarks-president-american-made-energy-0.

2. Tim Kiladze, "Economic Power Shifting from U.S. to China, Soros Says," *Globe and Mail*, November 15, 2010, archived at https://web.archive.org/web/201503170 33707/http://www.theglobeandmail.com/report-on-business/economic-power-shifting-from-us-to-china-soros-says/article1800333/.

3. Ibid.

4. "George Soros Says China's Financial Clout Is Growing," CNN Money, June 7, 2009, https://money.cnn.com/2009/06/07/news/international/soros_china.reut/index.htm.

5. Zhou Xin, "How Beijing and Hong Kong Sent Billionaire George Soros

Packing the Last Time He Attacked Asian Markets," *South China Morning Post*, January 28, 2016, https://www.scmp.com/news/china/economy/article/1906325/how-beijing -and-hong-kong-sent-billionaire-george-soros-packing.

6. "Soros Turns to China," *Forbes*, November 13, 2009. https://www.forbes. com/2009/11/13/soros-china-investments-markets-equity-billionaire.html?sh=60d7666 16e86; Dennis Eng, "Soros Praises HK for Blocking His Dollar 'Attacks,'" *South China Morning Post*, June 16, 2009, https://www.scmp.com/article/683788/soros-praises -hk-blocking-his-dollar-attacks.

7. "Current Market Crisis Is 'Worst in 60 Years': Soros," *Emirates 24/7*, January 23, 2008, https://www.emirates247.com/eb247/news/current-market-crisis-is -worst-in-60-years-soros-2008-01-23-1.217067.

8. Stephen Taub, "George Soros Is Even Richer Than We Thought," *Institutional Investor*, February 25, 2010, https://www.institutionalinvestor.com/article/b150z5zqz kzzm5/george-soros-is-even-richer-than-we-thought.

9. U.S. House of Representatives Committee on Oversight and Government Reform, "Statement of George Soros Before the U.S. House of Representatives Committee on Oversight and Government Reform," November 13, 2008, https:// oversightdemocrats.house.gov/sites/evo-subsites/democrats-oversight.house.gov/files /migrated/20081113120114.pdf.

10. Thomas L. Friedman, "Our One-Party Democracy," *New York Times*, September 8, 2009, https://www.nytimes.com/2009/09/09/opinion/09friedman.html.

11. Thomas L. Friedman, "Free Trade with China Will Bolster Democratization and Communication," *Tampa Bay Times*, May 17, 2000, https://www.tampabay .com/archive/2000/05/17/free-trade-with-china-will-bolster-democratization-and-com munication/.

12. Thomas L. Friedman, "Learning from Lance," *New York Times*, July 27, 2005, https://www.nytimes.com/2005/07/27/opinion/learning-from-lance.html.

13. Friedman, "Our One-Party Democracy."

14. Thomas L. Friedman, "Learning from Lance."

15. David E. Sanger, "Summit in New York: President Clinton and China Leader Meet, but with Little Gain," *New York Times*, September 9, 2000, https://www.nytimes .com/2000/09/09/world/summit-new-york-president-clinton-china-leader-meet -but-with-little-gain.html.

16. As a freelance contractor, I contributed articles to *The Epoch Times* for several years and also hosted a podcast.

17. Mark Landler, "China's Ban of Magazine Clouds Forum in Hong Kong," *New York Times*, May 6, 2001, https://www.nytimes.com/2001/05/06/world/china-s-ban-of -magazine-clouds-forum-in-hong-kong.html.

18. "In Jiang's Words: 'I Hope the Western World Can Understand,'" *New York Times*, August 9, 2001, https://www.nytimes.com/2001/08/09/international/asia /in-jiangs-words-i-hope-the-western-world-can-understand-200108099369423 4002.html.

19. Craig S. Smith, "*The New York Times* vs. the Great Firewall of China," *New*

York Times, March 31, 2017, https://www.nytimes.com/2017/03/31/insider/the-new -york-times-vs-the-great-firewall-of-china.html.

20. Craig S. Smith, "A Movement in Hiding: Special Report; Sect Clings to Web in Face of Beijing's Ban," *New York Times*, July 5, 2001, https://www.nytimes.com/2001/07/05 /world/movement-hiding-special-report-sect-clings-web-face-beijing-s-ban.html.

21. Erik Eckholm, "China's Leaders: Jiang's Views; Chinese President Optimistic About Relations with U.S.," *New York Times*, August 10, 2001, https://www.nytimes .com/2001/08/10/world/china-s-leaders-jiang-s-views-chinese-president-optimistic -about-relations-with.html.

22. Falun Dafa Information Center, "The *New York Times*' Falun Gong Distortion," March 21, 2024, https://faluninfo.net/new-york-times-falun-gong-distortion/.

23. *PBS NewsHour*, "President George W. Bush's Address to a Joint Session of Congress Following 9/11—Sept. 20, 2001," YouTube, September 3, 2021, video, https://www .youtube.com/watch?v=ZF7cPvaKFXM.

24. Barack Obama, "Transcript of Obama Speech," *Politico*, March 18, 2008, https:// www.politico.com/story/2008/03/transcript-of-obama-speech-009100.

25. Barack Obama, interview by Michel Martin, "Obama on Racial Issues During His Presidency Through Lens of His New Memoir," *All Things Considered*, NPR, November 16, 2020, https://www.npr.org/2020/11/16/935475339/obama-on-racial -issues-during-his-presidency-through-lens-of-his-new-memoir.

26. Barack Obama, "Remarks by President Obama to the Australian Parliament," Barack Obama *White House Archives*, November 17, 2011, https://obamawhite house.archives.gov/the-press-office/2011/11/17/remarks-president-obama-australian -parliament.

27. Hillary Clinton, "America's Pacific Century," *Foreign Policy*, October 11, 2011, https://foreignpolicy.com/2011/10/11/americas-pacific-century/.

28. White House, Office of the Press Secretary, "Fact Sheet: Advancing the Rebalance to Asia and the Pacific," Barack Obama *White House Archives*, November 16, 2015, https://obamawhitehouse.archives.gov/the-press-office/2015/11/16 /fact-sheet-advancing-rebalance-asia-and-pacific.

29. Bill Gertz, "State Department Calls Out Xi Jinping on S. China Sea Militarization," *Washington Times*, September 27, 2020, https://www.washingtontimes.com/news/2020 /sep/27/state-department-calls-out-xi-jinping-on-s-china-s/.

30. Michael Green, Kathleen Hicks, Zack Cooper, John Schaus, and Jake Douglas, "Counter-Coercion Series: Harassment of the USNS *Impeccable*," Asia Maritime Transparency Initiative, Center for Strategic and International Studies, May 9, 2017, https:// amti.csis.org/counter-co-harassment-usns-impeccable/.

31. Zachary Keck, "US Bombers Challenge China's Air Defense Identification Zone," *The Diplomat*, November 27, 2013, https://thediplomat.com/2013/11 /us-bombers-challenge-chinas-air-defense-identification-zone/.

32. Idrees Ali and Megha Rajagopalan, "China Demands End to U.S. Surveillance after Aircraft Intercept," Reuters, May 20, 2016, https://www.reuters.com/article/world /china-demands-end-to-us-surveillance-after-aircraft-intercept-idUSKCN0YA2BQ/.

33. Jackie Calmes, "Obama and Gillard Expand U.S.-Australia Military Ties," *New*

York Times, November 16, 2011, https://www.nytimes.com/2011/11/17/world/asia /obama-and-gillard-expand-us-australia-military-ties.html.

34. Central Committee of the Communist Party of China, "Document 9: A ChinaFile Translation," ChinaFile, November 8, 2013, https://www.chinafile.com/document -9-chinafile-translation.

35. Bethany Allen-Ebrahimian and Zach Dorfman, "Exclusive: Suspected Chinese Spy Targeted California Politicians," *Axios*, December 8, 2020, https://www.axios .com/2020/12/08/china-spy-california-politicians

36. Kathryn Watson, "House Ethics Committee Ends Investigation into Rep. Eric Swalwell, Taking No Action," *CBS News*, May 24, 2023, https://www.cbsnews.com /news/eric-swalwell-house-ethics-committee-investigation-closed/.

37. Garrett M. Graff, "China's Hacking Spree Will Have a Decades-Long Fallout," *Wired*, February 11, 2020, https://www.wired.com/story/china-equifax-anthem-marriott -opm-hacks-data/.

38. Derek B. Johnson, "Eight Years Since the Obama-Xi Agreement, Chinese Hacking Is Worse Than Ever," SC Media, April 24, 2023, https://www.scworld.com/news /eight-years-obama-xi-agreement-chinese-hacking-iworse-than-ever.

39. John Solomon, "China Isn't Complying with Obama-Era Stock Market Deal; Trump Urged to Intervene," *Just the News*, May 18, 2020, https://justthenews.com /government/white-house/china-isnt-complying-obama-era-stock-market-deal -trump-urged-intervene.

40. Glenn Kessler, "Biden's Repeated Claim He's 'Traveled 17,000 Miles with' Xi Jinping," *Washington Post*, February 19, 2021, https://www.washingtonpost .com/politics/2021/02/19/bidens-repeated-claim-hes-traveled-17000-miles-with-xi -jinping/.

41. Joe Biden and Xi Jinping, "Remarks by Vice President Biden and Chinese Vice President Xi at a U.S.-China Business Roundtable," Barack Obama *White House Archives*, August 19, 2011, https://obamawhitehouse.archives.gov/the-press-office/2011/08/19 /remarks-vice-president-biden-and-chinese-vice-president-xi-us-china-busi.

42. Ibid.

43. Solomon, "China Isn't Complying with Obama-Era Stock Market Deal."

44. Adam Entous, "Will Hunter Biden Jeopardize His Father's Campaign?" *New Yorker*, July 1, 2019, https://www.newyorker.com/magazine/2019/07/08/will-hunter -biden-jeopardize-his-fathers-campaign.

45. Aaron Mc Nicholas and Grady McGregor, "Hunting Biden's China Ties," *The Wire China*, August 20, 2023, https://www.thewirechina.com/2023/08/20 /hunting-bidens-china-ties-hunter-biden/.

46. "Trump's Claims and Hunter Biden's Dealings in China," Reuters, October 4, 2019, https://www.reuters.com/article/world/us-politics/trumps-claims -and-hunter-bidens-dealings-in-china-idUSKBN1WI2HK/.

47. Mc Nicholas and McGregor, "Hunting Biden's China Ties"; "Trump's Claims and Hunter Biden's Dealings in China."

48. Mc Nicholas and McGregor, "Hunting Biden's China Ties."

49. Ibid.

50. U.S. Senate Committee on Finance, "Grassley Raises Concerns over Obama Admin Approval of U.S. Tech Company Joint Sale to Chinese Government and Investment Firm Linked to Biden, Kerry Families," August 15, 2019, https://www.finance .senate.gov/chairmans-news/grassley-raises-concerns-over-obama-admin-approval-of -us-tech-company-joint-sale-to-chinese-government-and-investment-firm-linked -to-biden-kerry-families.

51. Ibid.

52. Ibid.

53. "Shares of China's classifieds website 58.com soar in debut," Reuters, October 31, 2013, https://www.reuters.com/article/58com-ipo-idUSL3N0IL5XP20131031/; Isabella Steger, "Baidu Unit Qunar Files for IPO," *Wall Street Journal*, October 30, 2013, https://www.wsj.com/articles/SB10001424052702303466450457910835080 2175842.

54. Elzio Barreto, "Alibaba IPO Ranks as World's Biggest After Additional Shares Sold," Reuters, September 22, 2014, https://www.reuters.com/article/world /alibaba-ipo-ranks-as-worlds-biggest-after-additional-shares-sold-idUSKCN0HH0A6/.

55. Kylie MacLellan, Olivia Oran, and Elzio Barreto, "Buoyant Stockmarkets Lift Year's Share Offerings by 24 Percent to $774 Billion," Reuters, December 20, 2013, https://www.reuters.com/article/business/buoyant-stockmarkets-lift-year-s-share -offerings-by-24-percent-to-774-billion-idUSBRE9BJ0BQ/.

56. Karen M. Sutter, Michael D. Sutherland, and Raj Gnanarajah, "U.S.-China Auditing Agreement and Issues for Congress," Congressional Research Service, In Focus Report IF12212, September 13, 2022, https://sgp.fas.org/crs/row/IF12212.pdf.

57. Rick Scott, "Sen. Rick Scott Calls on SEC Commissioner Nominee to Hold Chinese Companies on U.S. Exchanges Accountable," April 2, 2025, https://www .rickscott.senate.gov/2025/4/sen-rick-scott-calls-on-sec-commissioner-nominee-to-hold -chinese-companies-on-u-s-exchanges-accountable.

58. Ibid.

59. *Washington Free Beacon*, "Obama Adviser Likened Iran Nuclear Deal to ObamaCare," *Fox News*, November 2, 2014, https://www.foxnews.com/politics /obama-adviser-likened-iran-nuclear-deal-to-obamacare.

60. Lee Smith, "Obama Thinks Iran Can Rescue American Interests in the Middle East: He's Wrong," *Tablet Magazine*, June 18, 2014, https://www.tabletmag.com/sections /israel-middle-east/articles/obama-iran-american-interests.

Chapter Ten: The Thirty Tyrants

1. Donald Trump with Dave Shiflet, *The America We Deserve* (St. Martin's Press, 2000), 111, Kindle.

2. Lauren Hirsch, "The U.S. Investors Caught in the Scrum over TikTok," *New York Times*, March 26, 2024, https://www.nytimes.com/2024/03/26/technology /tiktok-investors-bytedance.html.

3. Arthur Waldron, "The Chamberlain Trap," *New Criterion*, September 2017, https:// newcriterion.com/issues/2017/9/the-chamberlain-trap-8757.

4. Council on Foreign Relations, "Jeb Bush on the Challenges for U.S. Foreign

Policy," January 19, 2016, video of event, https://www.cfr.org/event/jeb-bush-challenges -us-foreign-policy.

5. Ryan Teague Beckwith, "Read the Full Transcript of the Sixth Republican Debate in Charleston," *Time*, January 15, 2016, https://time.com/4182096 /republican-debate-charleston-transcript-full-text/.

6. Maggie Severns, "FEC Fines Jeb Bush Super PAC over Foreign Donation," *Politico*, March 11, 2019, https://www.politico.com/story/2019/03/11/jeb-bush -super-pac-china-1216590.

7. U.S. Department of Justice. "Harvard University Professor and Two Chinese Nationals Charged in Three Separate China Related Cases," press release, January 28, 2020, https://www.justice.gov/archives/opa/pr/harvard-university-professor-and-two-chinese -nationals-charged-three-separate-china-related; U.S. Department of Justice, "Former Harvard University Professor Sentenced for Lying About His Affiliation with Wuhan University of Technology; China's Thousand Talents Program; and Filing False Tax Returns," press release, April 26, 2023, https://www.justice.gov/usao-ma /pr/former-harvard-university-professor-sentenced-lying-about-his-affiliation-wuhan.

8. Jeff Pao, "US Canceling Chinese Student Visas Without Just Cause," *Asia Times*, April 19, 2025, https://asiatimes.com/2025/04/us-china-tensions-impact -visa-issuance-for-chinese-students/

9. Jon Feere, "Birth Tourists Come from Around the Globe," Center for Immigration Studies, August 26, 2015, https://cis.org/Feere/Birth-Tourists-Come-Around-Globe.

10. U.S. Immigration and Customs Enforcement, "Federal Prosecutors Unseal Indictments Naming 19 People Linked to Chinese 'Birth Tourism' Schemes," press release, January 31, 2019, https://www.ice.gov/news/releases/federal-prosecutors-unseal-indictments -naming-19-people-linked-chinese-birth-tourism.

11. "It's Not New, but Birth Tourism Is a Growing CNMI Industry," *Pacific Island Times*, December 5, 2017, https://www.pacificislandtimes.com/post/2017/12/05 /it-s-not-new-but-birth-tourism-is-a-growing-cnmi-industry.

12. U.S. Department of Justice, "Two U.S. Navy Servicemembers Arrested for Transmitting Military Information to the People's Republic of China," August 3, 2023, https:// www.justice.gov/archives/opa/pr/two-us-navy-servicemembers-arrested-transmitting -military-information-peoples-republic-china.

13. Julie Watson, "2 US Navy Sailors Accused of Providing Military Information to China," *AP News*, August 3, 2023, https://apnews.com/article/china-us-navy -espionage-sailors-64ba5d10fb39ef1a5313b940d8d9ae2a#.

14. "FBI Charges Chinese Nationals for Spying at Camp Grayling," Office of Congressman John Moolenaar, press release, October 2, 2024, https://moolenaar.house .gov/media-center/press-releases/fbi-charges-chinese-nationals-spying-camp-grayling.

15. Donald J. Trump, "Presidential Memorandum for the United States Trade Representative," Donald J. Trump White House Archives, August 14, 2017, https:// trumpwhitehouse.archives.gov/presidential-actions/presidential-memorandum -united-states-trade-representative/.

16. Cheng Ting-Fang and Lauly Li, "HP, Dell and Microsoft Look to Join

Electronics Exodus from China," *Nikkei Asia*, July 3, 2019, https://asia.nikkei.com /Economy/Trade-war/HP-Dell-and-Microsoft-look-to-join-electronics-exodus-from-China.

17. Isobel Asher Hamilton, "Amazon, Microsoft, and Google Plan to Move Production Away from China," *Business Insider*, July 3, 2019, https://www.businessinsider.com /amazon-microsoft-google-plan-to-move-production-away-from-china-2019-7.

18. Reuters, "Timeline: Key Dates in the U.S.-China Trade War," Reuters, January 15, 2020, https://www.reuters.com/article/business/timeline-key-dates-in-the-us -china-trade-war-idUSKBN1ZE1AA/.

19. Office of the United States Trade Representative, "Rebalancing United States-China Trade: United States-China Phase One Trade Agreement," https:// ustr.gov/phase-one; "What's in the U.S.-China Phase 1 Trade Deal," Reuters, January 15, 2020, https://www.reuters.com/article/business/whats-in-the-us-china -phase-1-trade-deal-idUSKBN1ZE2IF/.

20. Keith Bradsher, "Protests Erupt in Wuhan Over Waste Incinerator Plan," *New York Times*, July 5, 2019, https://www.nytimes.com/2019/07/05/world/asia/wuhan-china -protests.html.

21. "Wuhan Protest: China Incinerator Plan Sparks Mass Unrest," *BBC News*, July 8, 2019, https://www.bbc.com/news/blogs-china-blog-48904350.

22. Celia Hatton, "Armed Police Move in Against Anti-Plant Protestors," *BBC News*, June 29, 2015, https://www.bbc.com/news/blogs-china-blog-33308420.

23. Austin Ramzy and Chris Buckley, "'Absolutely No Mercy': Leaked Files Expose How China Organized Mass Detentions of Muslims," *New York Times*, November 16, 2019, https://www.nytimes.com/interactive/2019/11/16/world/asia/china-xinjiang -documents.html.

24. Masashi Crete-Nishihata et al., *Censored Contagion II: A Timeline of Information Control on Chinese Social Media During COVID-19*, The Citizen Lab Research Report No. 130, University of Toronto, August 25, 2020, https://citizenlab.ca/2020/08 /censored-contagion-ii-a-timeline-of-information-control-on-chinese-social-media -during-covid-19/.

25. U.S. Department of State, "Fact Sheet: Activity at the Wuhan Institute of Virology," January 15, 2021, https://2017-2021.state.gov/fact-sheet-activity -at-the-wuhan-institute-of-virology/.

26. Ibid.

27. Paulina Firozi, "Tom Cotton Keeps Repeating a Coronavirus Fringe Theory That Scientists Have Disputed," *Washington Post*, February 17, 2020, https://www.washington post.com/politics/2020/02/16/tom-cotton-coronavirus-conspiracy/.

28. Ted Cruz (@tedcruz), "China is the most significant geopolitical threat to the United States for the next century. The Chinese Communist Party is the greatest threat to our liberty, our security, and our way of life," X (formerly Twitter), April 30, 2020, https://x.com/tedcruz/status/1256252575176970240.

29. Brittany De Lea, "Nike Is 'a Brand of China and for China,' CEO Says During Earnings Call," *Fox Business*, June 25, 2021, https://www.foxbusiness.com/markets /nike-brand-of-china-ceo-says.

30. Lee Smith, *Disappearing the President: Trump, Truth Social, and Fight for the Republic* (Encounter, 2024), 61–79.

31. John Ratcliffe, "Views on Intelligence Community Election Security Analysis," Office of the Director of National Intelligence, memorandum, January 7, 2021, https://context-cdn.washingtonpost.com/notes/prod/default/documents/6d274110 -a84b-4694-96cd-6a902207d2bd/note/733364cf-0afb-412d-a5b4-ab797 a8ba154.#page=1; Jerry Dunleavy, "Intelligence Analysts Downplayed Chinese Election Influence to Avoid Supporting Trump Policies, Inspector Finds," *Washington Examiner*, January 7, 2021, https://www.washingtonexaminer.com/news/intelligence -analysts-downplayed-election-interference-trump-inspector.

32. Sarah Zheng, "Time for a Reset in US-China Relations, Foreign Minister Wang Yi Says," *South China Morning Post*, December 5, 2020, https://www.scmp.com/news /china/diplomacy/article/3112842/time-reset-us-china-relations-says-foreign-minister -wang-yi.

33. Hannah Beech, 'Trump Is Better': In Asia, Pro-Democracy Forces Worry About Biden," *New York Times*, November 30, 2020, https://www.nytimes.com/2020/11/30 /world/asia/biden-trump-china-asia.html.

34. Banned News, "CCP Expert: Biden Is the CCP'S Own," YouTube, December 4, 2020, video, 11:35, https://www.youtube.com/watch?v=acZXridt7wM.

Epilogue: Reversing Kissinger

1. Donald Trump with Dave Shiflett, *The America We Deserve* (St. Martin's Press, 2000), 108, Kindle.

2. "Conversation Between President Nixon and his Assistant for National Security Affairs," February 14, 1972, in U.S. Department of State, *Foreign Relations of the United States, 1969–1976, Volume XVII, China, 1969–1972*, Document 192, https://history. state.gov/historicaldocuments/frus1969-76v17/d192.

3. Asawin Suebsaeng, Gideon Resnick, and Erin Banco, "Henry Kissinger Pushed Trump to Work with Russia to Box In China," *The Daily Beast*, November 27, 2017, archived at https://archive.ph/F1jrE.

4. Donald J. Trump, "Remarks by President Trump in Joint Address to Congress," Donald J. Trump White House Archives, March 4, 2025,https://www.whitehouse.gov/ remarks/2025/03/remarks-by-president-trump-in-joint-address-to-congress/.

5. Adam Lehrer, "All the President's Men," *Tablet Magazine*, May 1, 2025, https:// www.tabletmag.com/sections/news/articles/trump-administration-staffing-sergio.

6. Trump with Shiflett, *The America We Deserve*, 108.

Index

About the Author

LEE SMITH IS A VETERAN JOURNALIST WHO WRITES FOR *TABLET* about national politics, foreign policy, and the press. Smith reported from the Middle East for a decade after the 9/11 attacks and wrote the critically acclaimed *The Strong Horse: Power, Politics, and the Clash of Arab Civilizations*. His 2019 book *The Plot Against the President: The True Story of How Congressman Devin Nunes Uncovered the Biggest Political Scandal in US History* was a *New York Times* bestseller and made into an Academy Award–nominated documentary film. Smith was born in San Juan, Puerto Rico, and was raised in New York City. He now lives in Charleston, South Carolina.